Great
Canadian Speeches

Selected and edited by
Dennis Gruending

Fitzhenry & Whiteside

Front cover design by David Drummond
Interior design by Kathy Aldous-Schleindl
Front cover image by David Drummond
Interior maple leaf icon by Kenneth Zirkel
Copyedited by Joan Tetrault
Proofread by Geri Rowlatt
Translated by Karima Afchar

The publisher gratefully acknowledges the support of The Canada Council for the Arts, the Department of Canadian Heritage, and the Ontario Arts Council.

THE CANADA COUNCIL | LE CONSEIL DES ARTS
FOR THE ARTS | DU CANADA
SINCE 1957 | DEPUIS 1957

We acknowledge the financial support of the Government of Canada through the Book Publishing Industry Development Program (BPIDP) for our publishing activities.

Printed in Canada by Friesens

05 06 07 08 / 5 4 3 2

National Library of Canada Cataloguing in Publication
          Great Canadian speeches / edited by Dennis Gruending.
Includes bibliographical references and index.
ISBN 1-55041-752-5
          1. Speeches, addresses, etc., Canadian. 2. Canada—History—Sources.
I. Gruending, Dennis, 1948-
PN4055.C3G74 2004   815'.008   C2004-902906-1

Publisher Cataloging-in-Publication Data (U.S)
          Great Canadian speeches / selected and edited by Dennis Gruending
—1st ed.
[320] p. : cm.
Includes bibliographical references and index.
Summary: A chronological collection of Canadian speeches, including the historical context of each, and an analysis of content and technique.
ISBN 1-55041-752-5
          1. Speeches, addresses, etc., Canadian.
I. Gruending, Dennis. II. Title.
815 dc22   PR9197.4.G74 2004

Fitzhenry & Whiteside Limited
195 Allstate Parkway
Markham, ON
L3R 4T8

First published in the United States in 2005 by
Fitzhenry & Whiteside Limited
121 Harvard Avenue, Suite 2
Allston, MA 02134

1–800–387–9776
www.fitzhenry.ca

Contents

For Martha, Maria, and Anna,

the women in my life

Acknowledgements

I began researching this book almost accidentally in 2001, while writing speeches for Saskatchewan's premier, Lorne Calvert. I found myself sitting at a keyboard day after day writing material for someone who maintained a prodigious speaking schedule.

I went for walks each lunch hour to clear my head, and those excursions most often ended at Saskatoon's public library. I began, almost absentmindedly, to look for books containing speeches that might inspire me in my task. There were various anthologies from the United States and Great Britain, and one from Australia, but to my surprise there was no collection of Canadian speeches.

I began to check on the Web and with other libraries. I did find one book, *Canadian Eloquence*, a small gem published in 1910 by Lawrence J. Burpee, who worked at the Ottawa Public Library at the time. Burpee collected eighteen speeches from the people he judged to be Canada's preeminent orators, including Joseph Howe, Wilfrid Laurier, Thomas D'Arcy McGee, John A. Macdonald, and a few others.

I became convinced that, ninety years after the publication of *Canadian Eloquence*, it was time for another anthology, containing both historical and contemporary speeches, but one that was more comprehensive in its choice of speakers and themes. I decided to direct my reading toward locating great Canadian speeches.

During my search I found several useful books (see Sources for complete information). *Who Speaks for Canada*, edited by Desmond Morton and Morton Weinfeld, contains a number of speeches, some reproduced here, but also includes selections from books of non-fiction, letters, poems, and other documents. Desmond Morton's *A Short History of Canada* was indispensable for general reference and fact checking, as was *The Canadian Encyclopedia*. *First People, First Voices*, edited by Penny Petrone, contains a valuable collection of speeches by Aboriginal people.

Although I have read collections of speeches by various prime ministers and others in public life, mostly I found myself poring over books of history and biography, paying close attention to source materials in my search for references to great speeches. The Library of Parliament in Ottawa proved to be a treasure trove for many of these books, and I thank the staff members for their friendly and competent service.

I read and enjoyed the following anthologies of speeches from other countries: *The Penguin Book of Twentieth-Century Speeches*, edited by Brian McArthur; *Australia Speaks*, edited by A. L. McLeod; *Lend Me Your Ears*, edited by William Safire; and *The Power of Eloquence*, a British collection edited by Andrew Scotland.

The following books were useful for their analysis of speeches and oratory: *Democratic Eloquence*, by Kenneth Cmiel; *Eloquence in an Electronic Age*, by Kathleen Hall Jamieson; *Simply Speaking*, by Peggy Noonan; and *Lincoln at Gettysburg*, by Garry Wills.

Canadian Speeches: Issues of the Day is a periodical that publishes speeches dating back to 1987, and it was an excellent contemporary source. Also, there are an increasing number of speeches available on-line. The best sources were the Empire Club, which has prepared digital copies of its speeches dating back to 1903, and Library and Archives Canada, a new institution combining the former National Library and the National Archives of Canada.

I made direct contact, usually via e-mail, with a number of people whose speeches appear in this collection. I thank them and others who agreed to have their speeches included.

Friends and colleagues too numerous to mention were generous with their time and comments regarding this project. I wish especially to thank Ian Wilson, Librarian and Archivist of Canada, Mike Graham, who has now retired from the Library of Parliament; and Marc Bosc, Clerk Assistant (Committees) for the House of Commons, and an anthologist in his own right. Mr. Bosc's book, *Canadian Parliamentary Anecdotes*, was another useful source.

Thanks as well to Charlene Dobmeier and her staff at Fitzhenry & Whiteside's subsidiary Fifth House Ltd. for their professionalism and good cheer.

Finally, I offer warm appreciation to my partner Martha Wiebe for her continuing love and support, and to our daughters Maria and Anna for tolerating their dad's literary and political obsessions.

Introduction

"Great oratory demands great issues"—Cicero

Throughout history great orators have moved their contemporaries to build nations, to make war or peace, to sway judges and juries, to inspire the living, and to mourn for the dead. Great speeches create history, but most often they, in turn, arise from times of crisis and opportunity.

During the Civil War, Abraham Lincoln used his address at Gettysburg to retrieve for America the vision of its founders for "a new nation, conceived in liberty, and dedicated to the proposition that all men are created equal." Adolph Hitler mesmerized his fellow citizens, inciting them to war. Winston Churchill turned the tide of that same war by powerfully exhorting his weary nation to action and sacrifice: "We shall fight on the beaches, we shall fight on the landing grounds, we shall fight in the fields and in the streets, we shall fight in the hills; we shall never surrender." Gandhi convinced millions of his fellow citizens to use peaceful means to confront India's British colonizers: "Non-violence is the first article of my faith. It is also the last article of my creed."

It is perhaps no surprise that some of Canada's finest orators gained prominence during the nineteenth century, a time of great political enterprises—the agitation for responsible government, then Confederation of the provinces. This collection of speeches begins with that period.

Joseph Howe, a self-taught Nova Scotia journalist, performed brilliantly in his own defence against libel in 1835, arguing that an unshackled press was essential for the public good. Thomas D'Arcy McGee, the "myth-maker of Confederation," was eloquent in his vision of a northern nation and a new Canadian nationality. John A. Macdonald drafted the resolutions that became the British North America Act, and it was he, more than anyone, who convinced a group of reluctant provincial politicians to accept Confederation.

Howe and McGee were both learned men who loved to speak about literature as well as about politics and public purpose. Arthur Meighen once agreed to speak to the Canadian Club about "the greatest Englishman of all time," and when the occasion arrived he talked about and quoted Shakespeare, all without any prepared notes. All three men would have agreed with the Roman scholar Cicero, who wrote that for an orator, "a knowledge of a vast number of things is necessary, without which volubility of words is empty and ridiculous."

The silver-tongued Wilfrid Laurier was equally eloquent in two languages, and he would have shone in any country's legislature or assembly. When John A. Macdonald died in 1891, Laurier told a hushed House of Commons that "the angel of death had touched him with his wing."

In addition to Laurier, Quebec has produced some of Canada's greatest orators—Henri Bourassa, Pierre Trudeau, René Lévesque, and Lucien Bouchard. Their eloquence owes in part to the classical education that reigned in the province's Catholic schools, where students were steeped in history, philosophy, literature, and language.

Confederation in 1867 thrust upon Canada the pride, but also the problems, of nationhood. Aboriginal peoples had lived here since time immemorial, but they were thrust aside by European settlement. They are often seen as passive victims who did not fully understand what was happening, but a speech by Mistawasis to a private gathering of his fellow chiefs during treaty negotiations in 1876 provides an eloquent and heart-rending analysis of their situation. A few years later, Louis Riel and the Cree chief Big Bear were in the prisoner's box, pleading for their own lives and for their people after being forced into a revolt that failed.

As the twentieth century dawned, new and powerful orators arrived on the scene. Lady Aberdeen, an unabashed progressive, used her position and her words to create a new space for women. It is all but impossible to find speeches given by women in the nineteenth century because they were not allowed to participate in public life. Men believed that women's place was in the home, and that they would be sullied by standing at the podium. The struggle by women for full participation was long and difficult, and is far from over even now.

But strong and articulate women did emerge. Nellie McClung used every available means, including the theatre in Winnipeg, to challenge Manitoba's obstinate and patronizing premier Rodmond Roblin on his opposition to women's right to vote. Her speeches during subsequent Manitoba elections were instrumental in his defeat and winning the vote for women.

McClung and other women, including Irene Parlby and Agnes Macphail, brought with them a new style of oratory that coincided with the rise of agrarian-based populist politics in Canada. Parlby became a member of the legislature in Alberta, and in 1921 Macphail became the first woman elected to the House of Commons. Their speech was direct and unadorned, and more self-revealing than that of their male contemporaries. "I suggest there is a splendid way out of the difficulty of marriage, and that is my way—stay out," Macphail said in a debate in 1925.

Irene Parlby's speech in a 1921 federal by-election was carried live on radio, a technology that was to have its own profound impact. Speakers in earlier times stood on a stump, a stage, or the steps of a train, and they had to speak loudly enough so that everyone in the audience could hear them. Radio technology, with its electronic magnification of the voice, created a much more casual atmosphere, and the message was received in the intimacy of the home rather than in a crowd. Radio signalled a shift in taste and sensibility from the florid style and fiery demeanour of the old eloquence to a new cooler and more conversational style.

Franklin Delano Roosevelt created his fireside chats for radio, and Canadian public figures became adept in its use as well. They included William Aberhart and Tommy Douglas, two preachers who became premiers. Aberhart was an evangelical minister with his own radio program, and when he discovered the economic doctrine of social credit, he promoted it on air. Douglas delivered his socialist parables "Mouseland" and "The Cream Separator" on radio as well as to live audiences, and as premier he frequently used radio to speak directly to citizens.

Prime Minister Richard Bedford Bennett gave a series of radio addresses during the depths of the Depression in 1935. He had been a rich and established businessman prior to entering politics, but he used radio to warn Canadians that the old order was gone, and that only interventionist government could save the country. Bennett's speeches were significant for another reason: his brother-in-law wrote them, and Bennett delivered them.

It is difficult to determine precisely when speechwriters came into vogue, because most speakers prefer to keep their ghosts in the closet. But speechwriters have become ubiquitous in the pressure-filled lives of most civic, business, and political leaders. Some observers, like academic Kathleen Hall Jamieson, argue that this "divorce between speech and thought" has fatally undermined both leadership and oratory, causing leaders to become actors who simply read lines that they do not own.

Louis Riel worked intensely in his jail cell for days on his address to the jury. Prime Minister John A. Macdonald made the time to write a set-speech for the "reciprocity" election in 1891. He carefully crafted the lines that have most come to identify him: "As for myself, my course is clear. A British subject I was born, a British subject I will die."

The pace of modern life and the demands placed on leaders means that they will have others do their writing, and much of their thinking, for them. Good speechwriters need not fear for their employment. But it is reassuring to know that, at times when the stakes are highest, leaders still think it through for themselves. Pierre Trudeau did just that in preparing his great speech in the May 1980 Quebec referendum campaign. Brian Mulroney did it a few years later, staying up late into the night to write his own speech on minority language rights.

A generation after radio became popular, television came along to change oratory once again. Television was as devastating for some public figures as it was beneficial to others. Prime Minister Louis St. Laurent was completely unable to adapt. The 1957 federal election was the first in which television was widely employed. The cameras intimidated St. Laurent, who looked old and tired, a man of yesterday's generation. By contrast, John Diefenbaker delivered speeches with an energy that inspired the nation. The result was an unexpected victory, a minority Conservative government, followed by a landslide in an election a year later.

Diefenbaker, however, was no match for Pierre Trudeau, the first political star of Canada's television age. Marshall McLuhan advised Trudeau that his face was the perfect mask for television and that he should exploit his persona. Trudeau did, with his fingers-in-the-belt gunslinger pose, his pirouettes behind the back of the Queen, and his fringed leather jackets.

McLuhan also observed that television is a "cool" and intimate medium, and not one that lends itself to fiery language and histrionics. Most public figures play it safe on television, believing, as their handlers tell them, that any gesture—the angry blush, the raised brow, or even the expressive hand—is exaggerated by the camera and small screen. Politicians and business leaders are usually advised to wear conservative suits and to be pleasant and reasonable at all costs.

Television has also replaced word with image. What could one say that would compete with the pictures of the Trade Tower air crashes? Television, with its insatiable demand for pictures and its penchant for brief news clips, has often been criticized for the decline of oratory, even the decline of public life itself. Yet people are making more speeches than ever—in Parliament, in boardrooms, at protest rallies, and at every manner of community organization. Public figures appear in interviews, on news and talk shows, phone-ins, panels, seminars, town hall meetings, and televised debates.

The best orators have always found ways to move and influence their peers, applying skills that they have learned, observed, and rehearsed to present their case persuasively for a specific purpose. These speeches may entertain through their creativity, logic, and passion, but the goal of each is action. Macdonald wants Confederation; McClung wants the vote for women; Lévesque wants independence for Quebecers; Pierre Trudeau wants a united Canada; David Suzuki wants us to wake up before it is too late. In the new century, Stephen Lewis pleads for the rich countries to fight the AIDS pandemic, and Thomas Homer-Dixon predicts that the world's existing systems of governance and commerce cannot easily adapt to the multiple challenges that confront us.

I have spent several years re-reading much of our history to prepare this collection, searching for the most powerful oratory that Canada has to offer. I have provided a historical context for these speeches, but have also probed their content and technique to find out what makes them great. They are windows through which we can review our common struggles and aspirations. This book is meant for anyone who treasures our country's history and its literature, but it is also intended to serve as an inspiration for thousands of people who either make speeches or write them for others.

Joseph Howe
1835

"What is right? What is just?
What is for the public good?"

Joseph Howe was a self-taught printer and journalist, steeped in a knowledge of Shakespeare, the Bible, and British history. He was Nova Scotia's finest orator, and also used his newspaper, the *Novascotian*, to criticize the British colonial administration, a tightly managed club controlled by the governor and his friends. Howe believed that intelligent public opinion informed by a free press was essential for the development of responsible government. As a result of his criticisms, Howe was indicted in 1835 for criminal libel, and made this eloquent speech to a Halifax jury in 1835.

Will you, my countrymen, the descendants of these men, warmed by their blood, inheriting their language, and having the principles for which they struggled confided to your care, allow them to be violated in your hands? Will you permit the sacred fire of liberty, brought by your fathers from the venerable temples of Britain, to be quenched and trodden out on the simple altars they have raised? Your verdict will be the most important in its consequences ever delivered before this tribunal; and I conjure you to judge me by the principles of English law, and to leave an unshackled press as a legacy to your children. You remember the press in your hours of conviviality and mirth—oh, do not desert it in this its day of trial.

If for a moment I could fancy that your verdict would stain me with crime, cramp my resources by fines, and cast my body into prison, even then I would not endeavour to seek elsewhere for consolation and support. Even then I would not desert my principles, nor abandon the path that the generous impulses of youth selected, and which my riper judgment sanctions and approves. I would toil on and hope for better times, till the principles of British liberty and British law had become more generally diffused, and had forced their way into the hearts of my countrymen. In the meantime I would endeavour to guard their interests, to protect their liberties; and, while Providence lent me health and strength, the independence of the press should never be violated in my hands. Nor is there a living thing beneath my roof that would not aid me in this struggle: the wife who sits by my fireside; the children who play around my hearth; the orphan boys in my office, whom it is my pride and pleasure to instruct from day to day in the obligations they owe to their profession and their country, would never suffer the press to be wounded through my side. We would wear the coarsest raiment, we would eat the poorest food, and crawl at night into the veriest hovel in the land to rest our weary limbs, but cheerful and undaunted hearts; and these jobbing justices should feel that one frugal and united family could withstand their persecution, defy their power, and maintain the freedom of the press. Yes, gentlemen, come what will, while I live, Nova Scotia shall have the blessing of an open and unshackled press. But you will not put me to such straits as these; you will send me home to the bosom of my family, with my conduct sanctioned and approved; your verdict will engraft upon our soil those invaluable principles that are our best security and defence.

Your verdict will, I trust, go far towards curing many of the evils which we have been compelled to review. Were you to condemn me, these men would say there is no truth in those charges, there is nothing wrong, and matters would continue in the old beaten track. If you acquit me, as I trust you will, they must form themselves into a court of inquiry for self-reformation; they must drive out from among them those men who bring disgrace on their ranks, and mischief on the community in which they reside. But, gentlemen, I fearlessly consign myself, and, what is of more consequence, your country's press, into your hands.

I do not ask for the impunity which the American press enjoys . . . but give me what a British subject has a right to claim—impartial justice, administered by those principles of the English law that our forefathers fixed and have bequeathed. Let not the sons of the rebels look across the border to the sons of the Loyalists, and reproach them that their press is not free.

If I wished to be tried by your sympathies I might safely appeal to you, who have known me from my childhood, and ask if you ever found malice in my heart or sedition in my hands? My public life is before you; and I know you will believe me when I say that when I sit down in solitude to the labours of my profession, the only questions I ask myself are What is right? What is just? What is for the public good? I am of no party, but I hold that when I am performing my duty to the country, I am sincerely doing that which I engaged to do when I took the press into my hands. You will hear the attorney general close this case on the part of the Crown, but do not allow yourselves to be won by his eloquence from the plain facts and simple principles I have stated. I must, however, do that gentleman the justice to acknowledge that in the conduct of this prosecution I have received nothing but courtesy at his hands. As an officer of the Crown he is bound to perform this public duty, but I well know that persecutions of the press are little to his taste. When urged at times by members of the Assembly, over which in his capacity of Speaker he presides, to resent attacks made on that body in the *Novascotian*, his answer had invariably been: "No, let the press alone; if we cannot stand against its assaults, we deserve to fall." That, I doubt not, would have been his advice to the magistrates had they deigned to consult him. But oh, had I his powers of oratory, how I could have set this case before you! "Were I Brutus, and Brutus Antony, there were an Antony that should move the very stones," not of Halifax to mutiny and sedition, but the broken stones in Bridewell to laughter and to scorn. The light of his penetrating intellect would have revealed the darkest recesses of municipal corruption; and with the hand of a master he would have sketched the portraits of these jobbing justices, and, hanging them around the walls of Bridewell, would have damned them to imperishable renown.

Howe was acquitted, and his brilliant self-defence attracted the attention of Reformers, and he was nominated as their representative for Halifax County in 1836. He became a major political force, and thanks in great measure to his efforts, Nova Scotia in 1848 became the first British colony to achieve responsible government. He was later to become a fierce opponent of confederation with Canada, preferring an imperial alliance with Britain.

Louis Joseph Papineau
23 October 1837

"We can no longer cling to the British Empire
for our happiness and prosperity"

Louis Joseph Papineau received a classical education at the Petit Sémi-naire de Quebec, and he became a lawyer, a liberal, and a great orator, who saw himself as a defender of Quebec's national heritage. The British defeated the French in the battle for Quebec in 1759, and were immedi-ately confronted by the challenge of consolidating military victory in political terms. In the Quebec Act of 1774, they restored Quebec to a semi-feudal status, with a seigneurial system of landholding and rule by an appointed governor. It was an arrangement pleasing to the church and most of the English-speaking merchant class.

The Constitutional Act of 1791 divided the province of Quebec into Upper and Lower Canada, and also provided for a governor with an appointed executive council, and an elected assembly, which had little power and no control. Although he was a seigneur himself, Papineau

demanded democratic reform, and became a leader of the Parti Patri-
ote. His speeches were suffused with contemporary liberal revolutionary ideas drawn from Europe, the U.S., and Latin America. Papineau
delivered this speech to a rally of four thousand people at Saint-Charles
on 23 October 1837.

When a people, even after expressing their views through all the avenues
recognized by constitutional procedure, through people's assemblies and
through their representatives in Parliament after mature deliberation, are
constantly exposed to systematic resistance; when their governors, instead of
redressing the various ills that they have themselves produced through their
bad government, solemnly record and declare their reprehensible determination to undermine and reverse the foundations of civil liberty, it becomes
the people's imperative duty to devote themselves seriously to considering
their unfortunate position and the dangers that surround them, and through
a well-designed organization to make the necessary arrangements to preserve intact their rights as citizens and their dignity as free human beings.

The wise and immortal writers of the American Declaration of Independence recorded in this document the principles on which the rights of
man are solely based, and demanded the advantageous establishment of the
institutions and form of government that alone can permanently ensure the
prosperity and social well-being of the inhabitants of this continent, whose
education and customs, linked to the circumstances of colonization, demand
a system of government that depends entirely on the people and is directly
responsible to the people.

In common with the various nations of North and South America that
have adopted the principles incorporated in this declaration, we regard the
doctrines that it contains as sacred and evident: that God did not create any
artificial distinctions between man and man; that government is only a simple human institution, formed by those who must be subject to its actions,
good or bad, and devoted to the benefit of all those who consent to come
or remain under its protection and control; and that therefore the form of
government can be changed when it no longer achieves the ends for which
it was established; that public authorities and men in power are only the
executors of the legitimately expressed wishes of the community, honoured
when they possess the confidence of the public and respected when they
enjoy public esteem; and that they must be removed from power when they

no longer give satisfaction to the people, the only legitimate source of all power.

In conformity with the treaties and capitulations drawn up with our ancestors and guaranteed by the imperial Parliament, the people of this province have for many years unceasingly submitted respectful petitions complaining of the intolerable abuses that poison their days and paralyze their industry. In response to our humble requests, instead of adjustments being granted, aggression has followed aggression, until finally it appears that we can no longer cling to the British Empire for our happiness and prosperity, our liberties, and the honour of the people and the Crown of England. The only aim has been to enrich a useless horde of officials who, not content with enjoying salaries that are hugely disproportionate to the duties of their position and to the resources of the country, have banded together in a faction driven purely by private interest to resist all reforms and defend all the iniquities of a government that is the enemy of the rights and liberties of this colony.

Papineau's speech led to an armed rebellion that was poorly organized and easily crushed by authorities. At approximately the same time, a similarly ill-fated revolt fired by the rhetoric of William Lyon Mackenzie was occurring in Upper Canada. Papineau fled to the United States, but later returned to become an elected member of the Assembly, advocating annexation to the United States. Mackenzie also fled to the United States, but was later pardoned and returned.

Louis-Hippolyte Lafontaine
25 August 1840

"The colonists must possess the management
of their own affairs"

As a youth Louis-Hippolyte Lafontaine was drawn to Papineau, but he disagreed with the armed revolt in 1837. He became a shrewd reformer who believed that Quebec could protect its French institutions, language, and culture within Canada. The competing tendencies of resistance and collaboration personified in Papineau and Lafontaine continue to characterize Quebec's public debate even today.

The British were embarrassed by the rebellions in 1837, and dispatched Lord Durham to Canada to study the situation. He had no respect for the Québécois and his clear intention was to assimilate them. He was, however, sympathetic to the argument that family compacts were abusing their privilege. His solution was to propose a single government for the two Canadas, with only English as the language of government. He recommended a measure of self-government, where the colonial administration would depend upon the confidence of an elected chamber. Britain responded with the Act of Union in 1841, which accepted a united Canada and assimilation of the French, but rejected responsible government.

Lafontaine had been elected as a deputy in Lower Canada, but now found himself in limbo with no elected assembly and no responsible government. He decided to continue the struggle, and significantly, to build an alliance with Reformers in Upper Canada, who were also agitating for responsible government.

His address to the Terrebonne electors on 25 August 1840 was seminal to the development of Canada as a democratic and multicultural state. His remarks obviously resonated in Upper Canada, because the address was quickly published in the *Toronto Examiner* in September 1840.

The union is at length decreed: Canada in the opinion of the imperial Parliament must henceforth be but one province . . . History will say that it was thrust by force upon the inhabitants of Lower and Upper Canada. To render the measure legitimate, their consent and approbation must be obtained. Their voice can make itself heard in the House of Assembly alone, where, nevertheless, the Imperial Act with its numerous injustices, will permit no more than a portion of their legitimate representatives to take their places in the first session of that new legislature.

The exercise of arbitrary power granted to the governor in chief may retard for a length of time the general election, as it may alike suddenly and unexpectedly call you to the hustings. Whether the event be near or distant, I shall not lose sight of my old engagements. Having been deputed to represent you in the Assembly of Lower Canada during two Parliaments if you have approved of my conduct and principles, as I have reason to believe, I proffer you once more my services in the united legislature . . .

The events which the future has in preparation for this country are of the highest importance—Canada is the land of our ancestors; it is our country as it must be the adopted country of the various populations which come from diverse portions of the globe, to make their way into its vast forests as the future resting place of their families and their hopes. Like us their paramount desire must be the happiness and prosperity of Canada, as the heritage which they should endeavour to transmit to their descendants in this young and hospitable country. Above all their children must be like ourselves, Canadians.

The greatest blessing enjoyed by the inhabitants of America is the social equality which reigns throughout this continent. If, in some of the old countries of another hemisphere, that equality should seem to suffice for the satisfaction of the wishes and wants of the inhabitants, it is insufficient alone to satisfy the vigorous populations of the new world. In addition to social equality, we must possess political liberty. Deprived of the latter, we might renounce all hope for the future; our wants would necessarily remain unsatisfied; and in vain would we strive to attain that state of well-being which the abundant resources of nature in America would seem to warrant . . .

But through what means is this political liberty, which is so essential to the peace, to the happiness and to the development of the vast resources of these colonies, to be obtained? Through the sanction of the popular will in the adoption of the laws; through the consent of the people in the voting and appropriation of the taxes; through the efficacious participation of the people in the action of government; through its influence legitimately exercised over the machinery of the administration, and its effective and constitutional control over those individuals to whom the direction of that administration is more immediately entrusted—in one word to the great question of the day: responsible government, such as it was recognized and promised to the Assembly of Upper Canada for the purpose of obtaining the consent of its members to the principle of the union, but not such as, in certain places, it may now perchance be defined . . .

For my part, I have no hesitation in declaring that I am in favour of this British principle of responsible government. I see in its operation the only guarantee we can have of a good and effective government. The colonists must possess the management of their own affairs. All their efforts must be directed toward this object in order to obtain which it will be necessary that the colonial administration be formed and controlled by and with the majority of the representatives of the people . . .

Another question not less important, is that which arises out of the union of the provinces—the union is an act of injustice and despotism; it is imposed upon us without our consent; it deprives Lower Canada of the legitimate number of its representatives; it wrests from us the use of our language in the legislature, contrary to the faith of treaties and the word of the governor general; it complies us to pay, without our consent, a debt which we have never contracted; and it empowers the executive to take illegal possession of an enormous portion of the revenues of the country, under the name of a civil list, without the consent of the representatives of the people.

Does it, therefore, follow that the representatives of Lower Canada should pledge themselves beforehand and unconditionally to demand the repeal of the union? No, they should not do so. They should wait before they adopt a determination, the immediate result of which might be to replace us, for an indefinite period under the legislation of a special council and leave us without any representation whatever . . .

The Reformers in the two provinces constitute an immense majority. Those of Upper Canada, or at least their representatives, have assumed the responsibility of the Union Bill, and of all its unjust and tyrannical conditions, by confiding, for all its details, in the discretion of the governor general. They will not, they cannot, approve of the manner in which the inhabitants of Lower Canada are treated by the bill. If they have been deceived in their expectations, they must protest against enactments which subject their political interests as well as ours to the caprice of the executive—if they should not do so, they would place the Reformers of Lower Canada in a false position in reference to them, and would thus incur the risk of retarding the progress of reform for long years to come.

They, as well as ourselves, would have to suffer from the internal divisions which such a state of things would inevitably give birth to. And yet theirs and ours is one common cause. It is the interest of the Reformers of both provinces to meet on the field of legislation, in a spirit of peace, of union, of friendship, and of fraternity. Unity of purpose is more necessary now than ever. I entertain no doubt that the Reformers of Upper Canada feel this necessity as deeply as ourselves, and that in the first session of the legislature, they will give us unequivocal proofs of that feeling, as a pledge of mutual and enduring confidence . . .

Such are my views of the leading features of our political position. If they are yours you will prove it on the day when, in common with your brother Reformers, you will be called upon to choose a member to represent you in the united legislature.

Lafontaine formed an administration with Robert Baldwin, an Upper Canadian Reformer, in 1842, and again in 1848, when the British finally accepted responsible government for the Canadas. Lafontaine became the first prime minister of Canada, albeit of only two provinces.

Joseph Howe

22 March 1841

"Start with the proposition that every child shall have the rudiments of education"

Joseph Howe believed that an unfettered press and the free flow of ideas were essential to the existence of responsible government. He believed that education was key to the ability to form ideas worthy of free citizens. Howe was a close observer of the United States, and was impressed by the results of a tax-assessed public school system in New England. He had been elected to the Nova Scotia Assembly in 1836, and in this speech he argues that education should be available to everyone. He is much more personal in his observations than was common in speeches of the day, and he clearly attempts to establish his motives as worthy and disinterested. His ideas about the value of universal education were not popular among his political opponents and the Anglican Church at the time.

If I could see a large majority of the House declare that education should be within the reach of every family in the province, that every child should get the rudiments of learning, I would willingly assume the responsibility and would cheerfully retire from the Assembly if that should be the penalty, satisfied that I, as one, have done good enough; that those with whom I have been associated have conferred great blessings on the country, and might leave subsequent legislation to our successors. I hope to see the day when that will carry, and to find, even now, in this committee, something like a free expression in favour of the principle. Members are apt to become so engaged with local interests as almost to unfit their minds for the calm consideration of great topics. But I appeal to gentlemen who are proud of the province that they are entrusted to represent whether anything is so calculated to excite attention as the question, whether the people shall be universally educated, or one-third be allowed to remain in lamentable ignorance?

I may turn for illustration to countries which we should be happy to follow—to those ancient systems which modern times are proud to imitate—and ask whether it is not the duty of Nova Scotians, in this early stage of the history of their country, to endeavour after similar advantages. Look to the United States; persons have said that the free institutions of that country have caused it to make the progress for which it has become remarkable. I honour those who founded the infant republic—under the circumstances they did wisely—but was it the mere political institutions that conferred superiority? Were not the boundless resources of a young country operated on by almost universal intelligence? What gave an active population to the valley of the Mississippi, to the territory of Texas, to the western prairies, except a surplus population which had been trained in the common schools of New England? Massachusetts, by its almost universal mental cultivation, could throw off its swarms to every point of the compass, which were ready to direct and lead the way among new communities.

In the olden time, it was well known, although the phrase is modern, that "knowledge is power." No people ever rose to eminence, no nation ever attained a brilliant rank in the pages of the past, which did not acknowledge the maxim. Who now runs over ancient story for the purpose of reading deeds of arms, of fields marked by carnage; who now tracks the steps of the rude destroyer, who made battles his pride and pleasure and set up a false standard of worth before a misled people? Is not the subject of study, rather, the progress of knowledge, the growth of art and science, and the elevation of nations in the moral and intellectual scale? If the fact that knowledge is power was known in ancient days and prized, how much more should it be now, and in a country such as Nova Scotia? Look at its size, its position, the number of its inhabitants and by whom they are surrounded, and strong inducements will be at once seen for the spread of intelligence and by it the multiplication of power. We are but two hundred thousand, in a narrow space, surrounded by millions. Are we not called on to increase our energies? And how? Is it by attempting to wrest power from those who constitutionally possess it—by assuming anything which a colonial condition renders inexpedient? No, but by increasing information and intellect—by adding to the intelligent minds who can illustrate the axiom that knowledge is power. Even when the Micmac roved unchecked through the wilderness, knowledge—the knowledge of the woods, native talent, energy, and acuteness—gave one man influence over another and proved the truth of the maxim. Classic history teems with evidences of the superiority of the educated over the mere physical mass. How much more is this the case in modern times. Now, instead of the wooden horse and the catapultae and the burning glass, there are the battering-train, the shell, and the army surrounded by all the appliances of modern science. Then, in the peaceful arts, they had but feeble attainments—now, there is the railroad, the steamship, the factory, and all that so vastly increases human capability.

It may be said that the province is only a small dependency of a great empire, and therefore it should be content with its present status. Would that be the reasoning of an intelligent youth, would he be satisfied with his father's character and acquirements and not seek reputation for himself? If that would be unwise and improper in the son of a family, so would it be in a colony, however small. The duty of the province is, so far as it can, to emulate the example of that great country from which it sprang, and if possible to go beyond it in the intellectual race. If I am asked what kind of knowledge I would cultivate here, my answer is, first give your civilization a base co-extensive with the province, and let, if you choose, its apex pierce the highest heaven of imagination and art. Start with the proposition that every child shall have the rudiments of education—that from Cape North to Cape Sable, there shall not be a family beyond the reach of common schools; not a child who is not acquainted with reading, writing, and arithmetic; give them the means for the highest progress, if you will, but make sure of the broad basis for all. Be certain that all have the rudiments, leaving the higher steps, in the sufficiently abundant seminaries of learning, to those who may be inclined to ascend them. How is the province to maintain its own station among surrounding multitudes? The mere boundaries may be protected by the armies of England; but the people will, of necessity, be influenced mentally and politically by those around them, as one portion of the human family operates on its neighbours—unless their intelligence and civilization are higher than those of the surrounding masses, in which case they will become the operating power. Leave education as at present, and the country must be influenced by the energy and talent of those around; make education co-extensive with the population, give the people a high position, and then they will exert an influence on all surrounding countries. Would not that be wise? Should we not emulate the bright example of the mother country, and prove that here the British blood and language and name have not degenerated? Although of necessity cut off from many means of information and stores of literature and learning, which time had accumulated there, we would show that we have made the most of our limited resources, and so far as we can, have elevated our portion of the people of America. Are there any who do not feel pride in the Nova Scotian enterprise which bridged the Atlantic with steamships and at other evidences of the provincial character and genius which made the country better known at home? Are any so careless of the character of the whole people as not to give them all the advantages which they ought to possess? This may not be the time—the gentlemen may not be prepared to go into all the details necessary for perfecting a measure founded on assessment—but we should exchange views on it and compare notes, and so hasten the hour at which it may be secured.

The triangle is a simple figure, yet by its properties oceans are traversed and planets measured. The three elements of reading, writing, and arithmetic are simple in themselves, yet the schoolboy, qualified with these, has the means of all knowledge; not of the mere information that is acquired by experience and observation, but of that which passes from hand to hand, and is the result of labour and genius and scientific inquiry. The gentlemen may feel the importance of what I am urging by asking what consideration they would allow these rudiments and all they had acquired by them to be stricken from their minds. We are but fifty men; yet if that blank were made, would not the country miss our varied information? Where would our families turn for the skill which wisely conducted their affairs? Where would we ourselves turn for the accumulated stores on which we now rely for the duties of mature life and for the solace of old age? We are only fifty men assembled on the floor of this House; and if the idea urged is painful, if we cannot bear the thought of being robbed of those sources of pleasure and power, if we would prefer parting with everything else than the knowledge and intelligence that distinguish us from the mass, we should ask ourselves, are there not ten thousand Nova Scotians growing up without the simplest rudiments of learning?

Peau de Chat

18 August 1848

"The Indians are uneasy seeing their lands occupied by the Whites"

Aboriginal people have lived in what is now Canada since time immemorial. Their early contacts with the arriving Europeans were not always positive ones, but for more than two hundred years they traded with them, practised diplomacy, participated in alliances, and at times fought in their wars on one side or the other. By the mid-1800s, Indians in Ontario were becoming alarmed at the apparently endless incursions by whites. Geologists searching for minerals on the north shores of Lake Huron discovered copper and the Bruce Mine opened in 1846. T. G. Anderson, vice-superintendent of Indian Affairs, held a council at Sault Ste. Marie in August 1848 to prepare for a treaty. Peau de Chat was chief of the Fort William Indians and here he attempts to answer Anderson's query about what justification Indians have to lay claim to lands. Consistent with Indian oratory, the chief's comments are rich in imagery and metaphor, and he invents or recalls conversations in an attributed way.

Father, you ask how we possess this land....You White people well know and we Red Skins know how we came in possession of this land. It was the Great Spirit who gave it to us, from the time my ancestors came upon this earth it has been considered ours. After a time, the Whites living on the other side of the Great Salt Lake found this part of the world inhabited by the Red Skins. The Whites asked us Indians, when there were many animals here, "Would you not sell the skins of these various animals for the goods I bring?" Our old ancestors said, "Yes, I will bring your goods." They, the Whites, did not say anything more, nor did the Indian say anything. I did not know that he said, "Come, I will buy your land, everything that is on it, under it." He, the White, said nothing about that to me, and this is the reason why I believe that we possess this land up to this day. When at last the Whites came to this country where now they are numerous, he, the English, did not say, "I will after a time get your land," or "Give me your land." He said indeed to our forefathers, when he fought with the French and conquered them, "Come on our side and fight them, and be our children." They did so, and every time you wanted to fight the Big Knives you said to the Indians, "Won't you assist me?" "Yes, we will help you." This man [pointing to Shinguaconse] was there and he was in much misery. The English were very strong when we gave our assistance. When the war was over, the English did not say, "I will have your land," nor did we say, "You may have it." And this, Father, you know, this is how we are in possession of this land. It will be known everywhere if the Whites get it from us.

Father, you ask in what instances the Whites prevent our farming. There are bad people among us who are continually saying to us, "Don't farm, live as Indians always did, you will be unhappy if you cultivate the land, take your gun, go and hunt, bring the skins to me, and leave off tilling the soil." And the Queen says to me, "Become Christian, my children." "Yes," I say, "we will become Christians." But when this bad man [the trader] sees me he says, "Leave it alone, do as you formerly did." And this is the way he destroys my religion and farming. This is the way I explain the question you have now asked me.

Father, the miners burn the land and drive away the animals, destroying the land. Game, much timber is destroyed, and I am very sorry for it. When they find mineral, they cover it once with clay so that the Indians may not see it and I now begin to think that the White man wishes to take away and to steal my land . . . I wish to let the governor have both land and mineral. I expect him to ask me for it, and this is what would be for our good. I do not wish to pass any reflections on the conduct of the Whites. Ask me then, send someone to ask for my land, my mineral. I won't be unwilling to let it go. The government shall have it if they give us good pay. I do not regret a word I have said. You, Father, you are a White man. Make yourself an Indian, take an Indian's heart, come assist me to root out the evil that has been among us and I will be glad. Answer me, is there anything that requires explanation?

Father, the Indians are uneasy seeing their lands occupied by the Whites, taking away the mineral, and they wish that our Great Father would at once settle the matter. Come and ask me for my land and mineral that there be no bad feelings left. I am sorry, my heart is troubled. I don't know what would be good for us. It will not do for me, an Indian, to say to the governor, "Come buy my land, yes, this is what I think would be very good, yes, very good for my people." Then the White man, the miner and trader could do what he liked with the land, and so could the Indian on that part which we would like to reserve. When we give our land up, we will reserve a piece for ourselves and we, with our families, will live happily on it, we will do what we please with it. There [pointing to Fort William], I will find out a place for myself. Perhaps you will come and arrange matters. It would be well if you could, and if an officer cannot come this autumn to settle our affairs, I will look out for one in the spring to do it for me and this is nearly all I have to say. Tell the governor at Montreal to send a letter and let us know what he will do and what our land is worth. In the meantime I will converse with my tribe on the subject. When I am going to sell my land, I will speak again and settle matters.

Thomas D'Arcy McGee
1860

"I call it a northern nation, for such it must become"

Historian Desmond Morton calls Thomas D'Arcy McGee the "image-maker of Confederation." Born in Ireland, he emigrated at age seventeen to the United States where he became a newspaper editor. He moved to Montreal in 1857. He was a man with many interests, a historian and poet, the author of many books, and he was the most accomplished orator among the pre-Confederation politicians. He had a wide knowledge and vocabulary, and took delight in exhibiting both. He became a proponent of a federation in British North America, casting an anxious eye to the territorial ambitions being expressed south of the border. He was elected from Montreal to the Legislative Assembly of the Canadas in 1858. He worked with John A. Macdonald and George-Étienne Cartier. While he lacked their political influence, he became the most eloquent proponent of a new northern nation.

I entreat the House to believe that I have spoken without respect of persons, and with a single desire for the increase, prosperity, freedom, and honour of this incipient northern nation. I call it a northern nation, for such it must become, if all of us do our duty to the last. Men do not talk on this continent of changes wrought by centuries, but of the events of years. Men do not vegetate in this age, as they did formerly, in one spot, occupying one portion. Thought outruns the steam car, and hope outflies the telegraph. We live more in ten years in this era than the patriarch did in a thousand. The patriarch might outlive the palm tree which was planted to commemorate his birth, and yet not see so many wonders as we have witnessed since the Constitution we are now discussing was formed. What marvels have not been wrought in Europe and America from 1840 to 1860! And who can say the world, or our own portion of it more particularly, is incapable of maintaining to the end of the century the ratio of the past progress? I for one cannot presume to say so. I look to the future of my adopted country with hope, though not without anxiety. I see in the not remote distance one great nationality, bound, like the shield of Achilles, by the blue rim of ocean. I see it quartered into many communities, each disposing of its internal affairs, but all bound together by free institutions, free intercourse, and free commerce. I see within the round of that shield the peaks of the western mountains and the crests of the eastern waves, the winding Assiniboine, the five-fold lakes: the St. Lawrence, the Ottawa, the Saguenay, the St. John, and the basin of Minas. By all these flowing rivers, in all the valleys they fertilize, in all the cities they visit in their courses, I see a generation of industrious, contented, moral men, free in name and in fact, men capable of maintaining, in peace and in war, a constitution worthy of such a country.

Thomas D'Arcy McGee

1862

"A Canadian nationality, not French-Canadian,
nor British-Canadian, nor Irish-Canadian: patriotism
rejects the prefix"

Thomas D'Arcy McGee's speech about a Canadian nationality was delivered three years prior to the conferences in Charlottetown and Quebec City, which negotiated the details of Confederation. In 1862, there was no sense of a pan-Canadian nationality. People considered themselves to be citizens of their locale (Nova Scotia, Quebec, or Upper Canada), or in some cases, simply citizens of the British Empire. Race and religion were great fault lines in the British colonies. McGee had been an Irish nationalist, but came to oppose that project, and in particular the Fenians who pursued Irish revolution and who were active in the United States, launching border raids into Canada. McGee was promoting what we might now call an un-hyphenated Canadianism, a concept echoed by others, including John Diefenbaker, a century later. This is probably McGee's most celebrated address.

It is upon this subject of the public spirit which can alone make Canada safe and secure, rich and renowned, which can alone attract population and augment capital, that I desire to say the few words with which I must endeavour to fulfill your expectations. I feel that it is a serious subject . . . but these are serious times, and they bring upon their wings most serious reflections. That shot fired at Fort Sumter on 12 April 1861, had a message for the North as well as for the South, and here in Quebec, if anywhere, by the light which history lends us, we should find those who can rightly read that eventful message. Here, from this rock for which the immortals have contended, here, from this rock over which Richelieu's wisdom and Chatham's genius, and the memory of heroic men, the glory of three great nations has hung its halo, we should look forth upon a continent convulsed, and ask of a ruler, "Watchman, what of the night?" That shot fired at Fort Sumter was the signal gun of a new epoch for North America, which told the people of Canada, more plainly than human speech can ever express it, to sleep no more, except on their arms, unless in their sleep they desire to be overtaken and subjugated. For one, I can safely say that if I know myself I have not a particle of prejudice against the United States; on the contrary, I am bound to declare that many things in the Constitution and the people I sincerely esteem and admire. What I contend for with myself, and what I would impress upon others, is that the lesson of the last few months furnished by America to the world should not be thrown away upon the inhabitants of Canada. I do not believe that it is our destiny to be engulfed into a Republican union, renovated and inflamed with the wine of victory, of which she now drinks so freely; it seems to me we have theatre enough under our feet to act another and a worthier part. We can hardly join the Americans on our own terms, and we never ought to join them on theirs. A Canadian nationality—not French-Canadian, nor British-Canadian, nor Irish-Canadian: patriotism rejects the prefix—is, in my opinion, what we should look forward to, that is what we ought to labour for, that is what we ought to be prepared to defend to the death. Heirs of one-seventh of the continent, inheritors of a long ancestral history—and no part of it dearer to us than the glorious tale of this last century—warned not by cold chronicles only but by living scenes passing before our eyes of the dangers of an unmixed democracy, we are here to vindicate our capacity by the test of a new political creation. What we most immediately want to carry on that work is men, more men, and still more men. The ladies, I dare say, will not object to that doctrine. We may not want more lawyers and doctors, but we want more men, in town and country. We want the signs of youth and growth in our young and growing country. One of our maxims should be: "Early marriages and death to old bachelors." I have long entertained a project of a special tax upon that most undesirable class of the population, and our friend the finance minister may perhaps have something of the kind among the agreeable surprises of his next budget.

Seriously . . . if we would make Canada safe and secure, rich and renowned, we must all liberalize, locally, sectionally, religiously, nationally. There is room enough in this country for one great free people; but there is not room enough, under the same flag and the same laws, for two or three angry, suspicious, obstructive nationalities. Dear, most justly dear to every land beneath the sun, are the children born in her bosom and nursed upon her breast; but when the man of another country, wherever born, speaking whatever speech, holding whatever creed, seeks out a country to serve and honour and cleave to, in weal or in woe, when he heaves up the anchor of his heart from its old moorings, and lays at the feet of the mistress of his choice—his new country—all the hopes of his ripe manhood, he establishes by such devotion a claim to consideration not second even to that of the children of the soil. He is their brother delivered by a new birth from the dark-wombed Atlantic ship that ushers him into existence in the new world; he stands by his own election among the children of the household; and narrow and unwise is that species of public spirit which, in the perverted name of patriotism, would refuse him all he asks . . . I am not about to talk politics . . . but I am so thoroughly convinced and assured that we are gliding along the currents of a new epoch, that if I break silence at all, in the presence of my fellow subjects, I cannot choose but speak of the immense issues which devolve upon us, at this moment, in this country. Though we are alike opposed to all invidious national distinctions on this soil, we are not opposed, I hope, to giving full credit to all the elements which at the present day compose our population . . .

We Irishmen, Protestant and Catholic, born and bred in a land of religious controversy, should never forget that we now live and act in a land of the fullest religious and civil liberty. All we have to do is, each for himself, to keep down dissensions which can only weaken, impoverish, and keep back the country; each for himself do all he can to increase its wealth, its strength, and its reputation; each for himself . . . to welcome every talent, to hail every invention, to cherish every gem of art, to foster every gleam of authorship, to honour every acquirement and every natural gift, to lift ourselves to the level of our destinies, to rise above all low limitations and narrow circumscriptions, to cultivate that true catholicity of spirit which embraces all creeds, all classes, and all races, in order to make of our boundless province, so rich in known and unknown resources, a great new northern nation.

On a spring evening in 1868, McGee was assassinated in Ottawa, and suspicion was that it was a Fenian plot.

John A. Macdonald
6 February 1865

"The best interests and present and future prosperity of British North America will be promoted by a federal union under the Crown of Great Britain"

The 1841 Act of Union brought Upper and Lower Canada together into one province, but it was a situation destined for deadlock. Governments came and went with regularity, and there were three general elections held from 1858 to 1864. Reformers fought Conservatives, and the French and English did not trust one another. George Brown, publisher of the *Globe* in Toronto, and John A. Macdonald's long-time political rival, led the Reformers. They demanded representation by population, a slogan that contained political logic, but which would, they knew, weaken Lower Canada because Upper Canada was growing more quickly. Brown was opposed by an alliance of Upper Canadian Conservatives and Quebec bleus, led, respectively, by John A. Macdonald and George-Étienne Cartier.

Great Britain wanted to be relieved of the expensive burden of protecting its colonies in Canada, and had come to believe, in any event, that Canada was not defensible against the Americans. The outbreak of the American Civil War in 1860 had a sobering effect on everyone.

By the time the Macdonald-Cartier government fell in 1864, Macdonald and George Brown had both concluded that the only way ahead for Canada lay in a federation that went beyond Upper and Lower Canada. In September 1864, the colonies of Nova Scotia, New Brunswick, Prince Edward Island, and Newfoundland planned to meet in Charlottetown to investigate a union among the Maritime colonies. Macdonald, Brown, and other representatives from Upper and Lower Canada had themselves invited to the meeting, and arrived by steamship.

It was Macdonald who prepared much of the Canadian material for the Charlottetown Conference in 1864, and another that followed in Quebec City in 1865. Macdonald's was the first of many speeches that occurred at the Quebec Conference to finalize a larger union. He was not in a league with Joseph Howe or D'Arcy McGee as an orator, but he was the drafter and deal-maker of Confederation, and was to remain the dominant presence in Canadian politics for many years.

This subject, which now absorbs the attention of the people of Canada, and of the whole of British North America, is not a new one. For years, it has more or less attracted the attention of every statesman and politician in these provinces, and has been looked upon by many far-seeing politicians as being eventually the means of deciding and settling very many of the vexed questions which have retarded the prosperity of the colonies as a whole, and particularly the prosperity of Canada . . .

The result was that when we met here on the 10th of October, on the first day on which we assembled after the full and free discussions which had taken place at Charlottetown, the first resolution now before this House was passed unanimously, being received with acclamation as, in the opinion of everyone who heard it, a proposition which ought to receive, and would receive, the sanction of each government and each people. The resolution is: "That the best interests and present and future prosperity of British North America will be promoted by a federal union under the Crown of Great Britain, provided such union can be effected on principles just to the several provinces."

It seemed to all the statesmen assembled—and there are great statesmen in the lower provinces, men who would do honour to any government and to any legislature of any free country enjoying representative institutions— it was clear to them all that the best interests and present and future prosperity of British North America would be promoted by a federal union under the Crown of Great Britain. And it seems to me, as to them, and I think it will so appear to the people of this country that, if we wish to be a great people; if we wish to form . . . a great nationality, commanding the respect of the world, able to hold our own against all opponents, and to defend those institutions we prize; if we wish to have one system of government, and to establish a commercial union with unrestricted free trade between people of the five provinces, belonging, as they do, to the same nation, obeying the same sovereign, owning the same allegiance, and being, for the most part, of the same blood and lineage; if we wish to be able to afford to each other the means of mutual defence and support against aggression and attack, this can only be obtained by a union of some kind between the scattered and weak boundaries composing the British North American provinces . . .

Now, as regards the comparative advantages of a legislative or a federal union, I have never hesitated to state my own opinions. I have again and again stated in the House that, if practicable, I thought a legislative union would be preferable. I have always contended that if we could agree to have one government and one Parliament legislating for the whole of these peoples, it would be the best, the cheapest, the most vigorous, and the strongest system of government we could adopt. But, on looking at the subject in the conference, and discussing the matter as we did, most unreservedly, and with a desire to arrive at a satisfactory conclusion, we found that such a system was impracticable. In the first place, it would not meet the assent of the people of Lower Canada, because they felt that in their peculiar position—being in a minority, with a different language, nationality, and religion from the majority—in case of a junction with the provinces, their institutions and their laws might be assailed, and their ancestral associations, on which they prided themselves, attacked and prejudiced; it was found that any proposition which involved the absorption of the individuality of Lower Canada, if I may use the expression, would not be received with favour by her people. We found too, that though their people speak the same language and enjoy the same system of law as the people of Upper Canada, a system founded on the common law of England, there was as great a disinclination on the part of the various Maritime provinces to lose their individuality, as separate political organizations, as we observed in the case of Lower Canada herself. Therefore, we were forced to the conclusion that we must either abandon the idea of union altogether, or devise a system of union in which the separate provincial organizations would be in some degree preserved. So that those who were, like myself, in favour of a legislative union, were obliged to modify their views and accept the project of a federal union as the only scheme practicable, even for the Maritime provinces . . .

I trust the scheme will be assented to as a whole. I am sure this House will not seek to alter it in its unimportant details; and, if altered in any important provisions, the result must be that the whole will be set aside, and we must begin *de novo*. If any important changes are made, every one of the colonies will feel itself absolved from the implied obligation to deal with it as a treaty, each province will feel itself at liberty to amend it *ad libitum* so as to suit its own views and interests; in fact, the whole of our labours will have been for naught, and we will have to renew our negotiations with all the colonies for the purpose of establishing some new scheme. I hope the House will not adopt any such a course as will postpone, perhaps forever, or at all events for a long period, all chances of union. All the statesmen and public men who have written or spoken on the subject admit the advantages of a union, if it were practicable, and now when it is proved to be practicable, if we do not embrace this opportunity the present favourable time will pass away, and we may never have it again . . .

If we are not blind to our present position, we must see the hazardous situation in which all the great interests of Canada stand in respect to the United States. I am no alarmist. I do not believe in the prospect of immediate war. I believe that the common sense of the two nations will prevent a war; still we cannot trust to probabilities. The government and legislature would be wanting in their duty to the people if they ran any risk. We know that the United States at this moment are engaged in a war of enormous dimensions, that the occasion of a war with Great Britain has again and again arisen, and may at any time in the future again arise. We cannot foresee what may be the result; we cannot say but that the two nations may drift into a war as other nations have done before. It would then be too late when war had commenced to think of measures for strengthening ourselves, or to begin negotiations for a union with the sister provinces . . .

The conference having come to the conclusion that a legislative union, pure and simple, was impracticable, our next attempt was to form a government upon federal principles, which would give to the general government the strength of a legislative and administrative union, while at the same time it preserved that liberty of action for the different sections which is allowed by a federal union. And I am strong in the belief that we have hit upon the happy medium in those resolutions, and that we have formed a scheme of government which unites the advantages of both, giving us the strength of a legislative union and the sectional freedom of a federal union, with protection to local interests . . .

In conclusion, I would again implore the House not to let this opportunity to pass. It is an opportunity that may never recur. At the risk of repeating myself, I would say, it was only by a happy concurrence of circumstances that we were enabled to bring this great question to its present position. If we do not take advantage of the time, if we show ourselves unequal to the occasion, it may never return, and we shall hereafter bitterly and unavailingly regret having failed to embrace the happy opportunity now offered of founding a great nation under the fostering care of Great Britain, and our sovereign lady, Queen Victoria.

George Brown
16 February 1865

"It may be that some among us will live to see the day when, as a result of this measure, a great and powerful people have grown up in these lands"

George Brown's Reform Party advocated free trade and representation by population, and he believed that any close union with Lower Canada was an obstacle to Upper Canada's future and prosperity. Brown either came to realize that the continuing political gridlock benefited no one and he was able to rise above his antipathies, or he saw in a pan-Canadian federation a solution that would eventually strengthen Protestant Upper Canada. Whatever his motive, Brown's speech during the 1865 Confederation debates was one of the best.

The scene presented by this Chamber at this moment, I venture to affirm, has few parallels in history. One hundred years have passed away since these provinces became by conquest part of the British Empire. I speak in no boastful spirit—what was then the fortune of war of the brave French nation might have been ours on that well-fought field. I recall those olden times merely to mark the fact that here sit today the descendents of the victors and the vanquished in the fight of 1759, with all the differences of language, religion, civil law, and social habit nearly as distinctly marked as they were a century ago. Here we sit today seeking amicably to find a remedy for constitutional evils and injustice complained of, by the vanquished? No, but complained of by the conquerors! Here sit the representatives of the British population claiming justice, only justice; and here sit the representatives of the French population discussing in the French tongue whether we shall have it. One hundred years have passed away since the conquest of Quebec, but here sit the children of the victor and the vanquished, all avowing hearty attachment to the British Crown, all earnestly deliberating how we shall best extend the blessings of British institutions, how a great people may be established on this continent in close and hearty connection with Great Britain.

No constitution ever framed was without defect; no act of human wisdom was ever free from imperfection; no amount of talent and wisdom and integrity combined in preparing such a scheme could have placed it beyond the reach of criticism. And the framers of this scheme had immense special difficulties to overcome. We had the prejudices of race and language and religion to deal with; and we had to encounter all the rivalries of trade and commerce, and all the jealousies of diversified local interests. To assert, then, that our scheme is without fault would be folly. It was necessarily the work of concession; not one of the thirty-three framers but had, on some points, to yield his opinions; and, for myself, I freely admit that I struggled earnestly, for days together, to have portions of the scheme amended. But admitting all this, admitting all the difficulties that beset us, admitting frankly that defects in the measure exist, I say that, taking the scheme as a whole, it has my cordial, enthusiastic support, without hesitation or reservation. I believe that it will accomplish all, and more than all, that we, who have so long fought the battle of parliamentary reform, ever hoped to see accomplished. I believe that, while granting security for local interests, it will give free scope for carrying out the will of the whole people in general matters; that it will draw closer the bonds that unite us to Great Britain; and that it will lay the foundations deep and strong of a powerful and prosperous people . . .

The interests to be affected by this scheme of union are very large and varied; but the pressure of circumstances upon all the colonies is so serious at this moment that if we cannot now banish partisanship and sectionalism and petty objections, and look at the matter on its broad intrinsic merits, what hope is there of our ever being able to do so? An appeal to the people of Canada on this measure simply means postponement of the question for a year, and who can tell how changed ere then may the circumstances surrounding us?

The man who strives for the postponement of this measure, on any ground, is doing what he can to kill it almost as effectually as if he voted against it. Let there be no mistake as to the manner in which the government presents this measure to the House. We do not present it as free from fault, but we do present it as a measure so advantageous to the people of Canada that all the blemishes, real or imaginary, averred against it sink into utter insignificance in presence of its merits. We present it, not in the precise shape we in Canada would desire it, but as in the best shape the five colonies to be united could agree upon it. We present it in the form in which the five governments have severally adopted it, in the form the imperial government has endorsed it, and in the form in which we believe all the legislatures of the province will accept it. We ask the House to pass it in the exact form in which we have presented it, for we know not how alterations may affect its safety in other places; and the process of alteration once commenced in four different legislatures, who can tell where that would end? Every member of this House is free as air to criticize it if he so wills, and amend it if he is able; but we warn him of the danger of amendment, and throw on him all the responsibility of the consequences. We feel confident of carrying this scheme as it stands, but we cannot tell what we can do if it be amended. Let not honourable gentlemen approach this measure as a sharp critic deals with an abstract question, striving to point out blemishes and display his ingenuity; but let us approach it as men having but one consideration before us, the establishment of the future peace and prosperity of our country. Let us look at it in the light of a few months back, in the light of the evils and injustice to which it applies a remedy, in the light of the years of discord and strife we have spent in seeking for that remedy, in the light with which the people of Canada would regard this measure were it to be lost and all the evils of past years to be brought back upon us again. Let honourable gentlemen look at the question in this view, and what one of them will take the responsibility of casting his vote against the measure?

The future destiny of these great provinces may be affected by the decision we are about to give to an extent which at this moment we may be unable to estimate, but assuredly the welfare for many years of four millions of people hangs on our decision. Shall we then rise equal to the occasion? Shall we approach this discussion without partisanship, and free from every personal feeling but the earnest resolution to discharge conscientiously the duty which an overruling Providence has placed upon us? It may be that some among us will live to see the day when, as the result of this measure, a great and powerful people have grown up in these lands, when all the boundless forests all around us shall have given way to smiling fields and thriving towns, and when one united government, under the British flag, shall extend from shore to shore. But who would desire to see that day if he could not recall with satisfaction the part he took in this discussion?

Antoine-Aimé Dorion
16 February 1865

"The people of Lower Canada are attached to
their institutions in a manner that defies any
attempt to change them"

Dorion was a Quebec lawyer and leader of the Parti Rouge (Liberals) in the 1850s, and he had served with George Brown in a short-lived government. He favoured a loose federation of Upper and Lower Canada, but was opposed to a wider confederation, as were a majority of the francophone delegates to the Quebec Conference. They feared that the English majority would inundate the French if the concept of representation by population, promoted by George Brown and other Reformers, were to be introduced. Dorion strongly opposed the motion prepared and promoted by John A. Macdonald for a legislative union, in which the central government held most of the power. Dorion's arguments in 1865 illustrate the historic conflict between French and English over the founding reality of Canada—was Confederation the union of two nations, or was it a federation of equal provinces? These conflicting views still exist.

Dorion also charged that Confederation was, as much as anything, a scheme by railway interests to have a new federal government pay for their grandiose schemes for new railway construction.

I should have desired to make my remarks to the House in French, but considering the large number of honourable members who are not familiar with that language, I think it my duty to speak at the present time in English. In rising on this occasion to address the House on the important question submitted to us, I must say I do so with an unusual degree of embarrassment, not only on account of the importance of the subject of our deliberations, but also because I have to differ from many of those with whom I have been in the habit of acting ever since I first entered into political life . . .

I should say that, when the Brown-Dorion administration was formed, the honourable president of the council urged very strongly that representation by population should be taken up as the method by which to settle the constitutional question; while, on the contrary, I saw the difficulty of so taking it up, even with such checks and guarantees as were spoken of, and made the counterproposition that a confederation of the two provinces should be formed . . .

I know that majorities are naturally aggressive and how the possession of power engenders despotism, and I can understand how a majority, animated this moment by the best feelings, might in six or nine months be willing to abuse its power and trample on the rights of the minority, while acting in good faith, and on what it considered to be its right. We know also the ill feelings that might be engendered by such a course. I think it but just that the Protestant minority should be protected in its rights in everything that was dear to it as a distinct nationality, and should not lie at the discretion of the majority in this respect, and for this reason I am ready to extend to my Protestant fellow citizens in Lower Canada of British origin the fullest justice in all things, and I wish to see their interests as a minority guaranteed and protected in every scheme which may be adopted.

With these views on the question of representation, I pronounced in favour of a confederation of the two provinces of Upper and Lower Canada as the best means of protecting the varied interests of the two sections. But the confederation I advocated was a real confederation, giving the largest powers to the local governments, and merely a delegated authority to the general government, in that respect differing *in toto* from the one now proposed which gives all the powers to the central government, and reserves for the local governments the smallest possible amount of freedom of action. There is nothing besides in what I have ever written or said that can be interpreted as favouring a confederation of all the provinces. This I always opposed . . .

This scheme proposes a union not only with Nova Scotia, New Brunswick, Prince Edward Island, and Newfoundland, but also with British Columbia and Vancouver's Island. Although I have not been able to get the information from the government, for they do not seem to be very ready to give information, yet I understand that there are dispatches to hand, stating that resolutions have been adopted in the legislature of British Columbia asking for admission into the confederation at once. I must confess . . . that it looks like a burlesque to speak as a means of defence of a scheme of confederation to unite the whole country extending from Newfoundland to Vancouver's Island, thousands of miles intervening without any communication, except through the United States or around Cape Horn . . .

So far as Lower Canada is concerned, I need hardly stop to point out the objections to the scheme. It is evident, from what has transpired, that it is intended eventually to form a legislative union of all the provinces. The local governments in addition to the general government will be found so burdensome that a majority of the people will appeal to the imperial government for the formation of a legislative union . . .

Honourable members from Lower Canada are made aware that the delegates all desired a legislative union, but it could not be accomplished at once. This confederation is the first necessary step towards it. The British government is ready to grant a federal union at once, and when that is accomplished the French element will be completely overwhelmed by the majority of British representatives. What then would prevent the federal government from passing a set of resolutions in a similar way to those we are called upon to pass, without submitting them to the people, calling upon the imperial government to set aside the federal form of government and give a legislative union instead of it?

Perhaps the people of Upper Canada think a legislative union a most desirable thing. I can tell those gentlemen that the people of Lower Canada are attached to their institutions in a manner that defies any attempt to change them in that way. They will not change their religious institutions, their laws, and their language, for any consideration whatever. A million of inhabitants may seem a small affair to the mind of a philosopher who sits down to write out a constitution. He may think it would be better that there should be but one religion, one language, and one system of laws, and he goes to work to frame institutions that will bring all to that desirable state; but I can tell honourable gentlemen that the history of every country goes to show that not even by the power of the sword can such changes be accomplished . . .

There is no hurry in regard to the scheme. We are now legislating for the future as well as for the present, and feeling that we ought to make a constitution as perfect as possible, and as far as possible in harmony with the views of the people, I maintain that we ought not to pass the measure now, but leave it to another year, in order to ascertain in the meantime what the views and sentiments of the people actually are.

George-Étienne Cartier
20 October 1866

"French Canadians have no need
to be afraid of the English"

George-Étienne Cartier came from a wealthy and influential Quebec family. He was involved, as a young man, in Papineau's 1837 rebellion, and in its aftermath escaped to Vermont. He returned to Canada in 1858 and came to believe that the rights and culture of the French could best be protected within a Canadian federation. When Canada received responsible government in 1848, he ran for election, and later served as co-premier with John A. Macdonald from 1857 to 1862. Together, they set in motion the movement toward Confederation. Cartier was to become Macdonald's key ally over many years. He gave the following speech in Montreal just prior to leaving for London in October 1866.

I, too, am a French Canadian, like many of those I see around me. I love my race, and of course I have a very natural predilection for it; but as a politician and as a citizen, I love others as well. And I am happy to see, in this meeting of fellow citizens of all classes, races, and religions, that my compatriots have recognized these feelings in me. I have already had the opportunity to declare in Parliament that the Protestant minority in Lower Canada has nothing to fear from the provincial legislature under Confederation. I have given my word and, I repeat, nothing will be done of such a nature as to harm the principles and rights of this minority. I take as my witnesses all the Protestant companions who are listening to me. I have given my word and I will keep it; it is the word of a man of honour . . .

Having told you that the Protestants of Lower Canada will have all possible guarantees, I must add that the Catholic minority of Upper Canada will have the same guarantees, and I give you my solemn word on this as well. The Catholic minority in Upper Canada will be protected equally with the Protestant minority in Lower Canada. Any fears on this score are empty and false. Don't dwell on this subject and, I say it again, all will be well . . .

A glorious era lies before us: we are entering Confederation. Let it not frighten you. After all, it is nothing but the realization of a plan designed by the first European to set foot in Canada, Jacques Cartier. Would Lower Canada want to limit the influence of the French race to the narrow confines of our province? When Jacques Cartier, in 1534, after landing in Newfoundland, discovered part of Canada and New Brunswick, he guaranteed its possession by France. François I, who claimed his share of America by virtue of Adam's will, sent Jacques Cartier out again, and the navigator extended his discoveries. What Jacques Cartier called Acadia comprises New Brunswick and Nova Scotia.

Thus, the lands that Jacques Cartier identified or discovered, at least in part, will soon be ruled by the same government. With Confederation, we will realize a vision of this great man: the coming together of all the provinces he discovered. If he rose from the grave today, he would undoubtedly look with satisfaction on this great country, enlightened by civilization and soon to enjoy an era of prosperity and happiness brought on by Confederation.

French Canadians have no need to be afraid of the English. After all, they are not so frightening. Instead, let us admire their energy and perseverance; let us imitate them. To be excellent French Canadians we need to have, along with the qualities of our race, the best qualities of the English

Canadians. We are partly descended from the Normans, and the blood of this heroic race is infused in the veins of the English as well, since the days of William the Conqueror.

I would like to say a word about the British institutions under which we are governed. This is the only form of government in the world that, while making use of the democratic element, has been able to keep it within reasonable limits. The democratic element has a fortunate effect in the political sphere when it is balanced by another force. We have this advantage over our neighbours the Americans, who have extreme democracy. It is the same in politics as it is in the physical world. The centripetal force has to be greater than the centrifugal force.

Jacques Cartier brought with him monarchical principles that I love and cherish. He is my namesake: I would like to walk in the footsteps of this illustrious man and I do not want to detract from his great plans. If, when three more centuries have passed, history remembers my name as someone who did something for his country, and if it says that one day I deviated from the virtue of my ancestors, it will hold my memory in abhorrence, and I do not wish it to be so.

John A. Macdonald
3 November 1873

"I have fought the battle of Confederation . . .
I throw myself upon this House, I throw
myself upon posterity"

John A. Macdonald and his Tories narrowly won the first post-Confederation election in 1872. With Confederation accomplished in 1867, the British wanted to withdraw their garrisons from Canada, but there were Anglo-American diplomatic grievances to settle. Macdonald had been forced to negotiate with the Americans from a position of weakness in talks that led to the Treaty of Washington in 1871, and many Canadians were unhappy with the results.

Macdonald had also promised to build a three-thousand-mile transcontinental railway to link central Canada with Manitoba and British Columbia. There was a nasty feud for the contract between rival developers based in Toronto and Montreal. Macdonald chose to go with Hugh Allan's Montreal group, providing them with a million-acre land grant and many other concessions for their labours. In 1873, someone broke into the office of Allan's solicitor and among the pilfered documents was a telegram sent from Macdonald to the solicitor during the previous year's election. "I must have another ten thousand," Macdonald had written. "Will be the last time of asking. Do not fail me." The release of this information caused a political firestorm, which Macdonald attempted to evade by shutting down the House of Commons in the summer of 1873. In November, he made a five-hour speech in the House, fortifying himself with tumblers of gin that he kept conveniently at hand. It was a masterful presentation in which he dealt with a panorama of issues, but never directly with his request for money from Allan.

I have to speak to the specific charges made against the government. Before the last elections took place, I knew what I had to face. I had a great, a strong and united opponent, I had showered upon my devoted head all kinds of opposition. I had been one of the high commissioners, one of the signers of the Treaty of Washington. It was said that I had betrayed the country, and the honourable gentlemen had described me in their speeches as a cross between Benedict Arnold and Judas Iscariot. But I met Parliament, and by a calm explanation of my course I won the approval of the House. Still the Opposition roared.

I knew that I must meet with a strong opposition in my native province from gentlemen of the opposite party. That province was the only province in the country that was not a gainer by that treaty, except as it was a gainer by the great gain which I think, overbalanced everything—that of a lasting peace between England and the United States. It gave to our children, and to our children's children, the assurance that we could enjoy our own comfort, that we could enjoy our own firesides, that we could sit under our own fig tree, without the possibility of the war cloud hanging over us; and if I was guilty of being a party to that treaty, I shall be glad to have it recorded on my tombstone . . .

I will state now what occurred with respect to the Pacific Railway. I was at Washington bartering my country, as some of the honourable gentlemen say, attending at all events to the Washington treaty, when the resolutions were carried which—happily I say for Canada—brought British Columbia into the union of British North American provinces. The proposition included the Pacific Railway, for British Columbia would not have come in unless the terms of the union had included a railway. Notwithstanding great opposition the resolutions were carried by my late honoured and lamented colleague [Sir George-Étienne Cartier], but he only carried them by promising to introduce resolutions by which the railway would be built, not by the government directly, but by private capital, aided by government grants . . .

As we could not succeed in going to the country with a perfect scheme for building the Pacific Railway, what else was left to us but to keep the amalgamation of these great capitalists open till after the elections, and then call them together, and the only word of preference for Montreal over Toronto was simply my expression that any influence the government might have in case of amalgamation, in the case of the two companies joining and electing a board of directors, would be fairly used in favour of Sir Hugh Allan for the presidency . . .

I made that promise, but I wish the House to remember that at the time of that telegram—in which I simply stated that as we could not form a company before the elections, we would form one afterwards out of the two, and would do what we could to make Sir Hugh Allan president— at that time there had been not one single word said about money, and there never was one said, as far as I was concerned, between Sir Hugh Allan and me.

I was fighting the battle in western Canada. I was getting subscriptions, as I have no doubt the honourable member for Lambton [Alexander MacKenzie] was getting subscriptions, and if he denies it I will be able to prove it. I state in my place that I will be able to prove it. I was doing what I could for the purpose of getting money to help the elections, and I was met not only by individual exertions, but by the whole force, power, and influence, legitimate and illegitimate, of the Ontario government.

I have no hesitation in saying that in all expenditure we were met by two dollars to one . . . If we had had the same means possessed by honourable gentlemen opposite, if we had spies, if we had thieves, if we had men who went to your desk, picked your lock, and stole your notebooks, we would have much stronger evidence than honourable gentlemen think they have now. We were fighting an uneven battle. We were simply subscribing as gentlemen, while they were stealing as burglars. We may trace it out as a conspiracy throughout. I use the word conspiracy advisedly, and I will use the word out of the House as well as in the House . . .

By their line of action, the gentlemen opposite have postponed for some years the building of that railway, and they have besmirched unjustly, dishonourably, the character of the Canadian government and of the Canadian people. If there be any delay, any postponement in the completion of that great system of railways, I charge it to the honourable gentlemen opposite. Long after this quarrel is over, it will be recorded in the history of this Dominion of Canada that there was one body of men in this country willing to forget self, to forget party, to forget section to build up a great interest and make a great country, and they will say that there was another party who fought section against section, province against province, who were unable to rise to the true position of affairs, and I say the history of the future will be our justification and their condemnation.

I have some more to say. I say this government has been traded with foul wrongs. I say this government has been treated as no government has ever been treated before. It has been met with an Opposition the like of which no government in any civilized country was ever met. I say we have been opposed not with fair weapons, not by fair argument, not by fair discussion as a government ought to be opposed, but opposed in a manner which will throw shame on honourable gentlemen opposite . . .

I say I am condemned. But I commit myself, the government commits itself, to the hands of this House, and far beyond the House, it commits itself to the country at large. We have faithfully done our duty. We have fought the battle of Confederation. We have fought the battle of union. We have had party strife setting province against province, and more than all, we have had in the greatest province, the preponderating province of the Dominion, every prejudice and sectional feeling that could be arrayed against us.

I have been the victim of that conduct to a great extent, but I have fought the battle of Confederation, the battle of union, the battle of the Dominion of Canada. I throw myself upon this House; I throw myself upon this country; I throw myself upon posterity, and I believe that I know that, notwithstanding the many failings in my life, I shall have the voice of this country and this House rallying round me. And, if I am mistaken in that, I can confidently appeal to a higher court, to the court of my own conscience, and to the court of posterity.

I leave it with this House with every confidence. I am equal to either fortune. I can see cast the decision of this House either for or against me, but whether it be against me or for me I know, and it is no vain boast to say so, for even my enemies will admit that I am no boaster, that there does not exist in Canada a man who has given more of his time, more of his heart, more of his wealth, or more of his intellect and power, such as it may be, for the good of this Dominion of Canada.

The *House of Commons Debates* of the day indicate that after the speech, "the right honourable gentleman resumed his seat amid loud and long continued cheering." Macdonald was exhausted by his oratorical exertion and took to his sickbed for several days. By the time he recovered, his government had collapsed, to be replaced by the Liberals. But his political career was far from over.

Mistawasis
17 August 1876

"I for one will take the hand that is offered"

Following Confederation, the Canadian government wanted to acquire the vast western lands of the Hudson's Bay Company, and to settle the west. The Aboriginal peoples living there had become an obstacle in the eyes of government, and Governor Edmond Morris was dispatched to sign treaties with them. In August 1876, Morris met with Cree and Saulteaux chiefs at Fort Carlton, near Prince Albert. It was a bitter and poignant moment for the chiefs. They had seen the buffalo all but exterminated, and hunger stalked the land. Their people had died in the thousands from smallpox and other European diseases, and their traditional way of life was doomed. Some, like Chiefs Mistawasis and Ahtukakup, believed it best to sign treaties and take reserves. Others, including Poundmaker and The Badger, did not trust the whites, and believed the treaty terms as described would be inadequate to feed and house their people. After preliminary talks with Governor Morris, the chiefs asked for a respite, and used a full day to hold a private caucus among themselves. They had taken pains to invite Peter Erasmus, a Métis interpreter, to their meeting, so that he could explain what the whites meant by their treaty terms. Erasmus was there as the chiefs agonized over their choice. Chief Mistawasis remained silent for hours, then rose to deliver this speech late in the day. Erasmus included his recollection of it in a book prepared many years later with his friend Henry Thompson.

I have heard my brothers speak, complaining of the hardships endured by our people. Some have bewailed the poverty and suffering that has come to Indians because of the destruction of the buffalo as the chief source of our living, the loss of the ancient glory of our forefathers; and with all that I agree, in the silence of my teepee and on the broad prairies where once our fathers could not pass for the great number of those animals that blocked their way; and even in our day, we have had to choose carefully our camp-ground for fear of being trampled in our teepees. With all these things, I think and feel intensely the sorrow my brothers express.

I speak directly to Poundmaker and The Badger and those others who object to signing this treaty. Have you anything better to offer our people? I ask, again, can you suggest anything that will bring these things back for tomorrow and all the tomorrows that face our people?

I for one think that the Great White Queen Mother has offered us a way of life when the buffalo are no more. Gone they will be before many snows have come to cover our heads or graves if such should be.

I speak the tongue of the Blackfoot. I have been in their lodges. I have seen with my eyes and listened with my ears to the sorrows of that once-proud nation; people whom we have known as our enemies, the Peigan and the Bloods who are their brothers. Pay attention, listen hard to what I am about to say. The Big Knives of the south came into Blackfoot territory as traders; though few in number they have conquered these nations, and that, all the Crees in the days of our fathers and their fathers before them failed to do. How did they do it? Listen closely, my brothers, and you will understand. What was done to them can be done to us if we throw away the hand that is extended to us by this treaty.

These traders, who were not of our land, with smooth talk and cheap goods persuaded the southern tribes it would be a good thing to have a place to trade products of the hunt, the hides and tanned goods. The traders came and built strong forts, and with their long rifles that can kill at twice the distance of our own and the short guns that can spout death six times quicker than you can tell about it, they had the people at their mercy. The Blackfoot soon found out the traders had nothing but whisky to exchange for their skins. Oh, yes, they were generous at first with their rotten whisky, but not for long. The traders demanded pay and got Blackfoot horses, buffalo robes, and all other things they had to offer. Those traders laughed at them for fools, and so they were, to sell their heritage for ruin and debauchery. Some of the bravest of the Blackfoot tried to get revenge for the losses, but they were shot down like dogs and dragged to the open plains on horses to rot or be eaten by wolves.

The Great Queen Mother, hearing of the sorrows of her children, sent out the Red Coats. Though these were only of a number you could count on your fingers and toes, yet the cutthroats and criminals who recognized no authority but their guns, who killed each other on the slightest pretence and murdered Indians without fear of reprisal, immediately abandoned their forts, strong as they were, and fled back to their own side of the line. I ask you why those few men could put to flight those bad men who for years have defied the whole of the southern Indian nations?

Surely these Red Coats are men of flesh and blood as ourselves and a bullet is just as effective on them as on any Blackfoot. Why of course, they are of flesh and blood. They could be killed as easily as any Blackfoot, but ask yourselves why the traders fled in fear from so few men. The southern tribes outnumbered this small police force one hundred to one, but they were helpless in spite of their numbers. Let me tell you why these things were so. It was the power that stands behind those few Red Coats that those men feared and wasted no time in getting out when they could; the power that is represented in all the Queen's people, and we the children are counted as important as even the governor who is her personal speaker.

The police are the Queen Mother's agents and have the same laws for whites as they have for the Indians. I have seen these things done and now the Blackfoot welcome these servants of the Queen Mother and invite her governor for a treaty with them next year. I, for one, look to the Queen's law and her Red Coat servants to protect our people against the evils of white man's firewater and to stop the senseless wars among our people, against the Blackfoot, Peigans, and Bloods. We have been in darkness; the

Blackfoot and the others are people as we are. They will starve as we will starve when the buffalo are gone. We will be brothers in misery when we could have been brothers in plenty in times when there was no need for any man, woman, or child to be hungry.

We speak of glory and our memories are all that is left to feed the widows and orphans of those who have died in its attainment. We are few in numbers compared to former times, by wars and the terrible ravages of smallpox. Our people have vanished too. Even if it were possible to gather all the tribes together, to throw away the hand that is offered to help us, we would be too weak to make our demands heard. Look to the great Indian nations in the Long Knives' country who have been fighting since the memory of their oldest men. They are being vanquished and swept into the most useless parts of their country. Their days are numbered like those of the buffalo. There is no law or justice for the Indians in Long Knives' country. The police followed two murderers to Montana and caught them but when they were brought to the Montana court they were turned free because it was not murder to kill an Indian.

The prairies have not been darkened by the blood of our white brothers in our time. Let this always be so. I for one will take the hand that is offered. For my band I have spoken.

Wilfrid Laurier
26 June 1877

"If it is a crime to be a Liberal, then I am guilty"

Wilfrid Laurier, a young lawyer, journalist, and parliamentarian, was by 1877 a rising political star in Quebec. He was a Liberal and in 1871 prominent bishops and clergy had worked against him in his first election. The British, after their victory over the French in 1759, made accommodation with the elites in Quebec, including the church hierarchy. The church was hostile to political liberalism, associating it with the revolutions that had occurred in nineteenth century Europe, stripping the church of much of its wealth and temporal power. In Quebec, many of the young men who had participated in the 1837 rebellion were fired by the tenets of liberalism. They were anticlerical and the church returned their hostility. Laurier accepted an invitation by Le Club Canadien in Quebec City to speak on liberalism on 26 June 1877. He delivered a masterful speech aimed at disarming his critics, both clerical and lay, and winning political space for Liberals in Quebec.

I do not deceive myself as to the standing of the Liberal Party in the province of Quebec; and I, at once, declare that it occupies a false position in the eyes of public opinion. I know that for a great many of my fellow citizens, the Liberal Party is a party composed of men holding perverse doctrines, with dangerous tendencies, and knowingly and deliberately progressing towards revolution. I know that in the opinion of a portion of our fellow countrymen, the Liberal Party is made up of men of good intentions, perhaps, but not the less dupes and victims of their principles, by which they are unconsciously but fatally led to revolution. I know that for yet another portion, not the least numerous, Liberalism is a new form of evil, in other words a heresy, carrying with it its own condemnation. I know all this, and it is because I do so that I consented to appear before you . . .

I belong to the Liberal Party. If to be a Liberal is a term of reproach, that reproach I accept. If it is a crime to be a Liberal, then I am guilty. One thing only I claim, that is that we be judged according to our principles . . .

Let us ascend to the very source and examine calmly what is, at bottom, the meaning of these two words, liberal and conservative. What idea is concealed beneath the word "liberal" which has been subjected to so many anathemas? What does the word "conservative" mean which seems so sacred that it is modestly applied to all that is good? Is the one, as it is pretended, as in fact it is affirmed everyday to be, a new form of error? Is the other, as it is constantly insinuated, synonymous of good, in all its phases? Is the one, revolution, anarchy, disorder? Is the other the sole safe principle of society? Such are the questions which are asked everyday in this country. These subtle distinctions, which are continually brought forward in our press are, nevertheless, old. They are but the repetition of the dreams of certain French publicists who, shut up in their studies, look only upon the past, and who bitterly criticize everything that now exists because existing things do not resemble those of old. Such people say that the liberal idea is a new one; and in this they are mistaken. The liberal idea as well as its opposite is not new. It is as old as the world, and it is to be found in every page of its history. But it is only today that we understand its forces and its laws and know how to utilize them. Steam existed before Fulton; but it is only since Fulton that we know the scope of its power and how to make it produce its marvellous results. It is the combination of the tube and piston that serves to utilize the steam. It is the form of representative government that has revealed to the world the principles of liberalism and conservatism; and it is that form of government that draws from each its full powers . . .

It is the habit of our adversaries to accuse us Liberals of irreligion. I am not here to parade my religious principles, but I proclaim that I have too much respect for the faith in which I was born ever to make it the foundation of a political organization.

You wish to organize a Catholic party, but have you never reflected that if, unfortunately, you were successful, you would bring on your country calamities, the consequence of which it is impossible to predict.

You wish to organize all Catholics into a single party without other tie, without other basis than that of religion, but you have not reflected that by that fact alone you organize the Protestant population as a single party, and that then instead of peace and harmony which now exists amongst the elements of our Canadian populations, you will bring on war—religious war, the most frightful of all wars . . .

Forty years ago, the country was in a state of feverish excitement and agitation which, in a few months later, culminated in rebellion. The British Crown was upheld in the country, but by powder and shot. And yet what did our forefathers demand? Nothing else than our present institutions; these institutions were granted and loyally applied, and behold the consequences: the English flag floats from the ancient Citadel of Quebec. It floats this evening above our heads and yet there is not a single English soldier in the country to defend it; its sole defence is the consciousness that we owe to it the liberty and security we find under it.

What Canadian is there who, comparing his own with even the freest of other countries, but feels proud of its institutions?

What Canadian is there who, in going through the streets of this old city, and seeing the monument a few feet from this place, erected to the memory of two brave men who fell on the same field of battle in fighting for the possession of this country, but feels proud of his country? In what country under the sun could you find a similar monument, erected to the memory of the conqueror and the conquered? In what country under the sun could you find the names of the victor and vanquished honoured in the same degree, occupying the same place in the sentiments of the population?

When in this last battle, commemorated by the monument erected to Wolfe and Montcalm, the cannon spread death among the French ranks; when the old heroes, whom victory had so often followed, saw her at last deserting them; when reclining on the sod, feeling their hearts' blood flowing and life departing they saw, as a consequence of their defeat, Quebec in the hands of the enemy and their country forever lost, no doubt their last thoughts turned towards their children, towards those whom they left without protection and without defence; doubtless they saw them persecuted, enslaved, humiliated; and then we may imagine their last breath to have been a cry of despair.

But if, on the other hand, Heaven had permitted the veil of the future to be raised before their expiring vision; if Heaven permitted them, before their eyes closed forever, to penetrate the unknown; if they could have seen their children free and happy, walking proudly in every rank of society; if they could have seen in the ancient cathedral the seat of honour of the French governors occupied by a French governor; if they could have seen the spires of churches piercing the azure in every valley from the waters of Gaspé to the plains of Red River; if they could have seen this old flag which reminds us of our greatest victory triumphantly borne in all our public ceremonies; finally, if they could have seen our free institutions, may we not believe that their last breath was softened to a murmur of thanks to Heaven, and that they found consolation as they died.

If the shades of those heroes yet move about this old city for which they died, and if they are on this evening in this hall, we Liberals may believe, at least we have the dear illusion, that their sympathies are entirely with us.

Louis Riel
Regina, 31 July–1 August 1885

"I found the Indians suffering. I found the half-breeds eating the rotten pork of the Hudson's Bay Company"

Louis Riel led the Métis agitation at Red River that resulted in Manitoba becoming a province in 1871. Elected as an MP, he was not allowed to sit, and was forced into a lonely fifteen-year exile in the United States. Many Métis moved west from Manitoba to the banks of the North Saskatchewan River to escape encroaching white settlement. In 1884, the Métis at Batoche, alarmed at the sight of land surveyors in their area, sent a delegation to Riel in Montana, asking him to come back to defend their rights against a government that ignored their requests. Riel returned, his agitation led to a short-lived rebellion, and he was captured and tried for treason. Riel's lawyers, despite his protests, pleaded insanity on his behalf. In his speech to the jury, delivered in English, Riel argued passionately that he was sane and had acted on behalf of people who needed his help.

Your Honours, gentlemen of the jury: It would be easy for me today to play insanity, because the circumstances are such as to excite any man, and under the natural excitement of what is taking place today (I cannot speak English very well, but am to do so, because most of those here speak English), under the excitement which my trial causes me would justify me not to appear as usual, but with my mind out of its ordinary condition. I hope with the help of God I will maintain calmness and decorum as suits this honorable court, this honorable jury.

You have seen by the papers in the hands of the Crown that I am naturally inclined to think of God at the beginning of my actions. I wish if I do it you won't take it as a mark of insanity, that you won't take it as part of a play of insanity. Oh, my God, help me through Thy grace and the divine influence of Jesus Christ. Oh, my God, bless me, bless this honorable court, bless this honorable jury, bless my good lawyers who have come seven hundred leagues to try to save my life, bless also the lawyers for the Crown, because they have done, I am sure, what they thought their duty. They have shown me fairness which at first I did not expect from them. Oh, my God, bless all those who are around me through the grace and influence of Jesus Christ our Savior. Change the curiosity of those who are paying attention to me, change that curiosity into sympathy with me.

The day of my birth I was helpless and my mother took care of me although she was not able to do it alone; there was someone to help her to take care of me and I lived. Today, although a man I am as helpless before this court, in the Dominion of Canada and in this world, as I was helpless on the knees of my mother the day of my birth. The Northwest is also my mother; it is my mother country and although my mother country is sick and confirmed in a certain way, there are some from Lower Canada who came to help her to take care of me during her sickness and I am sure that my mother country will not kill me more than my mother did forty years ago when I came into the world, because a mother is always a mother, and even if I have my faults, if she can see I am true, she will be full of love for me.

When I came into the Northwest in July, the 1st of July 1884, I found the Indians suffering. I found the half-breeds eating the rotten pork of the Hudson's Bay Company and getting sick and weak every day. Although a half-breed, and having no pretension to help the whites, I also paid attention to them. I saw they were deprived of responsible government, I saw that they were deprived of their public liberties. I remembered that half-breed meant white and Indian and while I paid attention to the suffering Indians and the half-breeds I remembered that the greatest part of my heart and blood was white and I have directed my attention to help the Indians, help the half-breeds and to help the whites to the best of my ability. We have made petitions, I have made petitions with others to the Canadian government asking to relieve the condition of this country.

We have taken time; we have tried to unite all classes, even may speak, all parties. Those who have been in close communication with me know I have suffered, that I have waited for months to bring some of the people of the Saskatchewan to an understanding of certain important points in our petition to the Canadian government and I have done my duty . . .

The agitation in the Northwest Territories would have been constitutional, and would certainly be constitutional today if, in my opinion, we had not been attacked. Perhaps the Crown has not been able to find out the particulars, that we were attacked, but as we were on the scene it was easy to understand. When we sent petitions to the government, they used to answer us by sending police, and when the rumors were increasing every day that Riel had been shot here or there, or that Riel was going to be shot by such and such a man, the police would not pay any attention to it. I am glad that I have mentioned the police, because of the testimony that has been given in the box during the examination of many of the witnesses. If I had been allowed to put questions to the witnesses, I would have asked them when it was I said a single word against a single policeman or a single officer . . .

As to religion, what is my belief? What is my insanity about that? My insanity, Your Honours, gentlemen of the jury, is that I wish to leave Rome aside, inasmuch as it is the cause of division between Catholics and Protestants. I did not wish to force my views, because in Batoche to the half-breeds that followed me I used the word, carte blanche. If I have any influence in the new world it is to help in that way and even if it takes two hundred years to become practical, then after my death that will bring out practical results, and then my children's children will shake hands with the Protestants of the new world in a friendly manner. I do not wish these evils which exist in Europe to be continued, as much as I can influence it, among the half-breeds. I do not wish that to be repeated in America. That work is not the work of some days or some years, it is the work of hundreds of years.

My condition is helpless, so helpless that my good lawyers, and they have done it by conviction—Mr. Fitzpatrick in his beautiful speech has proved he believed I was insane—my condition seems to be so helpless that they have recourse to try and prove insanity to try and save me in that way. If I am insane, of course I don't know it, it is a property of insanity to be unable to know it . . .

You have given me your attention, Your Honours; you have given me your attention, gentlemen of the jury, and this great audience. I see that if I go any further on that point I will lose the favour you have granted me up to this time, and as I am aiming all the time at practical results, I will stop here, master of myself, through the help of God. I have only a few more words to say, Your Honours. Gentlemen of the jury, my reputation, my liberty, my life, are at your discretion. So confident am I, that I have not the slightest anxiety, not even the slightest doubt, as to your verdict . . .

The only things I would like to call your attention to before you retire to deliberate are: first, that the House of Commons, Senate, and ministers of the Dominion, and who make laws for this land and govern it, are no representation whatever of the people of the Northwest.

Second, that the Northwest Council generated by the federal government has the great defect of its parent.

Third, the number of members elected for the council by the people make it only a sham representative legislature and no representative government at all . . .

If you take the plea of the defence that I am not responsible for my acts, acquit me completely since I have been quarrelling with an insane and irresponsible government. If you pronounce in favor of the Crown, which contends that I am responsible, acquit me all the same. You are perfectly justified in declaring that having my reason and sound mind, I have acted reasonably and in self-defence, while the government, my accuser, being irresponsible, and consequently insane, cannot but have acted wrong, and if high treason there is it must be on its side and not on my part.

HIS HONOUR: Are you done?

RIEL: Not yet, if you have the kindness to permit me your attention for a while.

HIS HONOUR: Well, proceed . . .

RIEL: I thank Your Honour for the favor you have granted me in speaking; I thank you for the attention you have given me, gentlemen of the jury, and I thank those who have had the kindness to encourage my imperfect way of speaking the English language by your good attention. I put my speech under the protection of my God, my Saviour, He is the only one who can make it effective. It is possible it should become effective, as it is proposed to good men, to good people, and to good ladies also.

Louis Riel was hanged in Regina on 16 November 1885. His execution caused a political and racial firestorm, creating a fault line in the new Dominion that was to persist for decades. Quebec was enraged, while in Ontario the press and Protestant organizations were just as insistent that Riel had been a traitor and deserved his fate.

Big Bear
25 September 1885

"Pity the children of my tribe.
Pity the old and helpless of my people"

Big Bear was a legendary Cree chief whose band roamed in search of buffalo from the parklands in what is now Saskatchewan to the Bear Paw Mountains in Montana. He feared what life on reservations would mean for his people, and he spurned offers of treaty, always holding out for better conditions, until he was starved into submission. When the Métis rebelled in 1885, the aging chief lost control of his young men and they killed nine people at the Hudson's Bay Company post at Frog Lake, near Fort Pitt. William Beasdell Cameron was a young clerk at the post, and he later testified against some of the perpetrators. Big Bear also was charged with treason. Cameron testified in the old chief's defence, saying that he had tried to prevent the killings. Big Bear spoke no English and the trial had to be interpreted for him. He was deemed guilty of treason, and asked if he had anything to say. He used his speech to

plead for members of his band, who had scattered while being pursued
by police and soldiers.

I think I should have something to say about the occurrences which brought me here in chains. I knew little of the killing at Frog Lake beyond hearing the shots fired. When any wrong was brewing I did my best to stop it in the beginning. The turbulent ones of the band got beyond my control and shed the blood of those I would have protected. I was away from Frog Lake a part of the winter, hunting and fishing, and the rebellion had commenced before I got back. When white men were few in the country I gave them the hand of brotherhood. I am sorry so few are here who can witness for my friendly acts.

Can anyone stand out and say that I ordered the death of a priest or an agent? You think I encouraged my people to take part in the trouble. I did not. I advised them against it. I felt sorry when they killed those men at Frog Lake, but the truth is when news of the fight at Duck Lake reached us my band ignored my authority and despised me because I did not side with the half-breeds. I did not so much as take a white man's horse. I always believed that by being the friend of the white man, I and my people would be helped by those of them who had wealth. I always thought it paid to do all the good I could. Now my heart is on the ground.

I look around me in this room and see it crowded with handsome faces, faces far handsomer than my own. I have ruled my country for a long time. Now I am in chains and will be sent to prison, but I have no doubt the handsome faces I admire about me will be competent to govern the land. At present I am dead to my people. Many of my band are hiding in the woods, paralyzed with terror. Cannot this court send them a pardon? My own children, perhaps they are starving and outcast, too, afraid to appear in the light of day. If the government does not come to them with help before the winter sets in, my band will surely perish.

But I have too much confidence in the Great Grandmother to fear that starvation will be allowed to overtake my people. The time will come when the Indians of the Northwest will be of much service to the Great Grandmother. I plead again to you, the chiefs of the white men's laws, for pity and help to the outcasts of my band.

I have only a few words more to say. Sometimes in the past I have spoken stiffly to the Indian agents, but when I did it was only in order to obtain my rights. The Northwest belonged to me, but I perhaps will not live to see it again. I ask the court to publish my speech and to scatter it among the white people. It is my defence. I am old and ugly, but I have tried to do good. Pity the children of my tribe. Pity the old and helpless of my people. I speak with a single tongue; and because Big Bear has always been the friend of the white man, send out and pardon and give them help.

How, Aquisanee, I have spoken.

Big Bear was sentenced to three years in Stony Mountain Penitentiary and left the courtroom in chains. He became ill in prison and died soon after his release, a lonely and broken man.

Goldwin Smith

20 November 1888

"Nature has manifestly made this
continent an economical whole"

The debate over free trade with the United States is older than Confederation itself. Canada had a reciprocity treaty with the U.S. beginning in 1854, but the Americans terminated it in 1856 and in the same year a bill introduced into Congress called for complete annexation. Torontonian Goldwin Smith and others continued to promote the idea of a commercial union with the Americans. Smith was a British expatriate who taught at Oxford and later at Cornell in the U.S. He settled in Toronto in 1871, writing and lecturing on Canadian and international affairs. He believed that Canada, particularly with the "French wedge in her heart," was not viable as a nation. He acted as a self-appointed proponent of commercial union, and created the Toronto Commercial Union Club. He made this speech to the Chamber of Commerce in New York on 20 November 1888.

I had the honour, some time ago, to receive from your president a letter of inquiry on the subject of commercial union. I believe I may say, with confidence, that the subject is taking a strong hold on the minds of our Canadian people. The eyes of our people have been opened as they have not been for a long time, if they ever were before, to the advantages of unrestricted trade with their own continent. All our great natural industries, those of the farmer, the lumberman, the shipowner, and the fisherman, desire the removal of the tariff wall. Even of our manufacturers, only the weaker classes object; the stronger are ready for the open market. You know that party ties, even when very irrational, are very strong, and at by-elections it is difficult to break them; but even at our by-elections, popular interest in the question has begun to tell, and at our next general election our trade relations with the United States are evidently going to be the main issue.

To me it has always seemed that the map settles the question. Nature has manifestly made this continent an economical whole, ordaining that its products, northern and southern, shall supplement each other, and that all its inhabitants, with their varied gifts and industries, shall combine in creating its common store of wealth. She has unified it by the great waterways, and where she has run chains of mountains, it has been from north to south, not from east to west. Her behest has been completed by the railway system which has bound us, and is daily binding us closer together, and which separatists help, with strange inconsistency, to develop, while they set themselves against the extension of commercial and general relations. To run a customs line across this continent, cutting off its northern margin commercially from the rest, is surely to fight against nature, and reject the benefits which she offers with outstretched hands. Viewed politically, the map of Canada presents a vast and unbroken domain, including the North Pole, and equaling in area the territory of the United States.

But, viewed economically, it presents four separate blocks of territory, having hardly any natural connection with each other, while each is naturally connected with the country immediately to the south of it. There are the Maritime provinces, cut off by a wide wilderness from old Canada, French and English; old Canada, cut off by another wilderness and by Lake Superior from the newly opened prairie region of the northwest; and the prairie region, cut off by a triple chain of mountains from British Columbia, while the Maritime provinces are economically connected with the northeastern states of the Union; old Canada, with New York and

Pennsylvania; the prairie region, with Dakota and Minnesota, which are divided from it only by a conventional line; and British Columbia, with the Pacific territories and states. If you happen to see the map prefixed to the *Handbook of Commercial Union*, published by the Toronto Commercial Union Club, the great facts of the economical case, and the conclusion to which they point, will be placed at once before your eyes. The attempt to force an interprovincial trade has failed, and each province practically is almost confined to its own market.

It is needless to tell you that Canada, if she could only be opened up and get access for her products to their natural market, is a great storehouse of wealth. She has minerals of almost every kind and in immense abundance, and more native copper than any other country in the world, all waiting for a market, and for the free ingress of American machinery and American capital. She has abundance of lumber, which, however, is being largely wasted, and will continue to be wasted till the lumber of this continent is brought into a common stock, assessed at its real value and husbanded accordingly. She has fish, not only in her seas, but in her great northwestern lakes, whence, if the trade were open, they would find their way to the tables of your middle states. She has barley and other special farm products, favoured by her soil and climate; she has healthy stock and horses, the demand for which among you is very large. She is a great treasure house of nature, which awaits the key of American capital and enterprise to unlock it. She is, as has been truly said, rich by nature, poor only by policy. She is far richer than Scotland was before her commercial union with England; yet England gained greatly by that union, though Scotland, perhaps, gained still more. It has been said that the products of the two countries, being similar, it is not likely that there would be much trade between them. Facts confute that assertion. Wherever an opening is made in the tariff wall by the remission of a duty, as in the case of eggs, trade rushes through; even when there is no remission, its tide beats against and overleaps the barrier with a force that shows how great the volume would be if the barrier were removed . . .

You cannot take up a Canadian newspaper, or read the Canadian correspondence of one of your own journals, without seeing that Canada is debating her political destiny, and that there is great diversity of opinion among us. Some, mostly of the official class, look forward to perpetual or, at least, indefinite continuance in the state of a dependency. Some cherish the hope that Canada, in spite of her want of compactness and the French wedge in her heart, will become an independent nation. Some think that the shadow can be made to go back on the dial of colonial history, and that Canada, in common with the other colonies, will surrender a part of her self-government to the government of an imperial federation.

Others there are who believe that the English-speaking race upon this continent will some day be one people. As it was one people before the civil war of the last century, so they believe that it will in time be one people again, and that England, well-advised as to her true interest, will applaud and bless the union. Without the consent of England, Canada will do nothing. To Canada, at all events, England, according to her lights, has been a good mother. What nobody in his senses desires is forcible annexation, which would give you disaffected citizens, and introduce discord into the vitals of the republic. A despot, when he annexes, can send down a viceroy; you would have to give the ballot, which would be used by unwilling citizens for the purposes of their discontent. If you want union at all, it is a free and equal union, a union of common interest and of the heart, such as a citizen of either country may advocate without treason, and welcome without dishonour. In the meantime, while the political destiny of the two countries is working itself out, why should not our industry and commerce enjoy the advantages of continental free trade? . . .

I almost feel that I have been presumptuous in addressing such an assembly as this on such a subject as the trade relations between the two countries, being, as I am, nothing but a private Canadian citizen. I have, however, at least no interest or motive other than the desire that our Canadian people should enjoy the fair earnings of their industry and the measure of prosperity which nature has designed for them.

John A. Macdonald
7 February 1891

"A British subject I was born, a British subject I will die."

As Goldwin Smith predicted, free trade did become the overriding issue in the 1891 election campaign. Reciprocity had long been dear to the Reformers (Liberals) of Upper Canada, and Wilfrid Laurier, the national leader, was a proponent as well. It appeared certain that the weary Conservatives and their leader were due for defeat. Macdonald was often ill during the campaign, but he rallied his party around the National Policy, ties to Britain, and the vision of a Canada distinct from the American republic. Macdonald called an election on 2 February and composed an election address that would become his set piece during the campaign. It is his most memorable speech.

When in 1878 we were called upon to administer the affairs of the Dominion, Canada occupied a position in the eyes of the world very different from that which she enjoys today. At that time, a profound depression hung like a pall over the whole country, from the Atlantic Ocean to the western limits of the province of Ontario, beyond which to the Rocky Mountains stretched a vast and almost unknown wilderness. Trade was depressed, manufactures languished and, exposed to ruinous competition, Canadians were fast sinking into the position of being mere hewers of wood and drawers of water for the great nation dwelling to the south of us. We determined to change this unhappy state of things. We felt that Canada, with its agricultural resources, rich in its fisheries, timber, and mineral wealth, was worthy of a nobler position than that of being a slaughter market for the United States. We said to the Americans, "We are perfectly willing to trade with you on equal terms. We are desirous of having a fair reciprocity treaty; but we will not consent to open our markets to you while yours remain closed to us."

So we inaugurated the National Policy. You all know what followed. Almost as if by magic the whole face of the country underwent a change. Stagnation and apathy and gloom, aye, and want and misery too, gave place to activity and enterprise and prosperity. The miners of Nova Scotia took courage; the manufacturing industries in our great centres revived and multiplied; the farmer found a market for his produce; the artisan and labourer employment at good wages; and all Canada rejoiced under the quickening impulse of a new-found life. The age of deficits was past, and an overflowing treasury gave to the government the means of carrying forward those great works necessary to the realization of our purpose to make this country a homogeneous whole.

To that end, we undertook that stupendous work, the Canadian Pacific Railway. Undeterred by the pessimistic views of our opponents, nay, in spite of their strenuous and even malignant opposition, we pushed forward that great enterprise through the wilds north of Lake Superior, across the western prairies, over the Rocky Mountains, to the shore of the Pacific, with such inflexible resolution that in seven years after the assumption of office by the present administration, the dream of our public men was an accomplished fact and I, myself, experienced the proud satisfaction of looking back from the steps of my car upon the Rocky Mountains fringing the eastern sky.

The Canadian Pacific Railway now extends from ocean to ocean, opening up and developing the country at a marvellous rate, and forming an imperial highway to the East, over which the trade of the Indies is destined to reach the markets of Europe. We have subsidized steamship lines on both sides of the ocean, to Europe, China, Japan, Australia, and the West Indies.

We have spent millions on the extension and improvement of our canal system. We have, by liberal grants of subsidies, promoted the building of railways, now become an absolute necessity, until the whole country is covered as with a network, and we have done all this with such prudence and caution that our credit in the money markets of the world is higher today than it has ever been, and the rate of interest on our debt, which is the true measure of the public burdens, is less than it was when we took office in 1878.

During all this time, what has been the attitude of the Reform Party? Vacillating in their policy and inconstancy itself as regards their leaders, they have at least been consistent in this particular, that they have uniformly opposed every measure which had for its object the development of our common country. The National Policy was a failure before it had been tried. Under it we could not possibly raise a revenue sufficient for the public requirements. Time exposed that fallacy. Then we were to pay more for the home-manufactured article than we used to when we imported everything from abroad. We were to be the prey of rings and of monopolies, and the manufacturers were to extort their own prices. When these fears had been proved unfounded, we were assured that overcompetition would inevitably prove the ruin of the manufacturing industries and thus bring about a state of affairs worse than that which the National Policy had been designed to meet. It was the same with the Canadian Pacific Railway. The whole project, according to our opponents, was a chimera. The engineering difficulties were insuperable; the road, even if constructed, would never pay. Well, gentlemen, the project was feasible, the engineering difficulties were overcome, and the road does pay.

Disappointed by the failure of all their predictions and convinced that nothing is to be gained by further opposition on the old lines, the Reform Party has taken a new departure and has announced its policy to be unrestricted reciprocity . . .

It would, in my opinion, inevitably result in the annexation of this Dominion to the United States. The advocates of unrestricted reciprocity on this side of the line deny that it would have such an effect, though its friends in the United States urge as the chief reason for its adoption that unrestricted reciprocity would be the first step in the direction of political union . . .

For a century and a half, this country has grown and flourished under the protecting aegis of the British Crown. The gallant race who first bore to our shores the blessings of civilization passed by an easy transition from

French to English rule and now form one of the most law-abiding portions of the community. These pioneers were speedily recruited by the advent of a loyal band of British subjects, who gave up everything that men most prize and were content to begin life anew in the wilderness rather than forego allegiance to their sovereign. To the descendents of these men and to the multitude of Englishmen, Irishmen, and Scotchmen who emigrated to Canada, that they might build up new homes without ceasing to be British subjects; to you, Canadians, I appeal, and I ask you what have you to gain by surrendering that which your fathers held most dear? Under the broad folds of the Union Jack, we enjoy the most ample liberty to govern ourselves as we please and at the same time we participate in the advantages which flow from association with the mightiest empire the world has ever seen. Not only are we free to manage our domestic concerns, but, practically, we possess the privilege of making our own treaties with foreign countries, and in our relations with the outside world, we enjoy the prestige inspired by a consciousness of the fact that behind us towers the majesty of England.

The question which you will shortly be called upon to determine resolves itself into this: shall we endanger our possession of the great heritage bequeathed to us by our fathers and submit ourselves to direct taxation for the privilege of having our tariff fixed at Washington, with a prospect of ultimately becoming a portion of the American union?

I commend these issues to your determination and to the judgment of the whole people of Canada with an unclouded confidence that you will proclaim to the world your resolve to show yourselves not unworthy of the proud distinction you enjoy, of being numbered among the most dutiful and loyal subjects of our beloved queen.

As for myself, my course is clear. A British subject I was born, a British subject I will die. With my utmost effort, with my latest breath, will I oppose the veiled treason which attempts, by sordid means and mercenary proffers, to lure our people from their allegiance. During my long public service of nearly half a century, I have been true to my country and its best interest, and I appeal with equal confidence to the men who have trusted me in the past and to the young hope of the country, with whom rests its destinies in the future, to give me their united and strenuous aid in this my last effort for the unity of the empire and the preservation of our commercial and political freedom.

Wilfrid Laurier
8 June 1891

"Sir John Macdonald now belongs to the ages"

In the 1891 election campaign, the elderly John A. Macdonald pushed himself beyond endurance and he had a series of strokes soon afterward. He died on Saturday, 6 June 1891, and on the following Monday he was eulogized in the House of Commons. Wilfrid Laurier, his political opponent of many years, spoke in the most moving of terms.

I fully appreciate the intensity of the grief which fills the souls of all those who were the friends and followers of Sir John Macdonald, at the loss of the great leader whose whole life has been so closely identified with their party, a party upon which he has thrown such brilliancy and lustre. We on this side of the House, who were his opponents, who did not believe in his policy nor in his methods of government, we take our full share of their grief, for the loss which they deplore today is far and away beyond and above the ordinary compass of party range. It is in every respect a great national loss, for he is no more who was, in many respects, Canada's most illustrious son, and in every sense Canada's foremost citizen and statesman.

At the period of life to which Sir John Macdonald had arrived, death, whenever it comes, cannot be said to come unexpectedly. Some few months ago, during the turmoil of the late election, when the country was made aware that on a certain day the physical strength of the veteran premier had not been equal to his courage, and that his intense labour for the time being had prostrated his singularly wiry frame, everybody, with the exception, perhaps, of his buoyant self, was painfully anxious lest perhaps the angel of death had touched him with his wing. When, a few days ago, in the heat of an angry discussion in this Parliament, news spread in this House that of a sudden his condition had become alarming, the surging waves of angry discussion were at once hushed, and everyone, friend and foe, realized that this time for a certainty the angel of death had appeared and had crossed the threshold of his home. Thus we were not taken by surprise and, although we were prepared for the sad event, yet it is almost impossible to convince the unwilling mind that it is true that Sir John Macdonald is no more, that the chair which we now see empty shall remain forever vacant, that the face so familiar in this Parliament for the last forty years shall be seen no more, and that the voice so well known shall be heard no more, whether in solemn debate or in pleasant and mirthful tones. In fact, the place of Sir John Macdonald in this country was so large and so absorbing that it is almost impossible to conceive that the political life of this country, the fate of this country, can continue without him. His loss overwhelms us. For my part, I say with all truth his loss overwhelms me, and it also overwhelms this Parliament, as if indeed one of the institutions of the land had given way. Sir John Macdonald now belongs to the ages, and it can be said with certainty that the career which has just been closed is one of the most remarkable careers of this century.

It would be premature at this time to attempt to fix or anticipate what will be the final judgment of history upon him; but there were in his career and his life features so prominent and so conspicuous that already they shine with a glow which time cannot alter, which even now appear before the eye such as they will appear to the end in history. I think it can be asserted that, for the supreme art of governing men, Sir John Macdonald was gifted as few men in any land or in any age were gifted, gifted with the most high of all qualities, qualities which would have made him famous wherever exercised, and which would have shone all the more conspicuously the larger the theatre. The fact that he could congregate together elements the most heterogeneous and blend them into one compact party, and to the end of his life keep them steadily under his hand, is perhaps altogether unprecedented. The fact that during all those years he retained unimpaired not only the confidence, but the devotion, the ardent devotion and affection of his party, is evidence that, besides those higher qualities of statesmanship to which we were the daily witnesses, he was also endowed with those inner, subtle, undefinable graces of soul which win and keep the hearts of men. As to his statesmanship, it is written in the history of Canada. It may be said without any exaggeration whatever, that the life of Sir John Macdonald, from the date he entered Parliament, is the history of Canada, for he was connected and associated with all the events, all the facts which brought Canada from the position it then occupied—the position of two small provinces, having nothing in common but their common allegiance, united by a bond of paper, and united by nothing else—to the present state of development which Canada has reached. Although my political views compel me to say that, in my judgment, his actions were not always the best that could have been taken in the interest of Canada, although my conscience compels me to say that of late he has imputed to his opponents motives which I must say in my heart he has misconceived, yet I am only too glad here to sink these differences, and to remember only the great services he has performed for our country, to remember that his actions always displayed great originality of view, unbounded fertility of resource, a high level of intellectual conception and, above all, a far-reaching vision beyond the event of the day, and still higher, permeating the whole, a broad patriotism, a devotion to Canada's welfare, Canada's advancement, and Canada's glory . . .

One after another we see those who have been instrumental in bringing Canada to its present stage of development removed from amongst us. Today we deplore the loss of him who, we all unite in saying, was the foremost Canadian of his time, and who filled the largest place in Canadian history. Only last week was buried in the city of Montreal another son of Canada, one who at one time had been a tower of strength to the Liberal Party, one who will ever be remembered as one of the noblest, purest, and greatest characters that Canada has ever produced, Sir Antoine-Aimé Dorion. He had not been in favour of Confederation—not that he was opposed to the principle; but he believed that the union of the provinces, at that day, was premature. When, however, Confederation had become a fact, he gave the best of his mind and heart to make it a success. It may indeed happen, sir, that when the Canadian people see the ranks thus gradually reduced and thinned of those upon whom they have been in the habit of relying for guidance, that a feeling of apprehension will creep into the heart lest, perhaps, the institutions of Canada may be imperilled. Before the grave of him who, above all, was the father of Confederation, let not grief be barren grief; but let grief be coupled with the resolution, the determination, that the work in which Liberals and Conservatives, in which Brown and Macdonald, united, shall not perish, but that though united Canada may be deprived of the services of her greatest men, still Canada shall and will live.

Lady Aberdeen
8 November 1894

"A golden link uniting women in bonds of sisterhood"

Lady Ishbel Maria Gordon, Marchioness of Aberdeen and Temair, was the spouse of Lord Aberdeen, Canada's governor general from 1893-98. She was a strong, impressive woman with many interests, a staunch democrat with a social conscience. She created the Victorian Order of Nurses in Canada, and she believed that women had a significant role to play in society. She was also instrumental in creating the National Council of Women, an endeavour that was opposed by conservative commentators and newspapers. In her address to the founding meeting of the Local Council of Women in Victoria, Lady Aberdeen accepted the Victorian concept that the primary role of women was as wives, mothers, and guardians of the social order, but she deftly pushed the existing boundaries.

I must thank you ladies, who have been good enough to come out and meet me this evening in such large numbers in response to the invitation of those who have asked me to tell you the aims and working of the National Council of Women of Canada. As for the gentlemen, will you forgive me if I ignore your presence here tonight, if I try, as best I can, to forget it? I look upon you only in the light of necessary evils in your capacity of escort to the ladies. But all the same that does not distract from the honour you have done me in being willing to be present in any capacity. Doubtless no movement affecting a considerable part of the community can prosper without the cordial support of both men and women. I trust that in this movement, the women of Victoria will be able to depend on the approval of their husbands, fathers, and brothers . . . There is likely to be a good deal of criticism of this movement, and I would earnestly ask you gentlemen spectators, though you are our critics in general, to try to understand our objects and to weigh the matter well before you oppose the council or divide it.

You will agree with us as to our ultimate objects, I know—unity, an endeavour to communicate mutual strength and sympathy between all women workers, and to stimulate all work for the good of others. Some may say that they do not see how the council is going to do all this. Let me ask them if they have a scheme of their own. If not, it is surely a solemn responsibility to try to hinder those who are at heart trying to do God's work and to reach after His idea of unity.

But now, ladies, I must set myself to my work and try to explain to you something of this National Council of Women of Canada, which is intended by its authors and promoters to forge, as it were, a golden link uniting all the women workers from ocean to ocean in bonds of sisterhood for the high and holy work which they are called on to undertake by virtue of their common womanhood, and their common responsibilities in this fair country.

I am afraid I must ask you to bear with me while I go through the dry details of our organization. But before doing this, I would like to remove some misapprehensions concerning the council by stating what it is not.

It is not a political association. Some English newspapers stated at one time that I was organizing a political association of women throughout Canada for the purpose of turning out the present government . . . Quite apart from the fact that I myself have forgotten for some time what politics mean, this council has nothing to do with politics; if there existed a political association of women in the Dominion, they could be represented on it.

The council is not a trades union, although trades unions or friendly societies of women can be represented on it. It is not a temperance association, although temperance societies can be and are represented on it. It is not a society for revolutionizing the relation of mistresses and servants, although we hope that the present difficulties in connection with domestic service will receive much consideration. It is not a religious body only, nor a philanthropic body only, nor an educational body only. It is none of these things, and yet it is all of them, and that I think is the keynote of the object of this meeting. We desire to form a body which will, as it were, focus the work and thought of women in Victoria, the work and thought of all the different activities being carried on. That is the object of the National Council of Women of Canada, and it is on the same principle that all the local councils throughout Canada are intended to be formed . . .

We all here agree that the home is woman's first mission. But what does that involve? Sometimes it is spoken of as if home duties meant a narrow life, a circumscribed life, but if we ask ourselves what home means to each of us, what it should mean to each of us, we shall see that it by no means involves a narrow life. If we ask ourselves each of us to think out what would be the ideal for ourselves, each in our own position in our own home, of what we could do and be, and if we could rise to that idea of character and influence and life and self-sacrifice, you will at once see how much it means and how much we have to learn. Sometimes people speak as though the power to be homemakers came by instinct to women, but do not we know, we who are in our homes as wives, mothers, sisters, daughters, that this is by no means the case? Do we not each of us realize our want of training and of knowledge in our contact with other lives, on which so much depends? Cannot we in these general conferences and meetings which are to bring us together as women who are wanting to fulfill their duty in the world, cannot we specially confer together on some of these matters which touch the very inmost springs of our lives? Do we not need to know much more of how to train our children, how to study our children, to understand the different characters of those little ones that have been confided to us, and whom we often damage because we do not understand and enter into the individuality, the different characteristics of each one, and the different training needed to fit them for their work in life? Cannot these subjects bearing upon the relations of parents and children be made, as I trust they will be, most important subjects in your councils . . .

But springing up from these home duties come our social duties, which come to every woman, her duties to society. We sometimes lament the low tone of society, but if there is that low tone anywhere, whose fault is it? Is it not that of the women of the place? And is not a very grave responsibility lying upon us, and especially now in these days when every opportunity is given to woman for thorough education and for the use of her influence for the heightening of the whole tone of society. If we see the young people in our midst making pleasure the main object of life, whose fault is that? If there are two standards of morality expected, one for man and the other for woman, one for Sundays and the other for weekdays, one for religion and the other for business, whose fault is it? Is it not the fault of those who set the tone in the home and in the social life? In these matters also, can we not unite in our conferences those of all churches and sections of thought who desire a lofty standard of morality, whether from the secular or religious point of view?

Can we not help one another to lift higher the ideal of life, whether in the home or social life, or the life of the country? Does it not depend upon us women, and especially upon those whom God has called to be mothers, to see that the children grow up with a high ideal of public life, that they should deem it to be a high privilege that they belong to this country, deem it a high honour to be trained to serve their country any way, however humble? These matters come home to us mothers, although I am not sure that the women of any country have realized the duty incumbent upon them to bring up their children with a distinct idea of what that service means. That brings us again to the further thought of a woman's duty to her country, and to mankind at large; to that wider idea of duty to which women are called in these days. The call comes to all of us in one way or another. There are few who can shroud themselves in the privacy of their homes without hearing in their hearts the summons to serve their fellow creatures in some way or another . . .

Let it be clearly understood that we are not demanding rights by this council; we are but seeking to help one another to perform our duties in a higher spirit and with a deeper motive than ever before, although, indeed, it may lead us to see duties where we never saw them before. But let us never seek to escape the discipline which has sanctified womanhood, but rather let us glorify in it. Let us make it yield us its full fruits, teaching us to give our very best and our very selves to whatever work for the common good God calls us . . .

Wilfrid Laurier

14 October 1904

"The twentieth century shall be the century of Canada"

Senator Grattan O'Leary said of Wilfrid Laurier, "No one in my experience touched him as an orator; he was the greatest I was privileged to hear in sixty years of observing Parliament." Laurier made the following campaign speech before a packed house in Toronto's Massey Hall on 14 October 1904. The speech, while not one of his best, was vintage Laurier—suave, playing to the audience, and attacking his political enemies. Near its end, he provided his grand vision for Canada, and his phrase about Canada's century remains attached to his name and his memory.

We have been in office now for eight years—our record is before the people of Canada. It is open for search, always open for search, and search under the most glaring light that can be found. To this I have no objection. This I rather welcome. I do not claim that we have been infallible; I do not claim that we not have made mistakes. On the contrary, I am prepared to admit that in some things purely departmental we may have been led into errors. But this I may tell you . . . we have given you a pure and honest government. We are assailed, it is true, and assailed with all the bitterness of the Tory party when they are in Opposition, but let me say this, and I put it to the judgment of all who are friends or foes, that the head and front of the charges that are brought against us is, after all, very small, very minute and very trivial. There are no serious charges against us. If those made are to be compared with the offences proved and charged against those who are now our traducers, when they were in office, they are simply as the weight of a feather against a mountain of iniquity.

It is easy to criticize; it is always easy to find fault. The problem is, the difficulty is, to construct and to build, and I submit again to the judgment of friend and foe, that after eight years in office there is no one here, there is not in the country, a man, a citizen, who does not feel prouder in his heart to call himself a Canadian than he was eight years ago. I do not claim credit for the prosperity, which this country has witnessed, but I assert that as a result of the policy followed by this government, the name of Canada has obtained a prominence which it had not eight years ago. I assert that the name of Canada during these eight years has far and wide and whether a man be a friend or be a foe, he knows he must admit that there are today in Europe thousands and thousands of men who had never heard the name Canada eight years ago, and who today, every day, turn their eyes toward this new star which has appeared in the western sky . . .

I hope to live to see the fertile west, into which thousands and thousands of men are crowding every year—I hope to see that goods of Ontario and Quebec carried into the new territory for the use of the settlers who are pouring in there—nay, I hope also to see the goods of Asia, of Japan, the new nation, and of China, the old nation, passing over the railway en route to the harbours of Great Britain. I hope to see that, and it is not a vain hope; if God spares me for years yet, I shall have the satisfaction of seeing it. Two years ago I was coming back from Europe, from England after the Imperial Conference which had taken place during the festivities of the coronation of His Majesty the king. I was in poor health and had to go down south, and then I for the first time took up this subject. And the more I looked at it the more enthusiastic I became, the more I satisfied myself that there was the grand highway from Europe to Asia for the twentieth century.

I tell you that the nineteenth century has been the century of United States' development. The past one hundred years has been filled with the pages of their history. Let me tell you, my fellow countrymen, that all the signs point this way, that the twentieth century shall be the century of Canada and of Canadian development. For the next seventy-five years, nay for the next one hundred years, Canada shall be the star towards which all men who love progress and freedom shall come.

I am simply a Canadian like yourselves, coming from another province, but trying the best I can to unite our common people. I ask you, and this is the prayer I want to convey to you, simply ask you to forever sink the petty differences which have divided you in the past and unite with us, and take your share of the grand future which lies before us. I give that prayer to you, but if there is one class to which above all others I would convey the appeal it is not to you older men, not to you middle-aged men, but to the young boys in the galley, the hope of the country.

To those who have life before them, let my prayer be this: Remember from this day forth never to look simply at the horizon, as it may be limited by the limits of the province, but look abroad all over the continent, wherever the British flag floats, and let your motto be Canada first, Canada last, and Canada always.

Henri Bourassa
5 July 1905

"These territories were acquired in the name
and with the money of the whole Canadian people,
French as well as English"

Henri Bourassa was a journalist and intellectual with an unrivalled influence in turn-of-the-century Quebec. He was for a time a Liberal in Laurier's caucus, but was increasingly bitter about Laurier's compromises over French language rights. Bourassa was pan-Canadian in his views, but he held the unshakeable opinion that Confederation had been a compact between the French and English, and that the two languages and cultures should be respected throughout the country. Bourassa made this speech in the House of Commons in 1905, when it was proposed that the French language rights should not be applied to the new provinces of Saskatchewan and Alberta. Those rights had been extended to Manitoba upon entry into Confederation in 1870, but had later been withdrawn, a development that Bourassa refused to accept.

Half a century later his arguments were echoed in Pierre Trudeau's approach to federalism, one that promoted bilingualism and bicultural-ism and used the Constitution to protect minority language rights.

I cannot bring myself to believe that in tracing the boundaries of Manitoba, the Dominion Parliament have thereby shown their intention of denying to the French-speaking people settled in the remainder of the territories the guarantees which they granted to that part of the population comprised within the limits of the new provinces . . . Would not the compact whereby the Dominion government is bound to guarantee to the Catholic minority in the Northwest their separate schools, bind them to maintain at the same time the official use of the French language, since these two constitutional rights were both included in the Bill of Rights presented by the delegates from the Red River and accepted by the Dominion Parliament? . . .

The Act of 1867 provided at the outset solely for the organization of the provinces then constitutional. Even before entering Confederation, these provinces enjoyed self-government; they had their own Parliament, their official tongue, their rules of parliamentary procedure. The idea did not occur to the fathers of Confederation to alter that condition of things; but in establishing the Dominion Parliament they did so on a basis in harmony with the rights and traditions of the two elements which make up the Canadian nation; and that is why they provided that the French and Eng-lish tongues would be, on equal terms, the official language of Canada. Later on, the Dominion Parliament acquired those immense western territories out of which were carved the province of Manitoba and those of Alberta and Saskatchewan. These territories were acquired in the name and with the money of the whole Canadian people, French as well as English, Catholic as well as Protestant. And when Parliament established the former of these provinces, they did not forget the rights of the French Canadian people; they deemed it fair and reasonable that the two official languages of Canada be so declared to be such in the province of Manitoba. Does the honourable member for St. John contend that the legislators of 1870, that the Macdon-alds, the Cartiers, the Holtons, the Huntingtons, that all these eminent statesmen who were then at the head of both parties, broke the Constitu-tion of 1867 when, in 1870, they recognized the rights of the French language in Manitoba?

MR. DEMERS: Circumstances have changed.

MR. BOURASSA: In what respect?

MR. DEMERS: As the prime minister has explained, the French Canadians were numerous enough at the time to warrant the official recognition of the French language in Manitoba; that reason does not exist in the territories today . . .

MR. BOURASSA: The honourable member for St. John has referred to the small numbers of French-speaking people in the territories. The solicitor general argued on the same lines when he stated that we had no right to claim the official recognition of the French language in the Northwest Territories, because the French-speaking people were not as numerous as the Germans, the Doukhobors, or the Mormons. The prime minister spoke in a similar strain when he stated that the French Canadians in Massachusetts have stronger claims to the official recognition of their tongue in that state than the French-speaking people have in our western provinces. Have we really reached that point? Are we, with one stroke of the pen, to blot out 150 years of our history; and on this Canadian soil, which our ancestors opened up to civilization under British flag, which we twice saved from the savage onslaughts on the part of Anglo-Saxon Protestants from the neighbouring republic; under this Constitution which is the mere outcome of the compact entered into by the two great groups of the Canadian nation; are we to be told that we are entitled to no more consideration than our fellow countrymen who have drifted into a foreign land? Is that really the reward coming to us after a century and a half of unfaltering loyalty to British institutions? Is that the result of the compact loyally gone into in 1867 between English- and French-speaking Canadians?

In order to do away with a proposal resting on the wide and solid foundation which I have mentioned, subterfuges are resorted to. It is argued that the original compact and the rights of the French language in the west have already been interfered with by Parliament in 1890. That is only a pretense. I have a higher notion of the duties and responsibilities devolving on the representatives of the Canadian nation. If the Parliament of 1890 has made a mistake, that is no reason for us to repeat it and aggravate it. If the Parliament of 1890 misapprehended the work of the fathers of Confederation and of the makers of the Manitoba Constitution, it is our bounden duty to correct that mistake. Parliament in 1890 abolished the use of the French language in the legislative assembly; and now that injustice becomes an argument for those who wish to carry through that sinister work and do away with the printing in French of statutes and legal proceedings. An effort is made to palliate that wrong by covering it up with a further crime. To that I answer boldly: instead of resuming the work initiated by Parliament in 1890, let us retrace our footsteps and take the stand taken formerly by the promoters of the Act of 1870 . . .

If we are anxious to carry on the work of the makers of the Manitoba Constitution, if we are anxious to maintain the constitutional basis which I have referred to, let us introduce in the bills submitted to us a clause guaranteeing the rights of the minority against any interference similar to that of which the English majority has been guilty in 1892. Instead of seeking in our past experience an excuse for our present inactivity, I find therein a lesson which should induce us to define clearly the rights of the minority and safeguard them by means of a precise and unmistakable enactment. Let us not delude ourselves in the matter. If the House rejects my proposal . . . then let us give up all hope as to the rights of the French language in the west. French-Canadian members who are fighting us are making for the downfall of our nationality; and should Parliament reject our amendment, I say an essential principle of our Constitution is being violated.

Let each one of us consult his conscience and realize what responsibility he is assuming just now. As for me, I refuse to take a hand in this unpatriotic work . . . I wish to blot out the wrong committed by the legislators of 1890, and to revert to the constitutional basis laid down by Parliament in 1870.

Bourassa broke with Laurier in 1910 over the government's naval policy, which Bourassa claimed would automatically involve Canada in any war declared by Great Britain. Bourassa founded the influential newspaper *Le Devoir*, and he encouraged Quebec nationalists to run in the 1911 election as independents. Enough of them won to deny a victory to Laurier and the Liberals, and to provide it to Robert Borden and the Conservatives.

Sundar Singh
25 January 1912

"We are subjects of the same empire"

At the turn of the century Canada wanted desperately to attract immigrants to populate its vast spaces and to produce and consume goods. The government prized immigrants from Britain, tolerated them from the rest of Europe, but did not want Asians as permanent residents, although they were needed as temporary workers. The government passed laws to prevent the citizenship of Chinese and South Asians, and to prevent Asian women and wives from coming to Canada. In January 1912, Sundar Singh spoke to the Empire Club, a bastion of anglophone privilege. He challenged the law and prevailing attitudes against Sikhs, although he did not appear to object to a similar treatment accorded to Chinese and Japanese in Canada.

Some few years ago a few troops of the Sikhs passed through Canada on their way to the jubilee of the late Queen Victoria ... These Sikhs went back home and they spoke of the vast prairies where they saw wheat growing the same as we grow wheat. The consequence was that a score of them came out in 1905, about forty of them came in that year and the next, and this went on till there was quite a strong body of them, about four thousand in all, engaged in agriculture; they were farmers in India, and of course they naturally took to farming when they came to this country.

They are British subjects; they have fought for the empire; many of these men have war medals; but, in spite of this fact, they are not allowed to have their families with them when they come to this country; in spite of their being British subjects, they are not allowed to have their wives here. People talk about these Oriental races, and the phrase is understood to include not only the Chinese and the Japanese, but the Sikhs as well, which is absurd. Letters giving inaccurate statements are appearing in the press all the time. I do not know why all this objection should be directed against the Sikhs, against that people, more than against any other Oriental people.

These people are here legally; they have satisfied every process of law; they have been here over five years; they have been good to their employers . . . their work is equal to that of other labourers; their quarters are better, and they are making more wages now; they have fitted into the situation here; they have made good.

In spite of this, there are these letters going through the papers, and there are attacks upon these men; although they are British subjects, nobody stands up for them. We appeal to you of the Empire Club, for we are only four thousand in number, to help us in this matter, and to see that justice is done to these subjects of our king.

We are subjects of the same empire; we have fought, we have sacrificed. We have fought for the empire, and we bear her medals; we have an interest in this country; we have bought property in British Columbia; we have our church and pay our pastor, and we mean to stay in this country. I understand that there is a society called the Home Reformation Society and that it says that it is better for a man to have a wife and family. To others you advance money to come here, and yet to us, British subjects, you refuse to let down the bars. All we are asking of you is justice and fair play, because the Sikhs have believed in fair play, and have believed all the time that they will get justice; that ultimately they will get justice from the British people.

Many people have been telling me that it is useless my trying to bring this question before the Canadian people, but I am firmly persuaded that, if the question is properly brought before right-minded Canadians, that they will say that the same rights should be given to the Sikh people as are given to any other British subjects . . .

It is only a matter of justice. If this empire is to be and continue to be a great empire, as it is sure to be, then it must be founded on righteousness and justice; your laws cannot be one thing for one set and a different thing for the rest of us.

These Sikhs are quite alone; they do the roughest labour; they do not come into competition with other labour, and yet this is the treatment they receive. They are plainly told: "We do not want you to bring your wives in." You cannot expect people to be moral, if you debar them from bringing in their wives and children. They can travel in Japan; they can travel in Europe; they can travel anywhere under the British flag, except here . . . We appeal to you, gentlemen, to say that in any country, under any conditions, the treatment that the Sikhs are receiving is not fair. We appeal to your good sense and to your humanity to see that justice is done, that this thing is not continued, for it has been going on for quite a long time.

Nellie McClung

28 January 1914

"Man was made for something higher than voting"

Nellie McClung was well known in western Canada as a writer and an activist for women's rights. On 27 January 1914, Manitoba Premier Rodmond Roblin met with McClung and a delegation of several hundred from the Political Equality League, which was seeking the vote for women. Roblin treated them condescendingly and flatly refused them, saying, "I believe woman suffrage would break up the home and send women to mix up in political meetings." The following evening McClung and others turned that meeting into a piece of guerrilla theatre, with McClung playing the part of the premier and making this mock speech to a fictitious group of men appearing before women legislators asking for the right to vote.

Gentlemen of the delegation, it gives me great pleasure to welcome you here today. We like delegations, and although this is the first time you have asked us for the vote, we hope it will not be the last. Come any time and ask for anything you like. We wish to congratulate you, too, on the quiet and ladylike way in which you have come into our presence; and we assure you that if the working men in England had fought for their franchise in such a pleasing and dignified way, the results would have been entirely different. If they had used these peaceful means and no other, they might still be enjoying the distinction and privilege of waiting on members of Parliament.

But I cannot do what you ask me to do, for the facts are all against you. Manhood suffrage has not been a success in the unhappy countries where it has been tried. They either do not vote at all, or else they vote too much, and the best men shrink away from the polls as from a pestilence . . .

Manhood suffrage would plunge our fair province into a perfect debauchery of extravagance, a perfect nightmare of expense. Think of the increased size of the voters list—we have trouble enough with it now. Of course, with the customary hot-headedness of reformers, you never thought of that, oh, no, just like a man, you never thought of the expense . . .

I tell you frankly, I won't do it, for I have always loved and reverenced men. Yet though I love them, I know their frailties. If once they are let vote, they become addicted to it, and even if the polls are only open once every four years, I tell you, I know men, they are creatures of habit, and they'll hang around the polls all the rest of the time . . .

Man was made for something higher and holier than voting. Men were made to support families and homes which are the bulwark of the nation. What is home without a father? What is home without a bank account? The man who pays the grocer rules the world. In this agricultural province, man's place is the farm. Shall I call men away from the useful plough and the necessary harrow to talk loud on street corners about things which do not concern them? Shall I cheat the farm by turning honest ploughmen into dishonest and scheming politicians? I tell you no, for I was born on the farm and I am not ashamed to say so—the farm, the farm, the dear, old farm— we'll never mortgage the farm.

In the United States of America, when men vote, there is one divorce for every marriage, for politics unsettle men, and that leads to unsettled bills, and broken furniture, and broken vows. When you ask me for the vote, you are asking me to break up peaceful and happy homes and wreck innocent lives, and I tell you again, frankly, I will not do it. I am an old-fashioned woman; I believe in the sanctity of marriage. Politics unsettles men, and enters every department of life, with its blighting influence. It even confuses our vital statistics. They tell me that where men vote, when the election is very close, men have been known to come back and vote years after they were dead. Now, do you think I am going to let the hallowed calm of our cemeteries be invaded by the raucous voice of politics? . . .

I know I am a factor in the affairs of this province. If it were not for this fatal modesty which on more than one occasion has almost blighted my career, I would say that I know I have written my name large across the province, so large indeed we had to move the boundaries to get it all in, and my most earnest wish for this bright land of promise is that I may long be spared to guide its destiny among the nations of the earth. I know there is no one but me who can guide the ship of state. I actually tremble when I think what might happen to these leaderless lambs. But I must not dwell on such an overwhelming calamity, but go forward in the strong hope that I may long be spared to be the proud standard-bearer of the grand old flag of this grand old party, which has gone down many times to disgrace but, thank God, never defeat.

McClung and others decided to take a more overtly political route, and McClung became a speaker in great demand during the 1914 and 1915 Manitoba provincial elections. The Liberals won in August 1915. Women received the vote in Manitoba in January 1916 and for federal elections in 1918.

Robert Borden
14 August 1914

"We stand shoulder to shoulder with Britain"

World War I began on 4 August 1914, when Britain's ultimatum for Germany to withdraw from occupied Belgium expired. The entire British Empire, including Canada, was automatically at war. The House of Commons was on summer break when the war broke out, and MPS had to be assembled from every corner of the country. Robert Borden, the Conservative prime minister, had defeated Laurier in the 1911 reciprocity election. Borden imposed the Emergency War Measures Act, providing the government with wide-ranging powers to act. Borden was not known as a grand orator. His speech in the House on 14 August was sombre and deliberate.

The war has come upon us in the end very suddenly indeed, and perhaps we have not all adequately considered the awful responsibility that must have rested upon the foreign secretary and the prime minister of the United

Kingdom when they and their colleagues took the issue which meant . . .
the first general European war for a hundred years, and beyond all question
the most appalling war history has ever known. We read in the press of the
haggard faces and the tremulous lips of Mr. Asquith and Sir Edward Grey
when they made their announcements; but there as here they were sustained
by the thought that for the time being party strife was stilled; and we do not
forget that those in the British Isles who had protested most strongly in the
first place against the participation of Great Britain in this war united in
upholding the hands of the government and in maintaining the interests and
duty of the empire . . .

We have absolutely no quarrel with the German people. I believe that
they are a peaceable people, that they are not naturally a warlike people,
although unfortunately they are dominated at the present time by a military
autocracy. No one can overestimate what civilization and the world owe to
Germany. In literature, in science, art, and philosophy, in almost every
department of human knowledge and activity, they have stood in the very
forefront of the world's advancement. Nearly half a million of the very best
citizens of Canada are of German origin, and I am sure that no one would
for one moment desire to utter any word or use any expression in debate
which would wound the self-respect or hurt the feelings of any of our fellow citizens of German descent . . .

Therefore we have declared by Order-in-Council and by proclamation
under the authority of His Royal Highness the governor general that those
people who were born in Germany or in Austria-Hungary and have come
to Canada as adopted citizens of this country, whether they have become
naturalized or not, are entitled to the protection of the law in Canada and
shall receive it, that they shall not be molested or interfered with, unless any
among them should desire to aid or abet the enemy or leave this country
for the purpose of fighting against Great Britain and her allies . . .

The men of Canada who are going to the front are going as free men
by voluntary enlistment, as free men in a free country. They are coming forward voluntarily for the purpose of serving this Dominion and this empire
in a time of peril. Already I am informed by the minister of militia that
thousands more than will be required have volunteered to go. I desire to
express my absolute concurrence in the view . . . that it is the duty of the
people of Canada, and of the government of Canada too, so far as may be
necessary, to make all suitable provision for the families and children of those

who are going to the front. We are giving to our country and our empire at this time of our best, and we are proud to do it; but we must not forget our duty to those who are left behind. Neither the people of Canada nor the government of Canada will ever for one moment forget that duty . . .

I desire to express appreciation at this moment of the action of the provinces of Canada and of individuals in Canada during the past week or ten days. From provinces and from individuals, gifts have come, great and small, showing the intense eagerness of the people and of every province in Canada to associate themselves in this great issue with what we are doing in the Dominion as a whole, and with all that is being done in every dominion of the empire. The people as a whole, not only here in Canada, but in the mother country itself and in every dominion will, I am sure, feel the most grateful appreciation and render the warmest thanks for all the aid thus tendered . . .

From every part of Canada, we have had most unmistakable evidence of the determination of the people of this Dominion to support the mother country and the other dominions which are bound together by the strongest possible ties, the ties of absolute British liberty and of perfect self-government. Those ties bind together the provinces of Canada in this Dominion. Those ties bind together the dominions of the empire with the mother country; and we rejoice to know that, in a time of stress and perhaps of peril such as this, they have proved the strongest possible ties that could be devised by any government throughout the world . . .

It is not fitting that I should prolong this debate. In the awful dawn of the greatest war the world has ever known, in the hour when peril confronts us such as this empire has not faced for a hundred years, every vain or unnecessary word seems a discord. As to our duty, all are agreed: we stand shoulder to shoulder with Britain and the other British dominions in this quarrel. And that duty we shall not fail to fulfill as the honour of Canada demands. Not for love of battle, not for lust of conquest, not for greed of possessions, but for the cause of honour, to maintain solemn pledges, to uphold principles of liberty, to withstand forces that would convert the world into an armed camp; yea, in the very name of the peace that we sought at any cost save that of dishonour, we have entered into this war; and, while gravely conscious of the tremendous issues involved and of all the sacrifices that they may entail, we do not shrink from them, but with firm hearts we abide the event.

Arthur Meighen
21 June 1917

"A choice between fidelity and desertion"

Brilliant, opinionated, and incisive, Arthur Meighen was one of Canada's great orators. He was one of the few twentieth century parliamentarians who were just as comfortable talking about Shakespeare and literature as about railroads and the military. Senator Grattan O'Leary wrote that, "In our own country, only Laurier, Howe and McGee dwelt on the same plane as him." Born in Ontario, he moved to Manitoba to practice law and was elected to the House of Commons in 1908. He served in the Borden government, where he was instrumental in writing legislation for conscription and other wartime measures.

Most Canadians believed the war in Europe would be a brief one, but it dragged on interminably in trench warfare and sporadic large battles that cost tens of thousands of lives. Initially, the Canadian government was confident that it could provide troops through voluntary enlistment, but by 1916 there was a growing demand, particularly among Canadians of British ancestry, for the government to impose conscription to raise more troops. That enthusiasm was not shared in Quebec, where people had little allegiance to Britain, and where Henri Bourassa and others were angry about the undermining of French language education throughout Canada. In 1916, British Prime Minister David Lloyd George summoned prime ministers of the dominions to London. Borden attended the meetings and visited with Canadians troops, particularly those wounded and in hospital. He was shocked and moved, and returned to Canada committed to conscripting men for compulsory military service. Meighen drafted the legislation, and he entered the debate on 17 June, responding to an amendment proposed by Opposition leader Wilfrid Laurier that the legislation be deferred and put to a national referendum.

I regard the forwarding of troops to the front on the scale now being undertaken as an all-essential, as something we cannot shirk. Does anybody really think otherwise? Whatever means are necessary to procure these men, they must be sent; and whatever action is necessary on our part to support our army at present in France, we must take. No one has seriously argued in this House, and in solemn truth no one seriously believes that we can dispatch, as we have done, three hundred and fifty thousand men overseas, commissioned by us to stand between our country and destruction, pledge them the undying fidelity of a grateful people, watch them through harrowing years of suffering, bathe ourselves in the reflected glory of their gallantry and devotion, and then leave them to be decimated and destroyed. Surely, an obligation of honour is upon us, and fortifying that obligation of honour is the primal, instinctive, eternal urge of every nation to protect its own security. There is no other way in which the security of our state can be to a maximum ensured, and certainly no other way in which its honour can be preserved . . .

I pass on to examine some contentions advanced in support of the amendment moved by the right honourable Opposition leader. It has been a matter of much interest, and indeed of curiosity, to observe the wonderful variety of opinions collected behind this referendum amendment. A referendum amendment is really not an amendment at all. Very definitely it is not a policy: it is a negation of policy. Why has it been adopted as party tactics? Merely as an expedient to avoid facing the issue, and to gather behind the Opposition leader all support, however incongruous, that can be got together. What kind of opinions are behind the amendment? It is moved by the leader of the Opposition, who complains that we have dashed this bill upon the House too suddenly and too soon. It is seconded by the honourable member for Edmonton (Mr. Oliver), who complains that we have already waited too long; that we should have taken this course and held a referendum a year ago. The leader of the Opposition argues that the bill will be met with opposition, if not with resistance, on the part of French Canada and will bring about disunion in our country. His seconder, the honourable member for Edmonton, wants in place of this bill another one which will take all of these one hundred thousand men out of French Canada alone . . .

Do honourable gentlemen realize where they are when they support this proposal? Do they recognize the company they are in? I make appeal to honourable gentlemen opposite, who at other times and under brighter skies may have felt there was some principle behind a referendum, to argue out for themselves whether that principle has any application in a crisis like this. Is the referendum peculiarly suited for war? Is it suited to a time when the best and most deserving of our electorate are overseas, shifting and surging along a battlefront of continental scale, and when only a mere fraction of their number may possibly be counted in the vote? Results of twelve months and more have proved that recruits in numbers anything like those required cannot be obtained by methods of the past.

The *Toronto Globe* has said that the voluntary system is as dead as Julius Caesar. Months ago the Liberal press of English-speaking Canada proclaimed that under it we could not get absolutely necessary troops. We have waited until we thought the public of Canada generally had realized that truth, and realized it with such overmastering conviction as to mean general consent to the enactment of a compulsory law. Why confuse the situation by a tricky referendum? Do not honourable gentlemen in their hearts admit that the passing of this amendment would bring joy to friends of Germany in every part of the world? It would be welcomed at Potsdam. It would be supported, were he here, by the head of the German nation himself. It would make headlines of elation in every German newspaper on this and other continents. Such is the company honourable gentlemen are in who support this proposal. Its passing would be a cause of rejoicing to every poolroom loafer, to every movie veteran, to every sporting fan, to all who have shrunk from duty; but it would be a subject of resentment, regret, and pain to men who have nobly done their part to preserve the liberty, and uphold the honour, of Canada . . .

We as a people have a right to deliberate, and in a constitutional way to vote, to negative, if we so desire, any policy which is still open for us to decide. But surely the prosecution of this war with the whole might of Canada is not in that category. That question has been passed upon. If there ever was a time for a referendum, which I deny, it was in August, 1914; it is not now. We have committed ourselves as a nation, we have signed the bond, it is for us to discharge the obligation. The prosecution of this war by every effective and honourable means is now a matter only of good faith: three hundred thousand living men and twenty thousand dead are over there, hostages of our good faith. All that remains for us is a choice between fidelity and desertion, between courage and poltroonery, between honour and everlasting shame.

We must rise to the level of our responsibilities. We must not be afraid to lead. Ministers of the Crown have been execrated from end to end of Canada for failure of leadership and all the rest. Many of those who have skulked at home, but who should be at the front, have lampooned the able and overburdened head of this government, crying out tiresome jargon about failure to lead. Newspaper after newspaper has done the same. Well, here is leadership. Let those who lagged behind and comforted themselves with this monotonous complaint—let them walk up now, close the gap, and stand beside the prime minister. The people of Canada, we have oft been told, call out to Parliament, to members of this House, for strong and fearless leadership. Are we going to answer that call with our hands in the air crying back to those people: "For heaven's sake, lead us." Such is the amendment we are now asked to support.

Lastly, the shadow of disunion is raised and we are pressed to turn back. One cannot help but observe that those who hold over us this threat are, one and all, opposed to the measure anyway, on other grounds. There will inevitably be difference of opinion, but quite plainly there will be nothing in the nature of schism unless honourable gentlemen are determined to create it. I am as confident as I have ever been of anything in my life that if members of this House, reading and studying this measure, and hearing it debated, will go to their constituents and tell them the meaning, purpose and spirit of this bill, there will be no possibility whatever of discord or resistance. Why should there be? There is not a clause that is unjust as between provinces, or races, or creeds. Very positively, and very obviously, there is neither intent, nor possibility, of unfairness to the province of Quebec. Never was more anxious care taken in drafting a law. The minister of justice, whose home is in Montreal, will be in charge of its administration . . .

I appeal to our friends opposite, and to those around me as well—for party divisions as we once had them are not just the same today—I appeal to all of every political faith to take the course which alone will command our self-respect, and which will entitle us to the regard of our own people, of our allies, and of generations to come.

Prime Minister Borden dissolved Parliament in October 1917 and named a union government committed to conscription. Quebec was adamantly opposed and the country was divided in ways that have never entirely healed. Laurier refused Borden's offer to participate in the government, although some of his Liberal members from English Canada did so. Meighen succeeded Borden in 1920 and served briefly as prime minister. He was later appointed to the Senate.

Joseph-Napoléon Francoeur
17 January 1918

"Quebec would accept the rupture
of the federative pact"

Joseph-Napoléon Francoeur was a member of the Quebec Assembly. In the tense period following the 1917 federal election, when English Canadians voted for conscription and Quebecers against, Francoeur introduced a motion that the province consider separation. That prospect had been discussed by some intellectuals in the nineteenth century, including writer Jules-Paul Tardivel, but it never had popular currency.

MR. JOSEPH-NAPOLÉON FRANCOEUR (L, Lotbinière): (proposes) . . . that this house believes that the province of Quebec would be ready to accept the rupture of the federative pact of 1867, if Quebec is believed to be, by other provinces, an obstacle to the union, the progress and the development of Canada . . .

Besides its intrinsic meaning, this motion is not a grievance against the results of this election, but a protest against this campaign of insults, deceit, and slander bestowed upon the province of Quebec, especially over the last few years, resulting in the election's outcome . . .

Have we answered the wishes of the fathers of Confederation? Has the province of Quebec respected the commitments comprised in this association contract? . . . With no fear of being contradicted, we can confirm that we have not shrunk from our duties nor eluded any responsibilities. We have been told that to propose this motion was to admit discouragement, and even defeat. We have wished to express the feelings of the great majority of the population, which is tired of being treated as such and which believes the time has come to either put an end to these sterile struggles or to accept all logical consequences. What this resolution means to its disparagers is that if the province of Quebec is one too many in the confederation, it is ready to discuss the matter and to assume responsibility for its actions . . .

What we want is to live and let live: to live by observing the letter of the Constitution and above all its spirit; to live according to our tastes, our temperament, and our mind-set; to live as free citizens, conscious of our duties and concerned about our responsibilities; to live by working on the progress and development of our province, convinced that we are thus ensuring the development of the country; to live by preserving our language, our beliefs, our traditions, our institutions, and our laws; finally to live as loyal Canadians devoted to the British Crown. Let live. Respect others the way we wish to be respected.

MR. ARTHUR SAUVÉ (C, Deux-Montagnes): Do the supporters of this motion want separation? Must we want, desire this separation? This is the question being asked everywhere ever since notice of this motion was given . . . Considering the overexcitement of spirits on the morrow of the electoral cyclone, it is in my humble opinion that I declared this motion to be inopportune and dangerous—inopportune because it would not have any practical results, and dangerous because it can only unleash a new tempest of revolting prejudices and disastrous accusations. On the morrow of the elections, I think we should have given the time to the great old man who represents his province in this country's Parliament and to the other most eminent leaders of our race to rigorously study the situation, to clear the path and find our key position. It came as no surprise to find that none of the leaders approved this motion. Should this question be raised, it should be submitted to the Parliament of Canada and not in our province where the English element only represents a minute minority in our legislature. Only then would we know if the rest of the country wishes for our isolation and the rupture of Confederation. Otherwise, how would we know?

Why speak of separation in Quebec's legislature? It is the federal Parliament, with the consent of the imperial government, who can dissolve the confederation ... Separation is against our national interests and also our economic interests, as, if we were separate, we would be bound to costly obligations, which would impede our development. We would be forced to reimburse part of the country's debt and our economic organization would be burdened with too heavy a task ...

MR. ATHANASE DAVID (L, Terrebonne): I am convinced that I have accomplished my duties towards the races, my province and my country, by stating that I stand by the Constitution of our country despite the dangers it presents, as the recent crisis has proven. I would not say it is a compelling attachment, but the respect owed to our governing Constitution when one is persuaded that its clauses contain enough justice and guarantees to recover from harm caused when it is breached ...

As far as I am concerned, this statement does not have the presumptuousness of representing anything more than my humble opinion, but I believe that it is preferable for a minority to be governed by a constitution that albeit may contain some dangers ... than to accept a new political system which ostensibly would offer a greater national satisfaction but that would conceal perhaps even greater misfortunes in the future ... I am confident that our confederation will emerge from this chaos like all nations of the world, educated by suffering, enlightened by new experience, and that by finding its way and by needing the efforts of each group and each race, it will make the necessary appeal to rally all groups and all races ...

MR. LAWRENCE ARTHUR CANNON (L, Quebec Centre): The shortcoming of this motion is the initiation of a debate over a hypothesis, an unsubstantial question. Never, neither today nor tomorrow, will the other provinces believe that we represent an obstacle to the development of Canada. It is impossible; we are at the center of it, the nucleus. Without Quebec, the confederation would cease to exist; it would be divided in two incapacitated parts. I do not like the wording. The day Quebec will attempt to step out of the confederation, the decision will be made by us and for our benefit and not because of the wishes or opinions of other provinces. Let us not be too preoccupied with the "What will they think?"...

For that matter, this attitude is not appropriate for a province whose population is, according to an expression coined by the premier at a memorable occasion, the most senior member of this country. It is not because certain newcomers to the western provinces and elsewhere, the last to arrive in our country, do not know how to apply the principles of the Constitution and treat us as equals, that the province must take a Cinderella attitude with one hand on the doorknob ready to tell its sister provinces, "I will leave if that is your wish." This attitude is undignified and it is not in the tradition of our race to give way to a stream of insults.

MR. LOMER GOUIN (L, Portneuf): I believe in the Canadian Confederation. A federal government seems to be the only option in Canada due to our differences in race and beliefs and also because of the variety and multitude of local needs of our immense territory...The confederation was neither the result of a whim nor an act lacking due thought, but the result of a necessity. This act was freely accepted by Quebec. It has benefited from it and will continue to do so and it is out of question to change such a good regime. What would happen if we were to separate?...

Landlocked as we are, with no access to the sea during all these winter months, in which position would we find ourselves? How would we defend our immense border? What duties would be applied to provinces with which we are presently trafficking freely? How much of the national debt would we have to assume? How would we pay for the debt that would rest on our shoulders?... Finally, in which position would our people find themselves outside of Quebec?... It is true that our province has often been the object of wrongful attacks and that we have rarely been spared insults. But should this be enough to justify a request to rupture a pact, which has allowed us to obtain the results that I summarized earlier?

MR. JOSEPH-NAPOLÉON FRANCOEUR (L, Lotbinière): All I wanted was for opinions to be expressed. I now declare that, given that my motion has had the desired effect, I do not wish for a vote to be registered.

Eventually, Francoeur withdrew his own motion, saying that it was a symbolic gesture. Nonetheless, it was an important historical moment, taking Quebec beyond the ideas of leaders such as Henri Bourassa, who were Quebec nationalists, but resolutely Canadian at the same time.

Arthur Meighen

3 July 1921

"They rest in the quiet of God's acre
with the brave of all the world"

World War I ended on 11 November 1918. Canada's fighting forces performed well, and it is said that Canada forged its identity as an independent nation in the horrible furnace of war. The costs were great—sixty thousand dead and thousands more who returned mutilated in mind and spirit. In 1921, Arthur Meighen, now prime minister, delivered this fine eulogy to the war dead at Vimy Ridge in France.

The Great War is past; the war that tried through and through every quality and mystery of the human mind and the might of the human spirit; the war that closed, we hope forever, the long, ghastly story of the arbitrament of men's differences by force; the last clash and crash of earth's millions is over now. There can be heard only sporadic conflicts, the moan of prostrate nations, the cries of the bereaved and desolate, the struggling of exhausted peoples to rise and stand and move onward. We live among the ruins and echoes of Armageddon. Its shadow is receding slowly backward into history.

At this time, the proper occupation of the living is, first, to honour our heroic dead; next, to repair the havoc, human and material, which surrounds us; and, lastly, to learn aright and apply with courage the lessons of the war.

Here in the heart of Europe, we meet to unveil a memorial to our country's dead. In earth which has resounded to the drums and tramplings of many conquests, they rest in the quiet of God's acre with the brave of all the world. At death, they sheathed in their hearts the sword of devotion, and now from oft-stricken fields they hold aloft its cross of sacrifice, mutely beckoning those who would share their immortality. No words can add to their fame, nor so long as gratitude holds a place in men's hearts can our forgetfulness be suffered to detract from their renown. For as the war dwarfed by its magnitude all contests of the past, so the wonder of human resource, the splendour of human heroism, reached a height never witnessed before.

Ours we thought prosaic days, when great causes of earlier times had lost their inspiration, leaving for attainment those things which demanded only the petty passing inconveniences of the hour, and yet the nobility of manhood had but to hear again the summons of duty and honour to make response which shook the world. Danger to the treasury of common things, for when challenged these are the most sacred of all, danger to them ever stirred our fathers to action, and it has not lost its appeal to their sons.

France lives and France is free, and Canada is the nobler for her sacrifice to help free France to live. In many hundreds of plots throughout these hills and valleys, all the way from Flanders to Picardy, lie fifty thousand of our dead. Their resting places have been dedicated to their memory forever by the kindly grateful heart of France, and will be tended and cared for by us in the measure of the love we bear them. Above them are being planted the maples of Canada, in the thought that her sons will rest the better in shade of trees they knew so well in life. Across the leagues of the Atlantic the heartstrings of our Canadian nation will reach through all time to these graves in France; we shall never let pass away the spirit bequeathed to us by those who fell; "their name liveth for evermore."

Irene Parlby
25 June 1921

"Strong party government does not interest us at all"

Following World War I, drought, low prices, and a general distrust of old line politicians gave rise to agrarian populist parties. By 1921 farmers' governments held power in Ontario, Manitoba, and Alberta, and candidates for the farmer-based Progressive Party were preparing to run in the next federal election. They were anti-politician, agitating against rigid party discipline and patronage, and advocated a form of corporatism in which all sectors would be involved in government. They argued against protective tariffs and for free trade. Irene Parlby was a cabinet minister in the United Farmers of Alberta government. She delivered this speech in Medicine Hat, Alberta, on 25 June 1921, on behalf of a Progressive candidate running in a federal by-election. Parlby and others like her brought a new voice to public discourse. Women had previously been excluded from politics, but during the war years they won the right to vote and to seek political office. The populist movements provided a political space for them, and for the first time Canadians heard female voices in their legislatures. In the case of Parlby and others, those voices were intense, plainspoken, and different, for example, from the Victorian flourishes of a Laurier or Meighen. This speech is also significant for being broadcast on radio, a new medium that allowed speeches to be carried far beyond the halls in which they were delivered, directly to thousands of farmsteads and city homes.

I feel honoured . . . to speak to this splendid gathering of men and women, and I feel thrilled to be taking even this small part in your fight for real representation in the government of this country. Many, many years ago I felt something like the same kind of thrill when I stood in the birthplace of the Magna Carta, the great *charta* of freedom of the British people, the cornerstone of the British Constitution. It is a long, long road from that cave in Surrey, where some of the independent-minded barons of old England met to discuss the thoughts which later led to the drawing up of the Great Charter at Runnymede, to the present time, but we are only continuing the work those men began. We also in this constituency of Medicine Hat are helping to make history, and are fighting for the independence of the people, not as then against the tyrannies of kings, but against the tyranny of the party machine and the government invisible . . .

This election is showing that the people are no longer content for the old party machine to nominate a representative who has been hand-picked as likely to make the most docile follower of the dictates of the party caucus. It is showing that the people are no longer content to vote meekly on election day for the man the machine nominates, and then, having by their votes elected him, send him to Ottawa with their blessing, while they go back to work and forget all about him (unless they are in the need of some patronage) until the next election comes around.

Today, the most mentally indolent of us are beginning to realize, are we not, that what these men down in Ottawa are doing concerns our welfare on the farm and home very closely? And having come to that degree of understanding, we are coming to the conclusion that the old theory of the virtue and necessity of the strong party government do not interest us at all, but that a government really representative of every section of the people is a matter of very great importance to all of us.

The two-party system has no doubt played a useful and important part in the development of government, but evolution does not stand still in government, any more than in any other phase of life. The old party contests and the old party cries are losing their hold on thinking people. We are watching in this contest a further development of government, the representation in Parliament of an economic group. Our critics say that this development is contrary to, and is a first step in the destruction of the British Constitution. On the contrary, it seems to me to be only another step in that long series of triumphs of the British Constitution, which through its elasticity has, during a long history, shown itself capable of adapting itself to new needs . . .

I notice in the press reports that the Opposition candidate has been showing his knowledge of the problems of the farming industry, by telling the farmers of this constituency that Canada is the only sure market for Canadian farmers. If that is true, God help the farm people—the sooner they get off their farms, the better. Surely there is no member of the electorate so ignorant that he or she can swallow such a statement as that even in an election campaign, when people so often get hysterical enough to swallow anything.

I believe that the farmers of Canada comprise something like 40 percent of the population. You people in the cities would no doubt be able to buy your food for a mere song, but on the other hand, we people on the farms would have no money to buy the products of your labour. This would again react on you.

We see this situation today. The present administration, since they have been in power, have been urging the farmers and other workers to produce, produce, produce, as the only way of salvation for the country.

Today we find the granaries overflowing, the packing houses overpacked, the farms overstocked, industrial plants and warehouses overflowing with unwanted goods, and this situation has been created principally by bankrupt statesmanship and by ignorance of the true principles of economics, by the greed of a few men who really control the destiny of the country. The farm people can hardly sell their produce even below the cost of production. Thousands of other workers cannot work, and yet with all the abundance, a high tariff wall keeps the necessities of life at a level at which the majority of people cannot afford to buy them.

With this situation before them our brilliant representatives, absolutely devoid of any sense of humour, sit at Ottawa solemnly voting large sums for the building of a merchant marine to carry goods to markets which they have done their utmost to destroy, ships which must necessarily sail the ocean on their return voyage with empty bottoms, because the people as patriots are told they must only buy made-in-Canada goods.

You would think a child would have sufficient sense to see through the folly of this combination of high protection—the buying of only Canadian-made goods by the Canadian people—and the development of an expensive merchant marine, which if the two previous policies are carried out, can only idly float in our harbours.

This policy of a protective tariff, although it has enriched a small percentage of the population, and has worked great hardships on many is, however, likely to act as a boomerang in the near future if continued, for in these days there is no getting away from the fundamental fact of community of interests and a policy which callously destroys the industry of agriculture in a country such as this brings the whole social structure to ruin, for agriculture in debt, its farms mortgaged, its purchasing power destroyed, means closed factories, hungry breadlines for other workers. So, if for no other reason than survival in the fight for existence, all other workers should join forces with the farmers in the fight for sending real representatives of their own to Ottawa . . .

The Opposition candidate says again that this is no day for novices to meddle with government. I say that this is no day for reaction to be in the saddle.

The world is staggering blind and maimed from the injuries of the Great War. It needs sympathy and understanding to heal its wounds. It needs imagination to reconstruct its ways. It needs the wide vision of true men and women working not for party and power, but for the welfare of the whole people. And it needs the spirit of tolerance and the loyalty of man to man.

Tolerance, imagination, sympathy with the electorate, breadth of vision, have not been known in the past as attributes of those who hold the political creed of the government now in power, yet if the country is ever to be brought back to health, is ever to fulfill the promises of her youth, all these qualities must be forthcoming in our legislators, and first and last and all the time, they must possess breadth of vision, for without vision surely the people shall perish.

Parlby later participated in the Persons case, in which five women fought a legal battle all the way to the Privy Council in Great Britain to be declared "persons" who could be appointed to Canada's Senate.

Agnes Macphail
26 February 1925, 4 June 1925, 9 May 1930

"I want for myself what I want for other women—
absolute equality"

Agnes Macphail was a female populist, representing the United Farmers of Ontario. She was the first woman elected to the House of Commons, and after she took her seat early in 1922, she was constantly scrutinized. She was treated with deference by some members and with undisguised contempt by others, who did not believe that women should be involved in politics. For years Macphail remained aloof from any party in the House, although she often co-operated with J. S. Woodsworth's progressive Ginger Group, and later she sat with the CCF. Macphail was quick, blunt, and at times sharply humorous, and almost always spoke without using prepared notes. She became one of Parliament's best orators, and during summer recesses she sometimes performed as a professional speaker on a Chautauqua circuit. Macphail was a passionate champion of many issues, but she was best known for her commitment to full equality for women. She and others were able to modify the conditions for divorce, which until that time had been tilted entirely toward husbands.

It is a fact that all women contribute more to marriage than men; for the most part they have to change their place of living, their method of work, a great many women today changing their occupation entirely on marriage; and they must even change their name. They then work continuously for many years until death happily releases them, and that without wages at all. They work without pay. No one can claim that a married woman is economically independent, for she is not; apart from some very rare exceptions, married women are dependent economically, and that is the last possible remaining bond on women. Women have struggled for ages now, and today they are ably championed in our country by the honourable member for West Calgary (Mr. Shaw) and his friends who in this House are demanding further rights for them. When I hear men talk about woman being the angel of the home I always, mentally at least, shrug my shoulders in doubt. I do not want to be the angel of any home; I want for myself what I want for other women—absolute equality. After that is secured, then men and women can take turns at being angels. I stress that angel part, because I remember that last year an honourable member who spoke from the opposite benches called a woman an angel and in the next breath said that men were superior. They must therefore be gods . . .

I believe it is the desire of everyone in this House that the home should be preserved. I believe the preservation of the home as an institution in the future lies almost entirely in the hands of the men. If they are willing to give to women economic freedom within that home; if they are willing to live by the standard that they wish the women to live by, the home will be preserved. If the preservation of the home means the enslavement of women, economically or morally, then we had better break it . . . I would ask men to think of that and think of it seriously. I do believe that the economic freedom of women is one of the things that is causing increasing divorces, because women will not tolerate what they once had to tolerate. You can smile about it if you like, but I know a lot of men who talk very learnedly on a subject like this and who want women to be very pure and very chaste when they themselves are not fit to associate with a chaste and pure woman. So, when we have a single standard for men and women, both morally and economically, we shall have a home that is well worth preserving, and I think we can be quite sure it will be preserved . . .

The thing we are discussing is this: a man and a woman get married and establish a home, a domicile. They may or may not have a family. The husband deserts the woman, clears out for two years or longer. The wife wants a divorce, but according to our law she must chase her husband over the face of Canada in order to sue for divorce . . . It is a humiliating thing. If domicile is a real thing, it must be the home that was created by the marriage. The husband deserts his wife and children, forsakes the home, and then the minister of justice asks that the man alone shall retain the domicile. If that is the law, it is a poor law, and let us change it . . . If the present law is based on injustice, and it clearly is, let us change it. All this bunk, if you will pardon the word, about equality between the sexes does not impress me very much. We are actually working towards equality, and clearly from the instances cited by the minister of justice tonight we have not yet got equality; woman is not yet a person, in spite of the judgment of the Privy Council that she is a person in regard to the Senate at least. We need very many changes in our laws. We can make them only one at a time. This is our chance at this one, and we will make the most of it.

William Aberhart
27 December 1934

"Social Credit at least treats the cause
of our present difficulty"

When the Great Depression hit Canada, it dealt an exceptionally cruel blow to the prairie provinces, which suffered a prolonged drought at the same time. Poverty and desperation led to agitation and a search for new political vehicles to replace the traditional parties. In Saskatchewan, the CCF gained ground, and in Alberta, William Aberhart won a following. He was already well known as Bible Bill, a fiery evangelical minister whose radio broadcasts were popular in the province. Aberhart embraced social credit in 1933, and used communications skills that he had honed on radio to promote the doctrine. Each citizen, he said, would receive a monthly allowance from the government. Aberhart believed that would both provide for basic needs and put money back into circulation. In some of his speeches, he even produced a chart showing the circulatory system of the human body, comparing the flow of blood to the flow of money in society. People flocked to him and his Social Credit Party swept to power in 1935.

Probably no subject has pressed itself upon the consciousness of the people of this province and of other parts of the world like that of social credit. From north to south and from east to west, no matter where you go, you can hear it discussed on every hand. That fact alone should challenge the interest of the intelligent citizens of this province.

As our speakers travel from place to place, and from district to district, they find that most of the interest in this subject is due to the fact that social credit claims to be a remedy for the present unnecessary suffering and dire privation that is prevalent everywhere . . .

If social credit is introduced into this province, it would pattern its procedure after the present method with the one exception that the credit would be issued by the provincial credit house instead of by the banks. The proposal is that the state credit house shall issue to each bona fide citizen of Alberta (the qualifications of citizenship will be prescribed), a monthly basic dividend credit (say twenty-five dollars) sufficient to purchase the bare necessities of food, clothing, and shelter, whether he works or does not work, and he will never be asked to pay it back.

If the government elected in Alberta is pledged to put social credit into operation in this province, it would likely take four main steps:

A complete, detailed, and most careful census of the province would be made, showing the name, the address, the district, probable occupation, age, length of residence, assets, liabilities, et cetera, of each person living within its boundaries.

The attorney general's department would be called upon to draft out, ready for adoption, the Social Credit Act.

A number of officials (chartered accountants, experienced bank officials, et cetera) would be trained to carry out, supervise, and inspect the work of the various branch credit houses to be situated in every district or neighbourhood in the province.

A commission would be appointed, consisting of expert members from every trade, calling, or profession to investigate carefully the price spread in our province and fix the just price for goods and services during the first three or six months of its operation. This just price would be changed from time to time to suit the exigencies of the case. I should judge that these steps might take from nine to fifteen months to accomplish . . .

Social credit at least treats the cause of our present difficulty, directly and continuously. This issuance of credit would immediately distribute the goods and services stored up, increasing the turnover of the retailer and wholesaler, putting the factories and producers back at work, and thus decreasing unemployment. The one great feature of the whole remedy was that men, women, and children would be guaranteed their food, clothing, and shelter. Giving purchasing power sufficient to buy the goods and services is not inflation. But some provision, it is true, must be made to direct and control the flow of profit . . .

To counteract, or cool off this boiling of the pot, two other features are suggested in social credit:

A just, equitable price of goods and services must be fixed. The commission of experts appointed by the government would investigate the price spread and fix an equitable, just price for all goods and services, one which was fair to the producer, manufacturer, and distributor, and which did not exploit the purchasing power of the consumer; in other words, give him value for this money . . .

The farmers today are being obligated to sell their goods below actual cost of production. In conversation with the retail grocers, I find that there could be probably a reduction of from 10 to 15 percent on groceries, when accounts are practically guaranteed and the turnover is greatly increased, as it would be under social credit. The same applies to many other lines. This also would give the small businessman a fair chance with the larger departmental or chain stores. Its main purpose, however, is to prevent the evil effects of uncontrolled inflation or deflation.

Provision must be made for a continuous flow of credit . . . The mighty, modern efficiency machinery has removed the burden from the backs of mankind, but has left them without purchasing power to obtain the goods made by the machines which they have invented. The goods and the services are available, the people really want them, but the consumers generally have not the wherewithal with which to purchase. Thus the retail storekeeper cannot sell his goods, and he is in difficulty to meet his payments and overhead charges. The wholesaler finds his warehouse packed with a surplus that he cannot dispose of, and he cannot collect from the retailer. The manufacturer and producer must therefore cease operations and dismiss the employees. Hence the country has to face the increasing problem of unemployment and relief.

These are all symptoms of the real trouble, a lack of purchasing power in the hands of the consumers. If the heart, with only 2 quarts of blood, can pump 135 gallons per hour, the state with $10 million credit should be quite easily able to distribute from $120 million to $160 million worth of goods and services. This would provide every one of the four hundred thousand adult bona fide citizens in the province with the bare necessities of food, clothing, and shelter during the year . . .

To keep this flow of credit properly directed and controlled, there might need to be a compulsory spending clause in the act, requiring that all saving or hoarding should be done by purchasing Alberta bonds.

There is but one other question that we will ask: Where will this $10 million credit come from? It will come from levy included in the just price of goods, much the same as the gasoline tax is secured today . . .

One objection to social credit is that it would make the women too independent. We hear a great deal about divorce and unhappy marriages, of white slave traffic and what not. Surely it is time that women were uplifted and made more independent. Women would no longer have to consider marriage from the present economic insecurity angle. They would not be induced to marry for a meal ticket. Do you think it would hurt the wife to have her own income with which to purchase her own clothes and not have to ask her husband when she wants anything? I am persuaded that social credit would tend to happier homes.

Richard Bedford Bennett
2 January 1935

"The old order is gone. It will not return"

This is the first in a dramatic series of radio addresses that Prime Minister Richard Bedford Bennett made to the nation early in 1935 while Canada was in the grip of the Great Depression. Bennett had been unapologetically conservative and anti-interventionist in his economic outlook, but by 1935 Canada was in deep trouble economically and unemployment was rampant. Bennett's brother-in-law, W. D. Herridge, convinced him that he must convert and follow the lead of Franklin Delano Roosevelt, who had introduced the New Deal in the United States to get the economy moving again. Herridge wrote Bennett's speeches and the prime minister delivered them directly to Canadians on a network of forty radio stations. Bennett was characteristically blunt in his remarks, but also unusually self-revealing. He appealed to Canadians directly in simple sentences and forceful language, but appeared uneasy with the radio medium.

The time has come when I must speak to you with the utmost frankness about our national affairs, for your understanding of them is essential to your welfare. This is a critical hour in the history of our country. Momentous questions await your decision. Our future course must now be charted. There is one course, I believe with all my heart, which will lead us to security. It is for you to decide whether we will take it. I am confident that your decision will be the right one, when, with care and diligence, you have studied the facts. Then you will support the action which your judgment decrees to be imperative; you will strive for its success, for its success will determine the future of Canada.

In the last five years, great changes have taken place in the world. The old order is gone. It will not return. We are living amidst conditions which are new and strange to us. Your prosperity demands changes in the old system, so that, in these new conditions, that old system may adequately serve you. The right time to bring about these changes has come. Further progress without them is improbable. To understand what changes and corrections should be made, you must first understand the facts of the present situation. To do that, you should have clearly in mind what has taken place in the past five years; the ways in which we have made progress, the ways in which we have not. To do that, to decide wisely, you must be in a position to judge those acts of government which have palliated your hardships, which have preserved intact our industrial and financial structure, and which have prepared the way for the reforms which must now take place . . .

Reform means government intervention; it means government control and regulation; it means the end of laissez faire. Reform heralds certain recovery; there can be no permanent recovery without reform. Reform or no reform, I raise that issue squarely. I nail the flag of progress to the masthead; I summon the power of the state to its support.

Who will oppose our plan of progress? It will be interesting and instructive to see. It seems to me that the party which supports laissez faire, which demands that government do not interfere with business, which says that the state has no such part to play in these critical times, it seems to me that that party may have a change of heart when it sees how the rest of us feel about the matter, and may decide to come along with you and me. Well, if it will denounce its hereditary chieftain, which is reaction, abandon its creed of inaction, and pledge its allegiance to action, to progress, to reform, it will be welcome if it is really sincere. For I am working, and working grimly, to one end only: to get results. And so, honest support from every quarter, from men and women of good will, of every party, race and creed, I hope for and heartily invite.

There must be unity of purpose. There can be no success without it. I earnestly entreat you, be in no doubt upon that point. I am not. If I cannot have your wholehearted support, it is wrong for me to assume the terrible responsibility of leadership in these times. I am willing to go on, if you make it possible for me still to serve you. But if there is anyone better able to do so, I shall gladly make way for him. And it is your duty to yourselves to support him, and not me. Your country's future is at stake. This is no time to indulge your personal prejudices or fancies. Carefully and calmly, look well into the situation, then pick the man and the policy best fitted to deal with it, and resolutely back that man and that policy. The nation should range itself behind them. In war you fought as one; fight now again as one, for the task ahead demands your war-time resolution and your war-time unity.

When my government came into power in 1930, the economic system of the world was rocking to its foundations. An economic disaster, unparalleled in the history of our civilization, had overtaken us. We were in the grip of something more than a serious illness. Its fatal termination was averted only by means never invoked before. We have been sick almost unto death, but we have survived. Given the right sort of treatment, we will completely recover.

In 1930 there was serious unemployment. Unemployment became greater and greater in the two years following. During the last year, we have been able to put large numbers of men to work. That was a real achievement. It is a fine beginning, but it is only a beginning. I told you in 1930 that I would end unemployment; that was a definite undertaking. By it I stand. Unemployment in Canada today is one of the consequences of this awful and unprecedented world depression. The continued faulty operation of the international economic machine has made re-employment impossible. I do not offer that as an excuse; I state a fact. Therefore, now that the time has come, I am determined to try with all my strength to correct the working of the system in Canada so that present unemployment conditions may be put an end to. When I say I will correct the system, I mean that I will reform it, and when the system is reformed and in full operation again, there will be work for all. We then can do away with relief measures; we then can put behind us the danger of the dole. I am against the dole; it mocks our claim to progress. Canada on the dole is like a young and vigorous man in the poorhouse. The dole is a condemnation, final and complete, of our economic system. If we cannot abolish the dole, we should abolish the system.

Bennett was defeated by the Liberals in an election later in 1935, before he could act on the activist government agenda that he promised.

Norman Bethune
16 June 1937

"Democratic Spain must live"

Dr. Norman Bethune left his medical practice in Montreal in 1936 to join the Republican forces fighting the fascists under General Franco in Spain. There Bethune pioneered a portable blood transfusion unit that was used at or near the front and it saved thousands of lives. In 1937, he was asked by the Republicans to return to Canada to raise money and support for their cause. He embarked on a speaking tour, and these remarks are taken from his speech in Montreal.

I went to Spain as a matter of honour. I have come back because there are some things that need to be said in reply to those outside of Spain who speak in the name of dishonour.

I am a doctor, a surgeon. My job is to sustain human life, in all its beauty and vigour. I am not a politician, but I went to Spain because the politicians betrayed Spain and tried to drag the rest of us into their betrayal. With varying accents, and with varying degrees of hypocrisy, the politicians ruled that democratic Spain must die. It was my belief, as it is now my conviction, that democratic Spain must live.

To the Spanish people, and to anyone who has seen Spain for himself, the position is clear. So clear, in fact, that Franco and his fascist backers urgently need a diversion to conceal their aggression, just as the Tory bleaters of non-intervention need a fig leaf to dress up the naked shanks of their miserable policy. They have found one, to their mutual relief. It is nothing more than the bastard child of the Austrian paperhanger and the Italian turncoat. It is "the menace of communism."

Fourteen years ago, Mussolini was shipped into Rome in a parlour car and installed in office to destroy the "communist menace." He promptly proceeded, in the name of his holy mission, to destroy the living standards of the people and the very right to life, liberty, and the pursuit of happiness. More recently, no doubt as part of the same holy mission, he has militarized Italy and brought Abyssinia into the grip of fascism and bloodshed.

Four short years ago, in Germany, Adolf Hitler was installed as chancellor, also to save Germany from the "communist menace." He proceeded, as you will remember, with even more dispatch than *Il Duce*. In the name of the holy war against Bolshevism, he made unholy war against every democratic German grouping, communist or anti-communist, ruined and murdered "non-Aryans," drove out some of the finest minds of the century, filled Germany with the horrors and brutality of the concentration camps, and fastened on the people the most terrible tyranny the world has ever seen. Herr Hitler is still raging against the "menace of communism," but already the guns of his new armies are pointing towards the territories of the leading noncommunist governments of Europe.

And now Franco and his Moors and his German and Italian backers announce the same theme: they, too, are saving Spain from the communist menace. And in Downing Street, and at our own capital, and among learned American senators, it is sagely opined that it is of course deplorable about Spain, but the Reds are back of it, after all, and the present fighting is merely an alleged national reaction to Moscow's connivings.

Now I am not the least bit interested tonight to discuss the merits or demerits of the communist program and philosophy. If the people of Spain wanted communism, it would be for them and nobody else to decide when and how they should have it. But I must say that the attempt to paint the invasion of Spain as a crusade to save the country from the "communist menace" is not only a wretched lie, it is a calculated and vicious insanity.

Is it not clear that if this insanity is to prevail, it will strike a mortal blow at all the rights and liberties of noncommunists as well as communists? For, if you are unfree, as the Spanish people were unfree, and you defend your freedom, you will be struck down as a communist. If you are hungry, as the Spanish people were hungry, you will be overwhelmed with cries of the "communist menace" when you ask for bread. If you long for a decent, peaceful life of minimum abundance, again like the Spanish people, you will have to face the vengefulness of those scouring the earth with fixed bayonets for the contamination of communism. Every sincere word, every desire for a better life, every protest against injustice, every plea to improve an imperfect world will be suspect, dangerous, an invitation to reprisals, an act to be put down as the rankest subversion.

There are some who argue, of course, that the Soviet Union is assisting the Loyalist regime and the communists inside and outside of Spain are supporting the Spanish government. This argument, presumably, is supposed to prove the existence of the "communist menace" in Spain and thereby to disqualify the Loyalists. I fail to follow the logic. I fail to follow the argument that because the Soviet Union, or the communists elsewhere, approve of something it is thereby necessarily proven bad. I further cannot accept the suggestion that because the fascists and their "neutral" Tory friends everywhere say something is good, it cannot therefore by quite bad.

Yes, the Soviet Union has sent aid to the Spanish Republic. So has Mexico, which is not communist. That is an undeniable fact. Is that to the discredit of Spain? I would revise the question: I would say that it is to the credit of the Soviet Union and Mexico that they have lived up to their obligations to the Spanish government, which represents Spain's people. The Soviet Union and Mexico, by according the Spanish government its legal rights, are aiding the government elected and supported by the people themselves. The western powers, by embargoing the Loyalists and shutting their eyes to the flow of arms and armies from Italy and Germany to Franco, are supporting the choice of Hitler, Mussolini, and the clique of Spanish financiers and feudalists who mint their wealth out of the poverty of the people.

Let us have done, then, with the miserable deception of anticommunism. It has served Hitler and Mussolini well, but not the enslaved German and Italian peoples. It may have a pleasing sound in Tory ears, and salve the consciences of some spinsterish British Labour leaders, but it is rank dishonesty nevertheless. It is the great lie of our decade. It is the last refuge of the reactionary whose political arsenal is empty, whose world is bankrupt, and whose patrons' thirst for power is desperate and undiminished. That is one of the lessons of Spain. I hope we will never forget it.

Spain *can* be the tomb of fascism. History will someday take full revenge on those who fail her.

Bethune later went to China to serve as a doctor with the communists in the civil war, and he died there of blood poisoning. He remains a hero and an icon in China and one of the most famous Canadians ever.

A. A. Heaps
30 January 1939

"Never have human beings been
treated so barbarously"

As Hitler attacked the Jews in the 1930s, many of them sought refuge in
other countries, including Canada. Prime Minister Mackenzie King
counselled Canadian Jewish groups and concerned MPs to work quietly
behind the scenes, implying that something would be done, but he took
no action. There was a significant public sentiment against Jewish
immigration, and Canada turned away a ship containing Jews fleeing
Germany. On 30 June 1939 a Quebec MP tabled a petition signed by thousands demanding that the government not allow Jews into Canada.
That prompted A. A. Heaps, a CCF MP from Winnipeg, who had accepted
King's advice about quiet diplomacy, to rise in the House and criticize
both the prime minister and his government's inaction.

During the twenty-two years that I have been in public life, thirteen of which have been spent in this Chamber, it has been always my aim to try to bring about a closer understanding and more harmonious relationship among the various component parts of our population, not merely of Winnipeg, but of the whole of the Dominion of Canada. I regret to say I have found that one of the main obstacles to that natural development of our people has been the fact that there are many politicians in the west, as there are probably in other parts of Canada, who are too ready to try to obtain political advantage by exploiting racial feelings and misunderstandings. I have always tried to avoid that in my public life . . .

During the past few days, there has been raised in this House the question of immigration and the question of the refugee. Representing as I do a constituency made up of a mixture of races, although it is preponderantly Anglo-Saxon, I feel I should be remiss in my duty if I did not make some statement with regard to these important questions, affecting as they do so many peoples, and touching principles with which I think most of the honourable members of this House are concerned.

So much has been said on this question of immigration that the facts, I believe, ought to be known and given consideration and prominence. Certain honourable members have been speaking of immigration and refugees as if they were one and the same problem, with the same meaning and the same implications. There is a great difference between immigration and the problem of refugees. No one to my knowledge has ever asked in these times for an influx of immigrants in the ordinary sense of the word. No one has even asked that the country should be flooded with refugees. In matters of this importance, people should not make rash statements without ascertaining the facts, nor should they deal in generalities.

What are the facts? Early last year, a delegation of members of this House met the prime minister (Mr. Mackenzie King) and discussed the question with him. Subsequently, a subcommittee of the Cabinet was appointed to consider the matter, and a number of the members of this House had an interview with the subcommittee . . .

What the delegation requested was that a reasonable number of refugees of all races and creeds be allowed to come forward to parts of Canada where it was considered most desirable that they should settle. The number suggested at the time was five thousand men, women, and children, approximately one thousand to twelve hundred families. All the members of the subcommittee at the time appeared to me to be sympathetic, and the members of the delegation present were prepared to give proper undertakings that none of the refugees would become a public charge. The number for which entry was requested was extremely small, in view of the need, but we felt that our government should show its sympathy in the matter; and to permit refugees to enter Canada and be freed from political, religious, or racial persecution was in strict accord with historic Liberal principles.

But a new phase has now been injected into the problem. Everyone who has kept himself informed as to recent events cannot help extending sympathy to the refugees for the plight in which they find themselves, whatever their race or creed may be. Never in the history of mankind have human beings been treated so barbarously as they are being treated at the present time by fascist powers. Men, women, and children, families which have been rooted for centuries in the land in which they lived, have been deprived and robbed of everything they possessed and ordered to leave the country, their only crime being that their racial origin or religious beliefs were distasteful to the powers that be or their democratic principles unwelcome in totalitarian states. The pitiful plight of all these people has aroused international concern. Almost every civilized country has definitely taken sympathetic action. Canada as yet has not done so, and I should like to see her take her rightful place with other democratic countries and show her sympathy in a practical manner. Great Britain, France, Holland, Australia, and many other countries are giving asylum to tens of thousands of refugees, and in no place, to my knowledge, have they been a burden to the governments that have received them.

In regard to employment, it might be well to mention that lately . . . in England, eleven thousand refugees had given employment to fifteen thousand Englishmen. Speaking now with a knowledge of the conditions, and not from mere hearsay, I say that if our government had shown the same sympathetic attitude on this question, the same conditions could have obtained here.

May I point out that the Right Honourable R. B. Bennett, speaking in Saint John, New Brunswick, only on Thursday last, said that we owed a debt of gratitude to those refugees and that we should accept our quota of them. There is in this country as a whole a very large body of opinion to the effect that the government should extend the hand of brotherhood and friendship to these people. It is they who have been the first victims of fascist tyranny and oppression; who knows who will be the next?

I make this plea on broad humanitarian grounds, not for any one sect or creed, but for all victims of persecution. It pained me last week to hear honourable members deny the plea of the refugee to the right of asylum. It seemed so inhuman. I am in a sense proud to have this opportunity of making such a plea and in a humble way to follow the teaching of ancient and modern religious thought so beautifully expressed in the words, "Do unto others as ye would have them do unto you," and if I may be permitted to add one further quotation familiar to us all, let us if possible have peace on earth, goodwill towards men.

Claris Edwin Silcox
January 1939

"Democracy must set its face like
flint against anti-Semitism"

While MP A. A. Heaps was criticizing Ottawa for its inaction on Jewish
immigration, a United Church clergyman named Claris Edwin Silcox
was speaking to Canadian Clubs in western Canada. Silcox represented
a group called The Committee on Jewish Gentile Relationships. They
were alarmed by the rise of anti-Semitism in Canada, and the government's lack of sympathy toward Jews being persecuted by Hitler.

I speak . . . as a Christian clergyman, conscious of the debt of the Christian
church to Judaism, conscious also of the fact that the treatment of the Jew
at the hands of the church has been the darkest blot on the escutcheon of
holy church for a thousand years, and resolved, insofar as I am able, to oblit-
erate that foul blot for all time to come . . .

I speak to you, moreover, as one who is devoted to the principles of democracy, who, while he is willing to recognize some values in both communism and fascism, is and never shall be reconciled to the fundamental ideas that create the totalitarian state, and who believes with all his heart that democracy, despite its apparent weakness, is still the only possible safeguard of the rights of conscience and the values of personality. I not only adhere to this faith in democracy with the passion of religious devotion, but I also believe that anti-Semitism is the spearhead of the totalitarian thrust against democracy, and that if we fail to repudiate anti-Semitism, we shall lose the first and most important round of the battle with dictatorships, and that the victory of totalitarianism will lead to the obliteration of the rights of conscience, the destruction of civil and religious liberty, and world chaos . . .

And that is why anti-Semitism today, wherever it is found, constitutes the great challenge of totalitarianism to democracy. Anti-Semitism is the spearhead of the totalitarian attack on democracy. If it succeeds, democracy will fail; if it fails, democracy stands a fair chance of weathering the storm. For if the authoritarian societies find it possible to crush the Jews—a vigorous if small minority of people inured to persecution, and peculiarly tenacious of their own way of life, and in some respects, judged by biological and practical standards, a superior people: intellectually keen, intensely realistic and practical, and backed by an ancient tradition that carries us to the very dawn of modern civilization, a cultural group to which the modern world owes more than it is willing to acknowledge in religion, in ethics, in law, in business, in finance, in art, in science, and in literature—then there will be little chance for any other minority to survive as a minority. The totalitarian steamroller will roll on, suppressing other forms of spiritual freedom or race persistence or cultural integrity.

The Jewish problem is, therefore, one of great moment to all of us who are Gentiles. The Jew cannot do a great deal today to save himself, if we Gentiles are resolved to annihilate him. In former times, he fled from the persecutors and took sanctuary elsewhere. Today, in a sense, he is trapped. The frontiers have been closed or next to closed to him. The possibilities of emigration and immigration have been rendered extremely difficult if not impossible by both the countries of emigration and those of immigration . . .

Democracy must set its face like flint against anti-Semitism. It must become more intelligent in its understanding of the way in which the Jewish problem arose; it must expose the lies on which anti-Semitism battens; it must watch the agents of foreign countries who seek to foment troubles and prevent our real national solidarity by drawing the red herring of anti-Semitism across the political and social scene; it must cultivate intellectual and spiritual relations with the members of the Jewish minority who suffer deeply in their souls and who, if they trust us to understand them, have more to offer us than we may have to offer them; and especially, it must take to itself some of these persecuted peoples who, after contributing more than their quota to the distinguished names of modern Germany in science, medicine, art, music, literature, and technical skill, after providing more than their share of Nobel prizewinners, are forced to seek a new sanctuary and a new fatherland in countries where the rights of personality are respected, where fair play is practiced, where democracy is not alone extolled in theory but lived, and where the contributions of minorities are not disdained . . .

As a Christian people, we do homage to the King of Kings and Lord of Lords. Let us show Him who was the Son of God and the son of a Jewish mother, Mary, and whose infant head was pillowed on a Jewish woman's breast, that for many of these poor people, His half-brothers and His half-sisters, there is yet room in the clamant and crowded inn of this world's complicated life, even in this vast and underpopulated Dominion, where these persecuted souls, weary of their wanderings and with no place to rest their heads, may at length find sanctuary—and understanding—and peace.

J. S. Woodsworth

8 September 1939

"I cannot give my consent to anything
that will drag us into another war"

James Shaver Woodsworth had an almost prophetic status among members of his CCF caucus and party. He was a pacifist. When Hitler invaded Poland and it became obvious that Canada would likely soon be at war, the caucus held a wrenching internal discussion in which most members disagreed with their leader. The following evening, when debate on Canada's course of action began in the House of Commons, only Woodsworth and two MPS from Quebec opposed Canada's participation. Woodsworth's remarks make it painfully clear that he had lost the ability to speak on behalf of his party regarding the war.

Tonight I find myself in rather an anomalous position. My own attitude towards war is fairly well known to the members of the House and, I think, throughout the country. My views on war became crystallized during the last war, long before the Co-operative Commonwealth Federation came into existence, but our Co-operative Commonwealth Federation is a democratic organization that decides matters of policy. My colleagues in the House and in the national council of the Co-operative Commonwealth Federation, which has been in session with us almost continuously for the last two days, have very generously urged that I take this opportunity of expressing my own opinions with regard to this matter.

The position of the Co-operative Commonwealth Federation will be stated at the earliest possible opportunity by one of my colleagues. I say, frankly, that with part of that policy I heartily agree, but with some portions of it I cannot agree. Yet I was never so proud to belong to the group with which I am associated. In the time at my disposal tonight, I shall try to give expression to my own personal views with regard to the war, to give my interpretation of the situation that exists today and perhaps suggest some things that should be done. From the scores of telegrams, letters, and communications of various kinds that have come to me in the last few days, and from my own knowledge of the Canadian people, I feel confident that there are thousands upon thousands who hold very much the views which I do.

In my judgment, an individual citizen in a democracy, and much more a representative of the citizens, can make his greatest contribution by expressing his own convictions as clearly as possible. I am trying to do that tonight. I consider that a great many of my colleagues in this House belonging to all parties are quite sincere in the policies which they advocate. I do not question their patriotism. Perhaps I am going too far when I ask them to believe that I and others who feel like I do are sincere in our convictions and are no less interested in the welfare of this country . . .

It is only a few months since we erected in Ottawa a memorial to the poor fellows who fell in the last war; it is hardly finished before we are into the next war.

After the last war, many of us dreamed a great dream of an ordered world, a world to be founded on justice. But, unfortunately, the covenant of the League of Nations was tied up with the Versailles treaty, which I regard as an absolutely iniquitous treaty. Under that treaty we tried to crush Germany. We imposed indemnities which have been acknowledged by all to be impossible. We took certain portions of territory. Even French black troops were put into the Rhineland, an indignity much resented at the time by the Germans. We took away colonies, sank ships, and all the rest of it. We know that long, sordid story. To no small extent, it was this kind of treatment which created Hitler. I am not seeking to vindicate the things that Hitler has done, not at all. He may be a very devil incarnate, and the prime minister might have read a great deal more than the extracts he read tonight. But you cannot indict a great nation and a great people such as the German people. The fact is we got rid of the Kaiser only to create conditions favourable to the development of a Hitler. Of course, Canada had her responsibility. But the great nations did not take the League of Nations very seriously . . .

It seems to me that, above all things, we in Canada must avoid hysteria and we are in a better position to do so than are the people in other places. We must devote our efforts to something constructive. Great Britain undoubtedly has heavy responsibilities at the present time, but I would ask whether we are to risk the lives of our Canadian sons to prevent the action of Hitler in Danzig and in the corridor. I would ask what it would mean if there were talk about giving up Gibraltar and the Suez and our control of our interest in Palestine or in the African colonies. What is the result? The League has been practically set aside and now we are back to power politics again . . .

I would ask, did the last war settle anything? I venture to say that it settled nothing; and the next war into which we are asked to enter, however big and bloody it may be, is not going to settle anything either. That is not the way in which settlements are brought about. While we are urged to fight for freedom and democracy, it should be remembered that war is the very negation of both. The victor may win; but if he does, it is by adopting the selfsame tactics which he condemns in his enemy. Canada must accept her share of responsibility for the existing state of affairs. It is true that we belong to the League, but anyone who has sat in this House knows how difficult it has been to secure any interest in the discussion of foreign affairs. More than that, we have been willing to allow Canadians to profit out of the situation. The prime minister may talk about preventing profiteering now, but Canada has shipped enormous quantities of nickel and scrap iron, copper and chromium to both Japan and Germany, who were potential enemies. We have done it right along. It may be possible now to prevent it, but I submit that if any shooting is to be done, the first people who should face the firing squad are those who have made money out of a potential enemy.

I am among a considerable number in this country who believe, and we hold it as a mature conviction, that war is the inevitable outcome of the present economic and international system with its injustices, exploitations, and class interests. I suggest that the common people of the country gain nothing by slaughtering the common people of any other country. As one who has tried for a good many years to take a stand for the common people, personally I cannot give my consent to anything that will drag us into another war. It may be said that the boys who stay out are cowards. I have every respect for the man who, with a sincere conviction, goes out to give his life if necessary in a cause which he believes to be right; but I have just as much respect for the man who refuses to enlist to kill his fellow men and, as under modern conditions, to kill women and children as well, as must be done on every front . . .

The world is a crowded community today; yet we are all of us more or less inclined to act as individualists. I remember during the last war adopting as a kind of motto this phrase: "Last century made the world a neighbourhood, this century must make it a brotherhood." The more I have studied history and economics, the more I have come to the conclusion that that is profoundly true. The choice is that or the deluge.

Few people knew that Woodsworth had suffered a stroke in the days prior to this debate. Tommy Douglas, who sat beside him in the House on that evening, recounted how Woodsworth's wife had written brief notes in inch-high letters in crayon, and Douglas passed them to him. "I knew that in a few minutes I would be voting against him," Douglas told a biographer, "but I never admired him more than I did that day."

Thérèse Casgrain

25 April 1941

"The right to vote is not an end in and of itself"

Thérèse Casgrain was born into an established and affluent Quebec family, but she became a relentless activist championing women's equality and social justice. Her speech to the League for the Rights of Women in 1941 occurred exactly one year after women won the right to vote in Quebec. Most politicians and the clergy had been staunchly opposed. Each year for more than a decade, Casgrain and other women found a sympathetic member of the Assembly to introduce a motion on female suffrage. Both movers and the women in the gallery were routinely subjected to ridicule. In this speech, Madame Casgrain makes reference to the long struggle for the vote, but places it in a broader context of justice for all.

We secured [the right to vote] a year ago today, after several years of what seemed a fruitless battle. At the time of this victory, several sources said to us: "Now that you have what you wanted, your struggle is over and you can relax." These words make me think of those romance novels in which the hero always marries the heroine at the end. What we forget is that the real story begins only after the wedding . . . This offer to relax was no doubt made with the best of intentions, but it shows, sadly, that there are those who have misunderstood the reason and the goal behind our struggle. The right to vote is not, and could never be, an end in and of itself: it is a means, a defensive weapon.

Now that we possess some means of action that were denied us in the past, our true mission becomes apparent, our responsibilities take shape, our duties are made clear . . . We acknowledge that a large number of our economic and social problems are, in fact, educational problems. The dangerous bias with which totalitarian states infiltrate early childhood education should motivate us to redouble our efforts in preparing our own youth, not for the blood-soaked tasks of war, nor for the violent technology of invasion, but rather for the responsibilities it consents to assume in the future. We must work closely with the schools to cultivate in our children's hearts love of family and of nation.

Plotting boundaries on geographic maps, praising a country of rhetoric and convention in your discourse—these will never shape a homeland: it is achieved by engraving those boundaries in the mind and soul of your children. Patriotism is not, has never been, a matter for rhetoric or convention. It is an undefined emotion that pulls at your heartstrings when a stranger utters the name of your country; it is an immeasurable exhilaration that sings within you when you tread native soil or when you breathe in its scent, and when its contours and relief seem like extensions of yourself. Education within the family and schools should instil this concept of a real and living homeland in our youth.

In these uncertain times, the heritage of a sound education is the only legacy we can be sure to pass on to our children. The post-war world—and I am not engaging in predictions of the future here, but rather considering facts simply and impersonally—the post-war world will have no tolerance for the weak, the underdeveloped, the irresolute; it will be a world where only intellectual and physical excellence will prevail. Will we have given our children the tools for their success and happiness . . .

Modern life has committed, as it were, working women to factories, clerical positions, and store clerk positions, as much in commerce as in industry. What kind of working conditions are women subjected to in our society? Exploitation of women's work is not speculation; it is in fact a sad reality all too often. We must take care of this problem. Equal pay for equal work. There is nothing in the world that justifies handling the women's workforce differently than the men's workforce; in fact, that goes for all things equal. As well, has it not been proven, notably by the textile industry survey report, that lowering women's salary results in a proportionately lowered salary for the men's workforce? Requesting just compensation for women's work not only safeguards a sacred right, but it also protects the security of the family unit. As for understanding the importance of working conditions, a Christian spirit or the simple respect of human dignity is all you should need.

The concern with which we safeguard human dignity will also inspire our discussions about social well-being. For example, there is so much wrong with the fact that a big city can give rise to the shameful existence of slums. What sources of physical and moral contagions arise out of these dark and dingy shelters, where neither sunlight nor fresh air ever penetrate. Must we reiterate that slums are the biggest cause of juvenile delinquency, and that most of the men and women that fill the prisons today lived, as children, in these holes without light? Can women, caretakers of the home, ignore the problem of slums, of a cancer that is inexorably eating away at the social fabric and attacks the very essence of the family?

We recognize today, more than ever before, our collective responsibility. This conference marks for us an anniversary; it shall, by the same token, be a starting point if our work truly begins today. I am certain that we will all perform our new duties with the fervour and patience we found within ourselves during our struggle to achieve the recognition of primordial rights.

William Lyon Mackenzie King

7 April 1942

"The government asks you to give it a free hand"

Ottawa's decision to invoke conscription in 1917 caused deep divisions between French and English Canada. When Canada went to war again in 1939, Prime Minister Mackenzie King promised there would be no conscription for overseas service. But, once again, the war dragged on with no apparent victory in sight. On 7 April 1942, King asked Canadians to vote in a referendum to relieve the government from its earlier promise. The plebiscite speech was carried on radio, and was vintage King in its complex logic and tortured diction.

I wish to speak to you tonight, my fellow Canadians, on a matter which, at this time of war, is of first importance to the present position of our country, and to its future security; and, therefore, of real concern to the homes and lives of all. On Monday, the 27th of this month, you will be asked to give the government a free hand in the discharge of its duty in carrying on the war . . .

The pledge from which the present government is asking to be freed is not related to any ordinary day-to-day matter of policy. It is a pledge which was made specifically in relation to the conduct of the present war. It is a pledge which was given, by government and Opposition alike, before and since the outbreak of the war, and to which, at the time it was made, no political party took exception. The present House of Commons was returned [in an election] in the light of that pledge.

The pledge to which I refer is, as you are all aware, that, as a method of raising men for military service overseas, resort would not be had to conscription. In other words, that voluntary enlistment would be the method by which men would be raised for service overseas . . .

The pledge not to impose conscription for service overseas was given in order to maintain the unity of Canada. Without this assurance, I do not believe that Parliament would have given, as it did, prompt and wholehearted approval to Canada's entry into the war. It was the trust of the people in the pledged word of the government which then maintained our national unity.

We must never lose sight of the importance of national unity. National unity is, I believe, more essential to the success of the war effort of any country than most other factors combined. "Every kingdom divided against itself is brought to desolation, and a house divided against a house falleth" . . .

I come now to the question: why have the government and Parliament not tackled this question on their own responsibility without resorting to a plebiscite? The answer is very simple. Had the government taken the position that, as conditions had changed, it did not intend longer to be bound by any pledge, it would immediately have been said that the government had violated the most sacred undertaking ever given in its name.

It would most certainly have been said that, before so deciding, we should have referred the matter to the people in a general election, or a referendum, or as we are doing, by means of a plebiscite, and asked to be relieved from all past commitments. It would have been asserted that we were no better than the Nazis; that we had ceased to have regard for the will of the people and were now relying upon force to give effect to policies which were the direct opposite of those on which we had been returned to power . . .

The truth, of course, is that our army today is just as large as it would have been if conscription for overseas service had been adopted. The absence of conscription for overseas service has not limited our war effort. The lack of power to impose such conscription has, however, placed our war effort in a wholly false light before our own citizens, and, what is worse, before our allies. In other words, conscription has been made the symbol of a total effort, regardless of all Canada is doing to help win the war.

The issue at present is not conscription; it is whether or not the government, subject to its responsibility to Parliament, is to be free to decide that question itself in the light of all national considerations . . .

The last thing I have been or would wish to be is an alarmist. I would, however, not be true to the trust the people of Canada have reposed in me did I not say that I believe the situation, for all free nations, is far more critical today than it has ever been. Canada's position is by no means an exception. Look at what has happened in the past two and a half years of war; look at what is happening today, and ask yourselves what other view is possible. Practically the whole of continental Europe, except Russia, is under the domination of Germany, and is compelled to serve her war machine. Despite Russia's magnificent campaign and the ground she has regained, much of her European territory is still in Nazi hands. Who can say what the outcome of the struggle between Russia and Germany may be? In the Middle East and in Africa, the situation is also desperately critical. In Asia and in the Pacific, Japan controls a large part of China, and has seized most of the strategic strongholds and territories formerly possessed by the Netherlands, France, Britain and the United States.

Across the Pacific, the tide of Japanese conquest has swept swiftly over thousands of miles of sea. A few weeks ago, it was Hong Kong, Singapore and the East Indies—attacked and taken; a little later, Burma and Australia attacked, with New Zealand also threatened. Today it is Ceylon and India . . .

Aggression has followed aggression with such speed in so many parts of the world that no one can now predict what new areas the war may reach next year, next month or next week. Danger threatens us from the east and from the west. It is in the face of this peril that for the defence of our freedom and of our country, the government asks you to give it a free hand.

In the plebiscite that followed, 64 percent agreed to relieve the government of its pledge, but in Quebec only 28 percent were in support. When Canada did introduce limited conscription in 1944, there was rioting in Montreal, and several of King's Quebec ministers resigned.

Lionel Groulx

29 November 1943

"Beware of the illusion of bilingualism"

Canon Lionel Groulx was a priest, a historian, and a leading Quebec intellectual from the early years of the century until his death in 1967. He was described by some as the spiritual father of Quebec and by others as a messianic nationalist. His interests, passions, and influence went well beyond the pulpit. He was a separatist in temperament, although he never described himself as one, perhaps to avoid offending the church's rule that priests should not be politicians. An ardent promoter of Quebec culture and the French language, Groulx preferred isolation to closer French-English relations, and was therefore opposed to any policy of bilingualism. He gave this speech in Montreal in 1943 during the height of World War II, and his references to the divisive conscription crisis are veiled, but obvious.

Why are we divided? The question is often asked, though in merely asking it one assumes a painful state of affairs. When a country's leaders are always talking about union and national unity, it shows that these things do not exist except as ideals. We are disunited, profoundly disunited. That is the hard fact. National union has never been so weak in Canada as during this war, and never before, we might add, have such clumsy attempts been made to preserve it . . .

The first obligation which English and French Canadians owe to each other, and I would also say, the primary condition for a *bonne-entente*, is frankness—I shall avoid subtlety. I say quite simply that so deep a division as that which separates the two races in Canada must have deep-lying causes, for it indicates disagreement on major issues. Let us say it: the two races do not get along well because one of them wants legal equality all right, but on condition that it keeps for itself the lion's share. I know there is nothing new about this truth. I know also that it is a crude truth, but it is true. In the final analysis, one category of Englishmen cannot forgive us for existing, and for claiming to exist, with the same rights as these gentlemen, the same liberty, the same dignity. In other words, what they do not wish to recognize nor accept in Canada, with its juridical and political consequences, is the French fact. There does exist a category of open-minded and generous Englishmen with whom we can get along, but there exists another which cannot realize that everybody does not think and feel *à l'anglosaxonne*, has not the same reactions as the Anglo-Saxons, as if the human race inhabited an Anglo-Saxon universe . . .

The last consecration of the French fact took place at the time of Confederation. This was its greatest consecration, completely categorical. No one can be ignorant of what this regime of 1867 was meant to be. In the minds of the fathers of Confederation, it was to be the legal expression of a free collaboration: collaboration between the races, collaboration between the provinces. They supposed that they had settled forever, beyond dispute, the French fact, the question of races and languages. An article of the Constitution proclaimed the legal and political equality of French and English. According to the statement of the most authorized leader of the English Canadians, there were no longer either conquerors nor conquered in Canada, but associates possessing equal rights in all domains. The new regime asserted the idea of political decentralization. The unitary state, or what was then called legislative union, was rejected in order to form a federation of autonomous provinces, which restored to old Lower Canada its complete political and national individuality. Quebec even attained, in this federation, a privileged situation, a supplement of guarantees . . .

These were the basic ideas which gave birth to Confederation; these were the masterly stipulations of the contract of 1867. But what has been the policy, in regard to the French fact, which has generally been followed in the English-Canadian provinces and at Ottawa for the past seventy-six years? The direct opposite of what it should have been. In all the provinces, the French minorities have been submitted to a rationing of their culture and to restrictions in the teaching of their religion. At Ottawa, the centre of Confederation, in the Parliament and the government which should protect minority rights, the French and Catholic minorities, one after another, have vainly implored protection against the despoilers of their rights. In the federal domain, the French language holds its position with difficulty only at the price of being constantly on the defensive. Canadians of French origin are forced to struggle with a voracious bureaucracy, without too much success, for a meagre share of positions and influence in the civil service. By its social legislation, the federal Parliament knowingly undermines our civil rights. Even in our own province, the federal bureaucracy undertakes to pervert and, at times, to demolish our type of workers' organization. What do I say? Ottawa does not respect even the fundamental principle of Confederation. The general tendency of its policy in regard to the provinces is to take over their autonomy. This policy, begun before the war, Ottawa has continued stubbornly with the war as an excuse . . .

Let us be frank. We are still divided on an extremely serious matter: the interpretation and the execution of the Confederation agreement. The increasing disagreement on the very principle of the federal state bodes ill for the future. A conviction is slowly developing in the uneasy mind of one of the mother provinces and of one nationality that she can no longer rely on the central power to be protective or impartial. More than that, placing itself at the head of the most hostile elements, this central power plots against the most sacred rights of one province and against the national future of almost a third of the Canadian population . . .

Let us beware . . . of the illusion of bilingualism, miracle worker of national union. English Canadians and French Canadians would need to talk more together only if their variances rested on misunderstanding. But we have seen that there is something very different from misunderstandings.

The Irish of Ireland eventually learned the language of their oppressors. Did they become reconciled thereby? In general, Irishmen and Englishmen speak the same language today. Do they get along any better? We ourselves have pushed bilingualism to the point of imprudence. We have scorned universal experience, forgetting that bilingualism generalized is usually the first phase of a nationality's pangs. We have been led into the imprudence in the name of economic liberation and national unity. However, bilingualism has not prevented us from becoming more than ever the servants of the minority in our province. I do not see our anglo-Canadian compatriots taking us more closely to their hearts for having learned their language more than they have learned ours.

Let us beware, for the same reasons, of enrolling en masse in Anglo-Saxon societies and clubs; infallible recipe, it appears, for ending all racial prejudices. I see clearly what French Canadians too often lose in these contacts; I have yet to discover what they gain. Whatever may come, we cannot enter like a herd into the societies of others, take part, by affiliation, in all the neutral associations, English or American, show ourselves consequently incapable of forming societies of our own, suited to our own spirit, and keep up any pretension to being a proud race—Catholics of initiative and creative imagination, and, in addition, leaders of social life in our province. We cannot play, dress, build, eat, think, feel like Englishmen or Americans and flatter ourselves that we shall remain indefinitely French. Enough of chimerical visions and vain dreams. To come to an understanding with the English, said Jacques Bainville, it is hardly necessary to cough or spit like them. We can unite; we cannot and we never should become unified. In the name of common sense, let us stop dreaming of a marriage of love where only a marriage of reason is possible . . .

The French Canada of tomorrow, an original creation, will be flesh of your flesh, the flower of your spirit. It will gush forth, resplendent with youth and beauty, from the breath of you young French Canadians, from your sociology as sons of Christ. Whatever may be said, we are a little people who have never had much happiness to spare. You will do these things for us in order that at last there may come an hour in our life, a day of wholesome retaliation, when it will be possible for us to say to ourselves as others do: "I have a land of my own; I have a soul of my own; I have a future of my own."

Tommy Douglas
circa 1944

"The Cream Separator" and "Mouseland"

Tommy Douglas had been involved in theatre and debating while studying for the Baptist ministry. He honed his speaking skills as a minister in Weyburn, Saskatchewan, during the Depression, an event that led him to look for political solutions to poverty and misery. He was elected to the House of Commons in 1935, but later returned to lead the CCF to victory in Saskatchewan in 1944. Douglas was a masterful orator who combined humour, sarcasm, irony, anecdote, and self-deprecation in ways that allowed him to become the country's most effective popularizer of socialist ideas. He created "The Cream Separator" after reading the social historian Lewis Mumford, and a friend told him the "Mouseland" story. He used both many times in speeches and radio broadcasts, employing their metaphor and allegory to analyze capitalism and the electoral system in a way that connected with his impoverished rural audiences.

The Cream Separator

I used to visit in farm homes, particularly around meal time, and if I got in around dinner time, of course, everybody in the family was busy. They were unhitching the horses. They were pumping the water. They were milking the cows. They were pitching down the hay and the oat sheaves. Somebody else was out gathering the eggs. Somebody else was feeding the pigs and the chickens. Everybody had something to do. Even the youngsters were given a job doing something, for instance, gathering the eggs or feeding the chickens.

And here I was, right off the city streets. I didn't know what to do, and I said "give me something to do." Well, nobody was going to trust this city boy with milking a good cow. They gave me the one job that anybody could do. They gave me the job of turning the handle of the cream separator.

Any of you ever turned the handle on the cream separator? Well, it's quite an experience. I got to be quite good at it. I got to the place where I could tell you how many verses of "Onward Christian Soldiers" it takes to put a pan of milk through this thing. And as I was turning the handle and they were pouring in the milk, and I could see the cream come out the one spout and the skim milk coming out of the other spout, one day it finally penetrated my thick Scotch head that this cream separator is exactly like our economic system.

Here are the primary producers: the farmers and the fishermen and the loggers. They are pouring in the milk. And here are the workers, whether they work on the railroad or go down to the mines or sail ships or work in a store or a bank, or teach school, clerk in the store, work in a hospital. They are the people whose services make the economy go round, and they're turning the handle. So here you have it: primary producer puts in the milk; people who work with hand and brain turn the handle. And then I thought, but there's another fellow here somewhere. There's a fellow who owns this cream separator. And he's sitting on a stool with the cream spout in his mouth. And the primary producer and the worker take turns on the skim milk spout. And they don't like skim milk. Nobody likes skim milk. And they blame it on each other. And the worker says, "If those farmers and fishermen, you know, would work a little harder, well I wouldn't be drinking this skim milk." And the fishermen and the farmers say, "If those workers didn't demand a forty hour week, didn't want such high wages, I wouldn't have to live on this blue milk." But you know, they're both wrong.

The farmers and the fishermen have produced so much we don't know what to do with it; we've got surpluses of foodstuffs. And the workers, they've produced so well that today nearly a million of them are unemployed. The fault is not with the worker. It is not with the primary producer. The fault is with this machine.

This machine was built to give skim milk to the worker and the primary producer, and to give cream to the corporate elite.

As a matter of fact, it doesn't always do that because every once in a while this little fellow sitting on the stool with the cream spout in his mouth gets indigestion. And he says, "Boys, stop this machine. We got a recession!" He says to the worker, "You're laid off. You can go on unemployment insurance and after that on welfare." And he says to the farmers and the fishermen, "You know, we don't need your stuff. Take it back home." And then he sits for a while, indigestion gets better, burps a couple of times, says, "Alright, boys, start the machine. Happy days are here again. Cream for me and skim milk for both of you."

Now what the democratic socialist party has been saying to Canadians for a long time is that the time has come in this land of ours for the worker and the primary producer to get their hands on the regulator of the machine so that it begins to produce homogenized milk in which everybody'll get a little cream.

Mouseland

Mouseland was a place where all the little mice lived and played, were born and died. And they lived much the same as you and I do. They even had a Parliament. And every four years they had an election. Used to walk to the polls and cast their ballots.

Some of them even got a ride to the polls. And got a ride for the next four years afterwards too. Just like you and me. And every time on election day all the little mice used to go to the ballot box and they used to elect a government. A government made up of big, fat, black cats.

Now if you think it strange that mice should elect a government made up of cats, you just look at the history of Canada for the last ninety years and maybe you'll see that they weren't any stupider then we are.

Now I'm not saying anything against the cats. They were nice fellows. They conducted their government with dignity. They passed good laws— that is, laws that were good for cats. But the laws that were good for cats weren't very good for mice. One of the laws said that mouse holes had to be big enough so a cat could get his paw in. Another law said that mice could only travel at certain speeds—so that a cat could get his breakfast without too much effort.

All the laws were good laws, for cats. But, oh, they were hard on the mice. And life was getting harder and harder. And when the mice couldn't put up with it any more, they decided that something had to be done about it. So they went en masse to the polls. They voted the black cats out. They put in the white cats.

Now the white cats had put up a terrific campaign. They said: "All that Mouseland needs is more vision." They said: "The trouble with Mouseland is those round mouse holes we got. If you put us in we'll establish square mouse holes." And they did. And the square mouse holes were twice as big as the round mouse holes, and now the cat could get both paws in. And life was tougher then ever.

And when they couldn't take that anymore, they voted the white cats out and put the black ones in again. Then they went back to the white cats. Then to the black cats. They even tried half black and half white cats. And they called that coalition. They even got one government made up of cats with spots on them: they were cats that tried to make a noise like a mouse but ate like a cat.

You see, my friends, the trouble wasn't with the colour of the cat. The trouble was that they were cats. And because they were cats, they naturally looked after cats instead of mice.

Presently there came along one little mouse who had an idea. My friends, watch out for the little fellow with an idea. And he said to the other mice, "Look, fellows, why do we keep electing a government made up of cats? Why don't we elect a government made up of mice?" "Oh," they said, "he's a Bolshevik. Lock him up!" So they put him in jail.

But I want to remind you: That you can lock up a mouse or a man but you can't lock up an idea.

Muriel Kitagawa
1945

"My people need the return of their properties"

During World War II, the government considered Canadians of Japanese origin to be security risks, and forcibly moved them away from coastal areas in British Columbia. The Japanese had few public defenders as wartime opinion formed against them. Muriel Kitagawa's family was stripped of its possessions and relocated. She later became an activist and called on Canadians to change their ways.

I stand here tonight to plead with you, not for myself alone, but for all of us . . . It's the rare person among us all, and I certainly include the Japanese people in this category, who will take time to worry over the affairs of other people less fortunate. We are much too busy with our own affairs to be bothered with what doesn't seem to concern us except in a vague and general way. We leave such worries to our representatives who are paid to worry and to act for us. Sometimes we do not make an effort to choose people who will really help us, and we carelessly choose people who do more harm than good. But we shrug, and let it go at that. We can get used to nearly everything . . .

Some good came out of the evacuation, not because the evacuation was good, but because the people had in them the guts to make good after misfortune. Let us not be fooled for one minute by the fact that many of my people are better off today than ever before, because evacuation cut the ropes that tied us to a past. If they did not rise above their suffering, if they did not try to get the best out of a bad situation, these people would not be better off. The ones who are better off had families of vigorous young people out to rescue their family by their united efforts. They also had that quality which would not be defeated by tough luck. Some of those who are worse off than before are in that state because the children are too young yet to work, or the breadwinner is too old, or too broken in spirit, or not physically able to start from nothing again. These are pitiful cases in any language.

The loss of a house, the loss of a few thousand dollars, the loss of a fishing boat, or a business, or a small shop . . . these items are big only in proportion to how much the victims could materially afford to lose. Many of my people actually need the return of their properties. They need badly the few hundreds or thousands of dollars that represent their loss, and it is only right that for their loss, since it was forced on them unjustly, they should be reimbursed.

But more than the return of lost property, reparation is the outward symbol acknowledging the loss of our rights. Time heals the details, but time cannot heal the fundamental wrong. My children will not remember the first violence of feeling, the intense bitterness I felt, but they will know that a house was lost through injustice. As long as restitution is not made, that knowledge will last throughout the generations to come . . . that a house, a home, was lost through injustice. It is important for you to remember that the loss of this property spelled the last indignity for a people deprived of the right to move freely, to live where they choose, to be what they can be best, deprived of participation in the life and events of their country, native or adopted, and deprived most of all of their integrity. Instead, it was taken for granted that we would be traitors given a chance . . .

The race-baiters always ask you to see twenty-three thousand saboteurs, but any sensible person knows how ridiculous that figure is. More than half that number were children, and the older children would much rather wear a Canadian uniform than sabotage their own country, and most of the adults thought more of their children's well-being and safety than the doubtful success of sabotage, and most of the adults wouldn't even think of sabotage. When it was taken for granted that we would all commit sabotage if left alone, we felt such a disgust as you cannot imagine. It made us spit that anyone could think such a thing of us, and made us wonder if, after all, Canadians did not have faith in their system of liberal education and Christian teaching. If you do not have faith enough in your system to be assured that the Japanese children could not be trained into good Canadians, do you blame us if we feel ashamed for you? Because we had faith in that education, we had faith in the Christian teachings . . . and what happened? That faith let us down.

What kept us afloat after the country let us down? Our faith in ourselves. We knew that our ideals and training were Canadian, even if you didn't. We knew that we had only to live up to our training and keep our integrity and self-respect intact, unsmeared by your lack of faith. It was hard work. Sometimes we almost gave up the struggle. Sometimes we wondered why we shouldn't get out and lick our sore wounds someplace else than here, but where could we go? To most of us, Japan is a foreign country full of all the things we learned to dislike, in spite of a lot of things that were good.

Still, through the strain and toil of a few enlightened people who gave their all towards securing us our lost freedom, we've managed to come through this far. On the way, we've lost dreams, and we've learned to distrust. We've also lost pride in Canada. But we know a deeper love for this, our native land, and would suffer much to stay here. Through bitterness we learned cynicism, and through frustration we gained new strength to fight for our rights . . .

Canada cannot be great until she *is* great. To that end, to be a great nation, Canada must destroy the virus of rot that affects our national life, and among other vices, race prejudice ranks high. It is the people, not the representatives, who can make this country great. For if all the people will not have corruptness in the governing of men, they will be sure to elect such people as would make greatness free, and secure in that freedom.

Joey Smallwood
October 1946

"An unbroken story of struggle"

Joey Smallwood grew up poor, and ambitious, in Newfoundland. After an eclectic career as a radio host and later a pig farmer, he found his issue in the confederation of Newfoundland to Canada. Most Newfoundlanders harboured no such idea, and were, if anything, friendlier towards Britain and the United States. Newfoundland decided against joining Confederation in 1867, preferring its status as a self-governing British colony. The island was bankrupt by 1934 and the British had to take direct control of its government. The Americans built and occupied large military bases there during World War II, but as they began to leave at war's end, Britain was looking for a way out. It was largely through Smallwood's efforts that confederation became an issue, as he travelled the colony using the communications skills he had perfected on radio. In 1946, Britain appointed the Newfoundland National Convention to meet and consider confederation. Delegates were elected to meet and debate the issue. Fortunately, the convention was recorded electronically, and the tapes provide a taste of a bare-knuckled debate where quarter was neither asked nor given.

The history of this island is an unbroken story of struggle. Our people's struggle to live commenced on the day they first landed here, four centuries and more ago, and has continued to this day. The struggle is more uneven now than it was then, and the people view the future now with more dread than they felt a century ago.

The newer conceptions of what life can be, of what life should be, have widened our horizons, and deepened our knowledge of the great gulf which separates what we have and are from what we feel we should have and be. We have been taught by newspapers, magazines, motion pictures, radios, and visitors something of the higher standards of well-being of the mainland of North America; we have become uncomfortably aware of the low standards of our country; and we are driven irresistibly to wonder whether our attempt to persist in isolation is the root cause of our condition.

We have often felt in the past, when we learned something of the higher standards of the mainland, that such things belonged to another world, that they were not for us. But today we are not so sure that two yardsticks were designed by the Almighty to measure the standards of well-being; one yardstick for the mainland of the continent, another for this island which lies beside it. Today we are not so sure, not so ready to take it for granted, that we Newfoundlanders are destined to accept much lower standards of life than our neighbours of Canada and the United States. Today we are more disposed to feel that our very manhood, our very creation by God, entitles us to standards of life no lower than our brothers on the mainland.

Our Newfoundland is known to possess natural wealth of considerable value and variety. Without at all exaggerating their extent we know that our fisheries are in the front rank of the world's marine wealth. We have considerable forest, water power, and mineral resources. Our Newfoundland people are industrious, hard-working, frugal, ingenious, and sober. The combination of such natural resources and such people should spell a prosperous country enjoying high standards, western world standards of living. This combination should spell fine, modern, well-equipped homes; lots of health-giving food; ample clothing; the amenities of modern New World civilization—good roads, good schools, good hospitals, high levels of public and private health. It should spell a vital, prosperous, progressive country.

It has not spelled any such things. Compared with the mainland of North America we are fifty years, in some things one hundred years, behind the times. We live more poorly, more shabbily, more meanly. Our life is more a struggle. Our struggle is tougher, more naked, more hopeless. In the North American family, Newfoundland bears the reputation of having the lowest standards of life, of being the least progressive and advanced of the whole family.

We all love this land. It has a charm that warms our hearts, go where we will—a charm, a magic, a mystical tug on our emotion that never dies. With all her faults we love her, but a metamorphosis steals over us the moment we cross the border that separates us from other lands. As we leave Newfoundland, our minds undergo a transformation. We expect, and we take for granted, a higher, a more modern way of life such as it would have seemed ridiculous or even avaricious to expect at home. And as we return to Newfoundland, we leave that higher standard behind, and our minds undergo a reverse transformation. We have grown so accustomed to our own lower standards and more antiquated methods and old-fashioned conveniences that we readjust ourselves unconsciously to the meaner standards under which we grew up. We are so used to our railway and our coastal boats that we scarcely see them; so used to our settlements, and roads, and homes, and schools, and hospitals, and hotels, and everything else, that we do not even see their inadequacy, their backwardness, their seaminess.

We have grown up in such an atmosphere of struggle, of adversity, of mean times, that we are never surprised, certainly never shocked, when we learn that we have one of the highest rates of tuberculosis in the world; one of the highest infant mortality rates in the world; one of the highest maternity mortality rates in the world; one of the highest rates of beriberi and rickets in the world. We take these shocking facts for granted. We take for granted our lower standards, our poverty. We are not indignant about them: we save our indignation for those who publish such facts, for with all our complacency, with all our readiness to receive, to take for granted, and even to justify these things amongst ourselves, we are, strange to say, angry and hurt when these shocking facts become known to the outside world ...

We have a perfect right to decide that we will turn away from North American standards of living and from North American standards of public services, and condemn ourselves as a people and government deliberately to long years of struggle to maintain even the little that we have. We may, if we wish, turn our backs upon the North American continent beside which God placed us, and resign ourselves to the meaner outlook and shabbier standards of Europe, two thousand miles across the ocean. We can do this, or we can face the fact that the very logic of our situation on the surface of the globe impels us to draw close to the progressive outlook and dynamic living standards of this continent.

Our danger, so it seems to me, is that of nursing delusions of grandeur. We remember the stories of small states that valiantly preserved their national independence and developed their own proud cultures, but we tend to over-look the fact that comparison of Newfoundland with them is ludicrous. We are not a nation. We are merely a medium size municipality, a mere minia-ture borough of a large city. Dr. Carson, Patrick Morris, and John Kent were sound in the first decades of the nineteenth century when they advocated cutting the apron strings that bound us to the government of the United Kingdom; but the same love of Newfoundland, the same Newfoundland patriotism, that inspired their agitation then, would now, if they lived, drive them to carry the agitation to its logical conclusion, to take the next step of linking Newfoundland closely to the democratic, developing mainland of the New World. There was indeed a time when tiny states lived gloriously. That time is now ancient European history. We are trying to live in the mid-twentieth century post-Hitler New World. We are living in a world in which small countries have less chance than ever before of surviving . . .

Confederation I will support if it means a lower cost of living for our people. Confederation I will support if it means a higher standard of life for our people. Confederation I will support if it means strength, stability, and security for Newfoundland. I will support confederation if it gives us dem-ocratic government. I will support confederation if it rids us of commission government. I will support confederation if it gives us responsible govern-ment under conditions that will give responsible government a real chance to succeed. Confederation I will support if it makes us a province enjoying privileges and rights no lower than any other province . . .

I believe that this move will lead to a brighter and happier life for our Newfoundland people. If you adopt this resolution, and Canada offers us generous terms, as I believe she will, and Newfoundland decides to shake off her ancient isolation, I believe with all my heart and mind that the people will bless the day this resolution was moved. With God's grace, let us move forward for a brighter and happier Newfoundland.

Peter Cashin

January 1948

"Newfoundland today is being conspired against from all sides"

Major Peter Cashin was a prominent Newfoundlander who served in the British army during World War I, and later as a cabinet minister in the colony's government. He despised Smallwood and opposed confederation, which he believed would submerge the centuries-old identity of Newfoundlanders and lead to economic ruin and dependency. He gave this speech to the Newfoundland National Convention in January 1948.

I am not speaking to hear the sound of my own voice, nor am I trying to warp the judgment of the delegates to this convention or the people of the country, or influence their minds with any more airy rhetoric or political spellbinding. My purpose has been . . . to give hard, cold facts which cannot be denied or talked away. What I have said emanates from my sincere political belief which is based on the solid and eternal doctrine: first, a country belongs to its people; second, it is the solemn duty of the people of that country to shoulder the responsibility of governing it. Any divergence or avoidance of that doctrine, any excuse for acting contrary to that fundamental truth is cowardly, unethical, and immoral. The challenge which faces the people of this country today is the patriotic and moral challenge to do their duty and to face their responsibilities like real men and women. It is a clear-cut issue, as clear and unambiguous as the challenge of right and wrong. But again I say, there are those amongst us who have shown that they are unwilling or have not the capabilities of facing their responsibilities and accepting obligations of democratic decency. They are prepared instead to assume the garb of mendicants and go begging at the back door of some outside country, asking to be taken in out of the rough world which they fear to face. Like Shakespeare's character, they are prepared to crawl under the huge legs of some foreign colossus and find themselves dishonourable graves. But I know that there are many thousands amongst us who are not prepared to form their opinions on mere moral or ethical grounds. They prefer to deal with matters from a more practical standpoint. They ask for facts. Well, I think I have given them the facts.

In my opinion, Canada is today in a position where she finds she has overreached herself. She reminds me of the frog in the fable who wanted to be as big as a bull and who puffed himself up until he burst. Canada is an ambitious country and in the thirties she got the idea that she wanted to become a big nation. She put on long pants before she became of age. She wanted an army, she wanted a navy and all the trimmings. How she might have gotten on if World War II had not come along we do not know. But like other countries, the blast of war hit her, and today she is left in an exhausted position, struggling for her life, and her financial bloodstream is fast running dry . . .

Canada wants this country and our Labrador possession, and the government of Great Britain has given her consent to this arrangement. There have been in this country since 1941, and are today, active agents whose business and object is to usher Newfoundland into confederation with Canada, and to induce our people to walk into the trap which has been baited. The outward evidence of the activities of these pro-confederate agents is shown in the foisting of this convention upon us, so that the agreement made with the Newfoundland government in 1933 could be evaded. It is shown in the act of exporting from this country a great portion of the people's treasury; in the reckless and deliberate squandering of our revenues to the tune of $40 million dollars a year; in the giving away of reckless concessions, and under disgraceful conditions, of our Labrador territory. It is evidenced by the false pictures of the fictitious prosperity which would be ours if we have confederation. It is shown by the actions of members of the Ottawa delegation, who in collaboration with the Canadian government, cooked up and brought back to us false estimates and misleading statements; by the existence of secret documents given to that delegation and the failure to produce them before this convention; by the circumstances under which the Canadian delegation was elected. All these things indicate to me at least beyond all doubt, that Newfoundland today is being conspired against from all sides. And if there was any doubt on this score, it must be dismissed when we see that the business of negotiating us into confederation has been entrusted to a body such as this, which has no power to negotiate, no power to speak for the people, which in the last analysis has neither the knowledge, the experience, nor the qualifications to pass on this matter, a matter which any sensible person knows is one for a properly constituted and elected government. This whole business is not alone illegal, it is worse—it is immoral . . .

I am convinced that although our country and our people are at present enshrouded in a pall of political darkness, they will eventually find their way into the light. This whole matter of bribes and promises will in the end be shown up for what it really is. And I say this not because our people would shrink from the new burden of taxation which confederation with Canada will place on their shoulders, not because of the vision of the thousands of homesteads which may have to be sold to satisfy the Canadian tax gatherers. No, it will not be for these things alone that our people will spurn this offer for them to sell out the land of their birth. I say our people will win through because of other, greater things. They will triumph, emerge from this ordeal, because there are still in this country such things as pride, courage, and faith—pride in the great traditions which have come down to us through centuries of independent living; courage to face up to life and hew out our individual fortunes; and finally, faith in our country and in the great destiny which I am convinced lies ahead of us.

Moses Coady

9 April 1950

"Democracy means equality of opportunity; it means
that each individual will have his fair share"

Father Moses Coady was a Roman Catholic priest who was born in Cape
Breton and lived there throughout his life, with the exception of time
away to study in Rome and Washington, D.C. Coady taught at St.
Francis Xavier University in Antigonish and eventually chaired its
department of extension. He was a fervent believer in using adult education to encourage people to improve their lot by organizing unions
and co-operatives. He founded the Coady Institute at St. Francis Xavier
University, and after his death, the Coady International Institute was
founded to continue his work in developing countries. Although in great
demand throughout North America, he gave this speech in Sydney,
Nova Scotia.

The basic problem of the world is the creation and distribution of wealth. This simple and apparently materialistic statement has many ramifications, but this is the storm centre, so to speak, and it is very necessary that this problem be solved. It is a bone of contention. It has caused a lot of trouble for all past time and will continue to cause trouble. It was the cause or at least the pretext of all past revolutions. We owe it to ourselves to solve this problem. We have solved other problems and our complacency, lack of interest, and general attitude towards this one look like stupid inconsistency.

Let us first get clear in our minds the norms or criteria which should guide us in this question of the creation and distribution of wealth. We are talking about the democratic solution, of course. Our democratic creed says that all men are equal, but this does not mean that they are all going to develop in the same way or have the same amount of wealth. Democracy means equality of opportunity; it means that each individual will have his fair share. How to get a formula by which democratic society will enable all men to get their fair share was and is the great question. We can lay down certain principles that will form, so to speak, a body of democratic doctrine, which we can all hold to be true.

The first principle is that any man is owner of the wealth created by the application of his physical and mental energies to natural resources to which he has undisputed title. This is exemplified in the case of the farmer who develops his piece of earth by his own energies.

If, on the other hand, a man has to use other human beings in the development of wealth or has to use natural resources that belong to other human beings, it matters not by what working arrangement he exploits them, he is not absolute owner of the wealth generated by such activities. This was always true, but it is particularly true of the modern industrial world. There is hardly any industrial operation or any modern business that can be conducted without the help of other human beings.

It is quite evident, too, that industries of all kinds use natural resources that were not in the first instance the property of the users. Gold, iron ore, coal, wood, land, and all the other varieties of natural resources were originally owned by all the people. If we go back far enough, it was true that the earth was for man. The story of how individuals or groups of individuals got the opportunity of exploiting these resources runs all the way from seizure by armed force, down through the devious ways of trickery, to accepted and legal methods of operation. It could be fairly said—especially in the case of nations—that human history is a story of "grab."

The second principle which constitutes a part of this body of democratic doctrine is that the financial remuneration for services in society should bear some relation to the economic level of the people served. This principle has direct bearing on the salaries of professional people—lawyers, engineers, doctors. It should determine also the amount of remuneration that business-men should get for their services to the public, and lastly it is the norm which governs remuneration for all kinds of social services. It is absurd and against the law of nature that individuals who rise out of the ranks of a poor people should get for their services financial returns out of all proportion to the gen-eral level of the wealth of the people. This has been the sin of all the ages—great wealth in the presence of dire poverty.

The third principle that should govern the distribution of wealth is the nature of the function which anybody performs in the system. If an individ-ual carries on a very difficult function calling for great ability, great learn-ing, which in turn demands long and costly training, then it is evident that that individual should be handsomely rewarded for his services. There are men in the world who are worth high salaries. It is good business for the people to hold out great rewards to their social servants. But sin comes in when people are able to fashion a system that will give them returns out of all proportion to their contribution. The great sin of the modern world is that stupid people, useless people, and bad people, by design and by luck and heredity, put themselves in a position to dominate the whole earth.

The fourth principle is that the remuneration of one vocational group in society should not be out of harmony with other groups. For example, it is possible for certain labour groups, on account of their strategic position, to get a share of the wealth out of all proportion to that which less fortu-nate groups of workers receive. Furthermore, the standard of living of one sector of a country which may not be as wealthy as another should not be too much out of harmony with the wealthier centres of the nation.

This, I believe, constitutes a body of doctrine which can build a new world.

John Diefenbaker
25 April 1957

"This party has a sacred trust"

John Diefenbaker was one of Canada's finest political orators and perhaps our greatest election campaigner. He became leader of the Progressive Conservatives late in 1956, and six months later Prime Minister St. Laurent called an election. Diefenbaker had met Merril Menzies, a young economist who came to believe that the long-serving Liberal government was incapable of new vision and unwilling to protect Canadian sovereignty against encroachments by the United States. Menzies sent Diefenbaker a series of memos in which he proposed a new national policy reminiscent of the nation-building John A. Macdonald. The ideas clicked with Diefenbaker, long an admirer of Macdonald, and he used them to create a set-piece speech, which he delivered with evangelical fervour to ever larger crowds during the 1957 campaign. He gave this speech in Toronto's Massey Hall. His references to "one Canada" and to a "sacred trust" were still being used more than thirty years later by Preston Manning, Brian Mulroney, and others.

My fellow Canadians, at the commencement of this national campaign you have come here to hear discussed the issues of the day. You have come here to have us lay before you a policy, a Canadian policy, to provide for an equality of rights everywhere in Canada and in every province in Canada . . .

I am of those who believe that this party has a sacred trust, a trust in accordance with the traditions of Macdonald. It has an appointment today with destiny, to plan and to build for a greater Canada. It has a sacred trust handed down to us in the tradition of Macdonald to bring about that Canada which is founded on a spirit of brotherhood, vision, and faith—one Canada, with equality of opportunity for every citizen and equality for every province from the Atlantic to the Pacific . . .

We intend to launch a national policy of development in the northern areas which may be called the New Frontier Policy. Macdonald was concerned with opening the west. We are concerned with developments in the provinces with provincial co-operation, and in our northern frontier in particular. The North, with all its vast resources of hidden wealth, the wonder and the challenge of the North must become our national consciousness. All that is needed, as I see it today, is an imaginative policy that will open its doors to Canadian initiative and enterprise. We believe in a positive national policy of development, in contrast with the negative and haphazard one of today. We believe that the welfare of Canada demands the adoption of such a policy, which will develop our natural resources for the maximum benefit of all parts of Canada, a policy which will encourage more processing of Canada's raw materials in Canada, and will foster a greater financial participation by Canadians. In short, we believe that Canadians must recognize that Canada's economic policy shall ensure and preserve for the people of Canada, and for future generations of Canada, the control of our economic destiny. That we believe . . .

I would be remiss . . . if I did not return to rediscuss something that affects the freedom of Canadians everywhere. I mean that institution that is one of the three pillars of democracy, those pillars being the Canadian people, the Canadian provinces, and the Canadian Parliament. I speak now of Parliament, I speak with my colleagues here from the House of Commons. Parliament, the place that I love . . .

I have seen the progressive restriction of the supremacy of Parliament in the last ten years. I have seen Parliament bludgeoned—and I say that is no pipe dream—bludgeoned by a majority. I have seen the hands of the Cabinet directing members and disciplining them into an abject servility. My friends, there is an issue that transcends all others—the preservation of freedom, its maintenance, the restoration of Parliament, and above everything else in that connection, an imperative and immediate necessity of a return to the two-party system in this country if freedom is to be preserved and political democracy maintained.

I love Parliament . . . I am one of those who does not form personal antagonisms with others who sit opposite to me; I hope I shall continue in that. But I witnessed scenes—my colleagues here witnessed scenes—that deny anything like it ever having taking place in all the history of a democracy. We say we will restore Parliament. Closure has its use. We have now found what its abuse means. We shall abolish closure to guard against its abuse in the days ahead . . .

In this opening meeting of the campaign, the first of several major speeches that I intend to make, what I have dealt with is the need of a national development policy to keep our young men and women in Canada, to build for Canada a Parliament that will be effective, a human betterment policy that will assure opportunity.

The platform, as it is revealed, will show that the policy of this party is based on its abiding faith in freedom; in the maintenance of our institutions which are the buttress of that freedom; in the sovereign independence of Canada; in the assurance of equal opportunity to all Canadians; in our dedication that the state shall be the servant and not the master of the people; that communism will be resisted from within and from without Canada by every means within our concepts of freedom of the individual . . .

My friends, this is a time for greatness in planning for Canada's future. Unity demands it; freedom requires it; vision will ensure it.

As far as the road on which the Liberal Party has travelled in recent years is concerned, if it is followed after the next election in the same direction, Canada would be led to the eventual extinction of its true parliamentary system.

I believe that if this nation is to have a new birth of unity and freedom, we must go back to the vision and the idealism of Canada's first nation builder. He led the way, Macdonald did, to national tolerance, dignity, and unity, as he joined with Cartier in brotherhood and in faith.

My pledge, on behalf of this party, will be to do my part to achieve one Canada. I don't think the people are asking for political carpentry today for both purposes. They are asking for something of a vision of a new Canada, the Canada that appears to me at this time, with its opportunity for Canadians. They ask for a lift in heart. They have a desire to serve. My purpose and my aim with my colleagues on this platform will be to bring to Canada and to Canadians a faith in their fellow Canadians, faith in the future in the destiny of this country . . .

We must make articulate the yearnings and the aspirations of Canadians everywhere, even unto the humblest of our people. If we are dedicated to this—and to this we are—you, my fellow Canadians, will require all the wisdom, all the power that comes from those spiritual springs that make freedom possible, all the wisdom, all the faith, and all the vision which the Conservative Party gave but yesterday under Macdonald, change to meet changing conditions, today having the responsibility of this party to lay the foundations of this nation for a great and a glorious future.

Lester Pearson

1957

"There can be no enduring and creative
peace if people are unfree"

Lester Pearson was a career diplomat during a golden age of Canadian
diplomacy, which he helped to create. He won the Nobel Peace Prize in
1957 for his role in defusing a tense situation in the Middle East, where
England and France threatened to take over the Suez Canal. Pearson
often appeared to be a reticent speaker, but in this, his Nobel acceptance speech in Stockholm, Sweden, in 1957, he is poised and confident.

During my lifetime greater and more spectacular progress has been made in
the physical sciences than in many centuries that preceded it. As a result, the
man who lived in 1507 would have felt more at home in 1907 than one who
died fifty years ago, if he came back to life today.

A great gulf, however, has been opened between man's material advance
and his social and moral progress; a gulf in which he may one day be lost if

it is not closed or narrowed. Man has conquered outer space. He has not conquered himself. If he had, we would not be worrying today as much as we are about the destructive possibilities of scientific achievements. In short, moral sense and physical power are out of proportion. This imbalance may well be the basic source of the conflicts of our time; of the dislocations of this "terrible twentieth century."

All of my adult life has been spent amidst these dislocations; in an atmosphere of international conflict; of fear and insecurity. As a soldier, I survived World War I when most of my comrades did not. As a civilian during the Second War, I was exposed to danger in circumstances which removed any distinction between the man in and the man out of uniform. And I have lived since, as you have, in a period of cold war, during which we have ensured by our achievements in the science and technology of destruction that a third act in this tragedy of war will result in the peace of extinction. I have, therefore, had compelling reason, and some opportunity, to think about peace, to ponder over our failures since 1914 to establish it, and to shudder at the possible consequences if we continue to fail . . .

Spinoza said that "peace is the vigour born of the virtue of the soul." He meant, of course, creative peace, the sum of individual virtue and vigour. In the past, however, man has unhappily often expressed this peace in ways which were more vigorous than virtuous. It has too often been too easy for rulers and governments to incite man to war. Indeed, when people have been free to express their views, they have as often condemned their governments for being too peaceful as for being too belligerent.

This may perhaps have been due to the fact that in the past men were more attracted by the excitements of conflict and the possibility of injury, pain and death. Furthermore, in earlier days, the drama of war was the more compelling and colorful because it seemed to have a romantic separation from the drabness of ordinary life. Many men have seemed to like war, each time, before it began . . .

Perhaps this has all changed now. Surely the glamour has gone out of war. The thin but heroic red line of the nineteenth century is now the production line. The warrior is the man with a test tube or the one who pushes the nuclear button. This should have a salutary effect on man's emotions. A realization of the consequences that must follow if and when he does push the button should have a salutary effect also on his reason . . .

May I express one final thought? There can be no enduring and creative peace if people are unfree. The instinct for personal and national freedom cannot be destroyed and the attempt to do so by totalitarian and despotic government will ultimately make not only for internal trouble but for international conflict. Authority under law must, I know, be respected as the foundation of society and as the protection of peace. The extension of state power, however, into every phase of man's life and thought is the abuse of authority, the destroyer of freedom, and the enemy of real peace.

In the end, the whole problem always returns to people; yes, to one person and his own individual response to the challenges that confront him.

In his response to the situations he has to meet as a person, the individual accepts the fact that his own single will cannot prevail against that of his group or his society. If he tries to make it prevail against the general will, he will be in trouble. So he compromises and agrees and tolerates. As a result, men normally live together in their own national society without war or chaos. So it must be one day in international society. If there is to be peace, there must be compromise, tolerance, agreement.

We are so far from that ideal that it is easy to give way to despair and defeatism. But there is no cause for such a course or for the opposite one that leads to rash and ill-judged action . . .

Above all we must find out why men with generous and understanding hearts and peaceful instincts in their normal individual behaviour can become fighting and even savage national animals under the incitements of collective action. This is the core of our problem: why men fight who aren't necessarily fighting men.

It was posed for me in a new and dramatic way one Christmas Eve in London during World War II. The air raid sirens had given their grim and accustomed warning. Almost before the last dismal moan had ended, the anti-aircraft guns began to crash. In between their bursts I could hear the deeper, more menacing sound of bombs. It wasn't much of a raid, really, but one or two of the bombs seemed to fall too close to my room. I was reading in bed and to drown out or at least take my mind off the bombs, I reached out and turned on the radio. I was fumbling aimlessly with the dial when the room was flooded with the beauty and peace of Christmas carol music. Glorious waves of it wiped out the sound of war and conjured up visions of happier peacetime Christmases. Then the announcer spoke, in German. For it was a German station and they were Germans who were singing those carols. Nazi bombs screaming through the air with their message of war and death; German music drafting through the air with its message of peace and salvation. When we resolve the paradox of those two sounds from a single national source, we will, at last, be in a good position to understand and solve the problem of peace and war.

Pearson later became leader of the Liberal Party and prime minister when he defeated John Diefenbaker in 1962.

Woodrow Lloyd

1962

"Medical care is not an optional
commodity, it is a necessity"

Woodrow Lloyd was premier when Saskatchewan introduced North America's first public, tax-funded health insurance program in July 1962. Although Tommy Douglas had been at the helm when the plan was devised, he left to lead the federal New Democratic Party in 1961, and it was his successor, Lloyd, who put the plan into action. Saskatchewan's doctors resisted, saying that it was state medicine and would interfere with their relationships with patients. The tension had reached an almost fevered pitch by May 1962, when the doctors held their annual meeting in a crowded ballroom in Regina. Lloyd, a rational and methodical man, walked into a hostile room and delivered this speech.

The people of Saskatchewan for many years have clearly expressed their concern for the provision of adequate health services. They have done so because experience has indicated the inability of most of us to adequately provide such services for ourselves and our families.

This has resulted in municipal doctor plans, designed to provide for rural medical service; in the construction of hospitals; in the control of tuberculosis; in widespread immunization for the prevention of communicable diseases that were once a scourge; in the cancer diagnostic and treatment program; in the mental health and psychiatric services; in the public assistance program for those on low income needing health care; and, of course, in the hospital insurance plan . . .

Doubtless many who are here today had misgivings when the Saskatchewan Hospital Services Plan was introduced in 1947. Probably there were institutions and communities as well who questioned the wisdom of the plan. Certainly some of the language used at that time, "regimentation," "government taking over," "unwarranted government action," "unbearable economic burden," is not unlike expressions currently used by some in respect to medical care insurance. Yet, today, the success of the Hospital Plan is beyond question and it is extremely popular. Every provincial government in Canada has followed suit and, moreover, as you know, the federal government has accepted a measure of financial responsibility.

I express confidence that in the same way the misgivings or fears which are now entertained by some regarding the medical care insurance program will be dissipated once you give the program a fair trial. Once this is done we are convinced that the satisfactory and productive partnership which has characterized the public program just mentioned can be expanded to the other fields of medical care.

Saskatchewan people have provided the funds to build and improve modern hospitals in which their physicians may work. They recognized the advisability of developing a full medical school in our province, and with it a first-rate teaching hospital. The desire of this same public of Saskatchewan for a method whereby the increasing costs of medical as well as hospital services may be lifted from the shoulders of individuals and families has been made abundantly clear in the public expression of the many organizations to which I referred earlier. The government has a responsibility to respond to this constructive attitude, and it would expect to be held to account if it did not meet its obligation . . .

May I now turn to the concern that seems to be evident, that the rights and privileges of doctors will be interfered with? As I gather from some statements made by the profession through their official spokesmen and from some comments made by individual physicians, there is a fear that the medical care insurance program will somehow severely restrict and limit the activities of the physicians. May I assure you again that the government has no intention or desire to influence the exercise of your professional judgment. In prescribing medical treatment, your knowledge and your word are supreme. The government has no wish or intention to change or to challenge that supremacy. We agree that nothing should interfere with your right to use your best judgment as to the treatment to be prescribed. We agree that you must have freedom to choose the patients you serve and the location of your practice. On the other hand, the patient must have the right to his choice of doctor. We have tried to include in the act the necessary provisions to make this abundantly clear.

I am aware of, and greatly respect, your concern for a proper doctor-patient relationship. If this relationship is adequately protected under existing voluntary plans, I am unable to see how its essential components can in any way be interfered with by the Medical Care Insurance Act. Patients will be free to select the doctor in whom they place their trust and doctors in turn will be free to accept this trust . . .

There is another side to the picture of services to the public. There has been a great deal of discussion recently over concepts of rights—the rights of individuals, the rights of groups, the rights of professions. I want to deal for a moment with what I consider to be the rights and proper expectations of the people of Saskatchewan. I repeat that, as patients, we are perfectly willing to place matters involving medical judgments entirely in the hands of a highly skilled group such as you are. In enacting the Medical Care Insurance Act, however, we have said that we, as consumers of medical services, and as taxpayers, have a right to a say in how we pay our medical bills. We have a right to construct an administrative agency, responsible to us, to arrange for such payment. The act deals, therefore, not with medicine, but with economics and the administration of public finance. The act provides medical consumers with a voice in those economics and that administration.

Medical services are essential to health and to life itself. Good medical services are part of the basis for a healthy, productive economy. Medical care is not an optional commodity, it is a necessity. When medical services are needed, they should not in the interests of each of us or all of us be denied to any of us. When a commodity or service is essential, our society has long since accepted that consumers have a legitimate right to a voice in making the essential governing decisions in such matters. That voice has been for medical care, embodied in the Saskatchewan Medical Care Insurance Act, an act passed by a properly elected legislature in the province of Saskatchewan.

Saskatchewan's doctors staged a bitter twenty-three-day strike in July 1962 before accepting the new public health insurance plan. Within a decade similar health plans were in place in all Canadian provinces.

Jean Lesage
5 April 1963

"We have launched a vast project of national renewal"

Jean Lesage became the Liberal premier of Quebec in 1960 after a long reign by Maurice Duplessis and the Union Nationale. Lesage led a reform government that insisted Quebec had new expectations about its powers and responsibilities within Confederation. The new programs that accompanied reform of the health, education, and social service systems were expensive. Lesage argued that Ottawa had taken control of the levers of the economy during World War II and that the balance had never shifted back to the provinces as he believed it should. Lesage was also finance minister, and on 5 April 1963, just five days prior to a federal election, he delivered an ultimatum in his budget speech. Historian Ramsay Cook describes it as "a shrewd declaration of independence." It shocked federal politicians, especially Lesage's federal Liberal cousins. Lesage's speech was at once a demand for more power and control for Quebec, and a response to a burgeoning nationalist sentiment in the new Quebec.

The state of Quebec has fiscal powers and it exercises them. From the start of Confederation, there has been change and development in this field; I need not today go into its causes and trends. I shall merely look at the facts as they are; and the situation I find arouses in me thoughts that I would like to share with this House.

Anyone involved in government knows that nonexistent or inadequate fiscal powers sharply curtail its scope of action. In other words, the fiscal system can in itself be an instrument of economic growth. Economic planning, as practised in certain European countries, provides telling proof of this.

Now, the fiscal system is one tool of economic growth over which Quebec has relatively little control. The share of income tax collected by the province is greater now than it has ever been, for several generations back, but it is still clearly inadequate.

At federal-provincial conferences I have time and again put forward Quebec's legitimate claims, basing myself, with reason, on what I have called Quebec's prior needs. Last year in my budget speech, I dealt with this subject at length . . .

We have launched, in Quebec, a vast project of national renewal; and, whichever party may take office on Monday, we will not put up with a denial, for reasons we cannot go along with, of our right to the means of action we still lack.

I may even add that, by so often giving short shrift to Quebec's pleas up to now, the federal government has acted as though it meant to put a brake on our province's social and economic development. In running some of the joint programs, the federal government's attitude has only provided further grounds for the lurking suspicions of a growing number of Quebecers. Unless there is, within the next few months, a marked shift in federal policies bearing on fiscal matters and on the redistribution of federal powers, we shall not soon recover our faith that the federal government correctly understands the workings of our federal system.

Three days from now, federal elections are to be held. We do not yet know which political group the Canadian people will choose to put at the helm of the country. Whatever the results of the election, however, it will be absolutely essential that the new government meet Quebec's demands. For the benefit of the government to be elected on April 8, let me briefly recall that Quebec for the time being requires the following minimum fiscal powers: 25 percent of the personal income tax, 25 percent of the corporation income tax, and 100 percent of succession duties. Moreover, we want equalization payments to be computed on the basis of the yield of personal and corporate income tax in the province where that yield is highest. These are, for the moment, our minimum requirements. It will later be necessary, on the basis of the work of the Royal Commission on Taxation that has just been set up, to reconsider the whole question of the division of fiscal powers between the central government and the government of the state of Quebec . . .

As to joint programs, I recall what I said on the subject at the federal-provincial conference of July 1960. The federal government should stop being a party to them; it should withdraw. The joint programs were introduced at a time when they were likely to serve the Canadian economy; they are no longer warranted now. The flagrant unfairness with which Quebec was recently treated in the matter of vocational and technical training shows that not only has the federal government deprived us of what we needed and were entitled to, it actually used the joint programs to favour other provinces at our expense . . .

At a time when many of our fellow citizens are wondering about the advantages that Confederation holds for Quebec, the attitude of the present federal government is doing little to dissipate the existing backlog of both ancient bitterness and new uneasiness.

In an event, the true solution, within Confederation, is to get the joint programs replaced by reinstating the provinces' own fiscal powers. Joint programs on matters within exclusive provincial jurisdiction, such as education, are inadmissible. Provinces can only endanger their autonomy by participating in them. In fact, such programs involve the channeling of public funds through the federal treasury for specifically provincial ends. Moreover, since it is the federal government that sets the goals and priorities, it is also the federal government that defines the conditions under which provinces will be invited to work toward these goals. Such conditions impose a definite framework upon the exercise of provincial powers. This situation is totally unacceptable to Quebec.

In the normal course of events, present fiscal arrangements between the federal and provincial governments would fall due for renewal by 1967. Quebec, cannot, however, wait until then. While there might, in the past, have been some faith in the effectiveness of joint programs, the groundlessness of such faith is now proven: the system is not only rickety, it is inequitable. It must be dropped at once, especially in the field of education; and it must make room for the recovery of fiscal rights by the province, which will thus be able to make full use of her resources in terms of the specific needs of her population . . .

I will not continue indefinitely to speak for Quebec's needs, nor will I be content to go on submitting her requests to the central government in some vague hope that it may condescend to meet them. The matter is a vital one; and I do not intend, as premier, to minister of finance, to go on repeating myself year after year without tangible results. This then is the last time I am putting the case in these terms in a budget speech.

Twelve months will elapse before the next budget. By then, either the central government, whichever party is elected on April 8, will have taken advantage of the twelve intervening months to take Quebec's requirements into account; or else we in Quebec, shall, on our side, during the same twelve months, have seen to it that the necessary steps are taken in fiscal matters. These decisions will be governed by the goals of economic, social, and cultural self-assertion that we have set for ourselves at the express desire of the people of Quebec.

François Aquin
3 August 1967

"Vive le Québec libre"

The nationalist movement in Quebec continued to grow throughout the 1960s, even as Canada held elaborate celebrations for its centennial year in 1967. French President General Charles de Gaulle paid a state visit to Canada in that same year to convey the greetings of France on the one hundredth anniversary of Confederation. From a balcony in old Montreal he uttered his famous phrase, "vive le Québec libre," a message unmistakable in its support of Quebec separatism. Prime Minister Pearson watched the speech on television in stunned disbelief. He issued a statement on behalf of the Canadian government that said in part, "The people of Canada are free. Every province of Canada is free. Canadians do not need to be liberated." De Gaulle left for home without completing his visit. The Quebec Liberals, now in Opposition, also issued a statement critical of de Gaulle's actions. A few days later, François Aquin, a Liberal member of the Quebec Assembly, resigned to sit as an independent, and made this statement.

Last Friday, I resigned as a member of the Liberal caucus and as a member of the Liberal Party. I could not, in conscience, approve the party declaration concerning President de Gaulle's visit on Quebec land. The president's visit, the words he spoke, the candour with which he went to the heart of matters here constitute an historic event and a step forward in the fulfilment of our destiny.

After having known the conqueror's occupation, foreign tutelage and treasons within their borders, Quebecers as a people have for some years considered the Quebec state a singular instrument of their progress. Yet the Quebec state lacks international recognition, as vital for a people as is a man's need to communicate with others. The Quebec state lacks the maturity of its own constitution that would give it the tools necessary to transform its situation, in human terms and in the direction of freedom.

General de Gaulle did not come here to tell us what to think or what to do. He came here to offer France's support for our national evolution. Why refuse the offered hand? Why brandish the myth of Quebec's abandonment by France, a myth fabricated to mask the francophobia of our public figures and to absolve a conqueror that, over the course of nearly a century, prevented by force communication with the motherland? Why seek refuge in the standard arguments of diplomatic interference? Why be frightened by the reaction of forces who want to keep Quebec in servitude? I am with those who have accepted the offered hand. Charles de Gaulle understood the profound aspirations of the Quebec people desirous of liberation and emancipation. He grasped the depth of the drama lived by our countrymen, poor in a rich country, second-class citizens in their own city, forced to work in the language of their masters, foreigners on the soil of their own land, torn between what they are and what they want to be.

At the cry of "vive le Québec libre," the soul of an oppressed and bullied people rose up in unison with triumphal cheers on July 24. It would now be exorcised, this word freedom, that before only some dared to barely whisper, this word freedom that rightfully belongs to all of humanity, that belongs to nations, that belongs to man.

That day, the president revealed Quebec to many Québécois and he revealed les Québécois to the world. Awareness of our situation can only coincide with the awareness of peoples in the Third World who, like us, march toward their reality. It is with peoples as it is with individuals pursuing their own freedom; little by little the road opens toward others.

President de Gaulle, in consolidating the cultural unity of the *francophonie*, has for a long time pleaded the cause of modern nationalism, progressive nationalism, open and peaceful, that will one day prevail over the territorial and warlike bourgeois nationalism of colonial powers. He pleaded this cause again along all the roads of Quebec. And our people, who are so often said to be drowning in a sea of two hundred million anglophones, are still standing. They did not fear the eddies; they did not fear the undertow.

They responded to the message of decolonization with enthusiasm. But evidently, for those who destroy a people in Vietnam and for those who back them under so-called military accords, for those who kill in Aden and for those who back them under the Commonwealth, for those who oppress in Angola and for those who back them under NATO, for those who are scandalized by the so-called interference of brotherly talk while preferring to send armies or to supply arms, the very presence of General de Gaulle in America was a living reproach and his words became unacceptable . . .

I now sit here alone, free of all parties, but the hour is near when every free man of Quebec will have to go to the heart of these matters and speak his mind. The work of liberating Quebec, imprisoned as it is by an obsolete constitution, has never been so pressing. What is an obstacle for us has become a springboard for the government of Canada. Let's abandon these masks of the status quo: the changing of the Canadian constitution and the conservative evolutionism of this statute. It is not on points of tax that the destiny of a people will be built. Beyond the quibbles, notably of lawyers and fiscal experts, Quebec in its soul has chosen freedom. Freedom supposes that the state of Quebec possesses its own totality of powers essential for radical economic, social and cultural transformation. There is more than one road to freedom, but if the incomprehension of the communities with which we are yet ready to negotiate as equals leave us no other option, tomorrow we will have to choose independence. In the building of this freedom, economic and social structures must change and evolve so that the Quebec man and woman will become collectively responsible for our revolution, in peace, justice and love.

Vive le Québec libre, Mr. Speaker. I ask you for the privilege to occupy another seat in this Chamber.

Pierre Trudeau
16 October 1970

"Violent and fanatical men are attempting to destroy Canada"

In October 1970, the Front de Libération du Québec kidnapped Pierre Laporte, the province's labour minister, and James Cross, a British diplomat. The FLQ was a separatist group infused with the ideology of Third World resistance groups. Pierre Trudeau responded by invoking the War Measures Act, which curtailed normal civil and human rights. The army arrived in the streets, rounding up hundreds of Quebecers and putting them into jail. On 16 October 1970 a sombre Trudeau appeared on national television to explain and defend his decision directly to citizens of the nation.

I am speaking to you at a moment of grave crisis, when violent and fanatical men are attempting to destroy the unity and the freedom of Canada. One aspect of that crisis is the threat which has been made on the lives of two innocent men. These are matters of the utmost gravity and I want to tell you what the government is doing to deal with them. What has taken place in Montreal in the past two weeks is not unprecedented. It has happened elsewhere in the world on several recent occasions; it could happen elsewhere within Canada. But Canadians have always assumed that it could not happen here and as a result we are doubly shocked that it has.

Our assumption may have been naive, but it was understandable; understandable because democracy flourishes in Canada; understandable because individual liberty is cherished in Canada. Notwithstanding these conditions, partly because of them, it has now been demonstrated to us by a few misguided persons just how fragile a democratic society can be, if democracy is not prepared to defend itself, and just how vulnerable to blackmail are tolerant, compassionate people.

Because the kidnappings and the blackmail are most familiar to you, I shall deal with them first. The governments of Canada and Quebec have been told by groups of self-styled revolutionaries that they intend to murder in cold blood two innocent men unless their demands are met. The kidnappers claim they act as they do in order to draw attention to instances of social injustice. But I ask them, whose attention are they seeking to attract? The government of Canada? The government of Quebec? Every government in this country is well aware of the existence of deep and important social problems. And every government to the limit of its resources and ability is deeply committed to their solution, but not by kidnappings and bombings—by hard work. And if any doubt exists about the good faith or the ability of any government, there are Opposition parties ready and willing to be given an opportunity to govern. In short, there is available everywhere in Canada an effective mechanism to change governments by peaceful means. It has been employed by disenchanted voters again and again.

Who are the kidnap victims? To the victims' families they are husbands and fathers. To the kidnappers their identity is immaterial. The kidnappers' purposes would be served equally well by having in their grip you or me, or perhaps some child. Their purpose is to exploit the normal, human feelings of Canadians and to bend those feelings of sympathy into instruments for their own violent and revolutionary ends.

What are the kidnappers demanding in return for the lives of these men? Several things:

For one, they want their grievances aired by force in public on the assumption, no doubt, that all right-thinking persons would be persuaded that the problems of the world can be solved by shouting slogans and insults.

They want more—they want the police to offer up as a sacrificial lamb a person whom they assume assisted in the lawful arrest and proper conviction of certain of their criminal friends. They also want money—ransom money. They want still more. They demand the release from prison of seventeen criminals, and the dropping of charges against six other men, all of whom they refer to as political prisoners. Who are these men who are held out as latter-day patriots and martyrs? Let me describe them to you.

Three are convicted murderers; five others were jailed for manslaughter; one is serving a life imprisonment after having pleaded guilty to numerous charges related to bombings; another has been convicted of seventeen armed robberies; two were once paroled but are now back in jail awaiting trial on charges of robberies. Yet we are being asked to believe that these persons have been unjustly dealt with, that they have been imprisoned as a result of their political opinions, and that they deserve to be freed immediately, without recourse to due process of law.

The responsibility of deciding whether to release one or other of these criminals is that of the federal government. It is a responsibility that the government will discharge according to law. To bow to the pressures of these kidnappers who demand that the prisoners be released would be not only an abdication of responsibility, it would lead to an increase in terrorist activities in Quebec. It would be as well an invitation to terrorism and kidnapping across the country. We might well find ourselves facing an endless series of demands for the release of criminals from jails, from coast to coast, and we would find that the hostages could be innocent members of your family or mine.

At the moment the FLQ is holding hostage two men in the Montreal area, one a British diplomat, the other a Quebec cabinet minister. They are threatened with murder. Should governments give in to this crude blackmail we would be facing the breakdown of the legal system, and its replacement by the law of the jungle. The government's decision to prevent this from happening is not taken just to defend an important principle, it is taken to protect the lives of Canadians from dangers of the sort I have mentioned. Freedom and personal security are safeguarded by laws; those laws must be respected in order to be effective.

If it is the responsibility of government to deny the demands of the kidnappers, the safety of the hostages is without question the responsibility of the kidnappers. Only the most twisted form of logic could conclude otherwise. Nothing that either the government of Canada or the government of Quebec has done or failed to do, now or in the future, could possibly excuse any injury to either of these two innocent men. The guns pointed at their heads have FLQ fingers on the triggers. Should any injury result, there is no explanation that could condone the acts. Should there be harm done to these men, the government promises unceasing pursuit of those responsible.

If a democratic society is to continue to exist, it must be able to root out the cancer of an armed, revolutionary movement that is bent on destroying the very basis of our freedom. For that reason the government, following an analysis of the facts, including requests of the government of Quebec and the city of Montreal for urgent action, decided to proclaim the War Measures Act. It did so at 4:00 AM this morning, in order to permit the full weight of government to be brought quickly to bear on all those persons advocating or practising violence as a means of achieving political ends.

The War Measures Act gives sweeping powers to the government. It also suspends the operation of the Canadian Bill of Rights. I can assure you that the government is most reluctant to seek such powers, and did so only when it became crystal clear that the situation could not be controlled unless some extraordinary assistance was made available on an urgent basis.

The authority contained in the act will permit governments to deal effectively with the nebulous yet dangerous challenge to society represented by the terrorist organizations. The criminal law as it stands is simply not adequate to deal with systematic terrorism.

The police have therefore been given certain extraordinary powers necessary for the effective detection and elimination of conspiratorial organizations which advocate the use of violence. These organizations, and membership in them, have been declared illegal.

The powers include the right to search and arrest without warrant, to detain suspected persons without the necessity of laying specific charges immediately, and to detain persons without bail. These are strong powers and I find them as distasteful as I am sure do you. They are necessary, however, to permit the police to deal with persons who advocate or promote the violent overthrow of our democratic system. In short, I assure you that the government recognizes its grave responsibilities in interfering in certain cases with civil liberties, and that it remains answerable to the people of Canada for its actions. The government will revoke this proclamation as soon as possible.

Tommy Douglas
16 October 1970

"A black Friday for civil liberties in Canada"

Most Canadians supported Pierre Trudeau on the War Measures Act, accepting his contention that there was an insurrection occurring, and that it called for the imposition of war measures in peacetime. An overwhelming majority of MPS supported Trudeau as well, but NDP leader Tommy Douglas and most of his caucus were opposed. Douglas said he was appalled by the kidnappings, but he believed that the government had enough powers to deal with the crisis without invoking the draconian War Measures Act. Douglas was vilified at the time, as can be seen from the frequent heckling during this controversial speech in the House of Commons on 16 October 1970.

These last few days have been days of anxiety for all the people of Canada, and particularly for the members of this House who sit on the treasury benches. We have all been appalled and disgusted by the abduction of two innocent men who are being held as hostages in an attempt to blackmail the government into releasing convicted criminals and to do certain other things which, in my opinion, are completely unreasonable.

Because this situation is so delicate, we in this party have carefully refrained from making any statements or from asking any provocative questions. Because we felt that the government should be given every opportunity to deal with what was an extremely difficult situation, we have gone along with the government on at least two or three matters.

We have agreed with the government's refusal to accede to the outrageous demands of the kidnappers. I can understand the feelings of those sensitive individuals whose first reaction was that the government should deal with the kidnappers and should be prepared to accede to their demands. I would not go so far as the prime minister as to call them weak-kneed and bleeding hearts. I think they are people with a great sensitivity and a great sense of the value of human life. But I think such people overlook two important facts.

The first fact is that compliance with the demands of the abductors would not necessarily guarantee the safe return of the two men who they have taken as hostages. The second, and even more important, is that acceding to the demands of the kidnappers would only set in motion a whole series of similar incidents, and nobody knows where the road would end . . .

Now we come to a point on which we cannot support the government. The government is now convinced that there is a state of civil disturbance and anticipated sabotage which requires prompt and vigorous action. The government, of course, undoubtedly has in its possession information that is not available to us. I suggest that if the government has information that civil disturbances are likely to break out on a large scale and that sabotage is anticipated in menacing proportions, then the government, of course, has the responsibility to deal with it.

I submit that, properly, the government had two options in dealing with the situation. The first was to deal with it under the powers which it now has under the laws of Canada, to utilize all the powers under the treason sections of the Criminal Code and the sections dealing with seditious intention. There are very considerable powers there. I think the government deserves some criticism because some of those sections have not been used. There have been indications of seditious intent upon which the government could have acted. There is also the offensive weapons provision, and in dealing with the matter the government could have acted under that authority. The government had the power to call in the armed forces, and did so, and there was no criticism of the government for using these extraordinary powers if they, in their opinion, on the basis of information which they and they alone had, considered the situation serious enough to warrant such action.

The second option which was open to the government was that if it came to the conclusion that the powers it now enjoys under the Criminal Code and various other statutes were not sufficient to cope with this situation, the magnitude of which the rest of us are not fully aware of, the government had the option of coming to Parliament and asking Parliament, in a democratic way, to clothe it with the authority to deal with this unusual situation.

Certainly I can say, so far as this party is concerned, we would have been prepared to facilitate very quickly such matters coming before Parliament in order that the government might be able to indicate the areas in which it had not sufficient power and the justification for requiring greater powers and greater authority. But the government has not utilized this option. Instead, the government has taken the unusual step of invoking the War Measures Act. In my opinion, the government has overreacted to what is undoubtedly a critical situation. Does civil disturbance constitute apprehended insurrection?

AN HONOURABLE MEMBER: Yes . . .

DOUGLAS: The government, I submit, is using a sledgehammer to crack a peanut.

SOME HONOURABLE MEMBERS: Oh, oh!

DOUGLAS: This is overkill on a gargantuan scale. Why has the government invoked the War Measures Act? May I point out that the FLQ have been around for some six or seven years? For several years now, it is well known that they have committed and been found guilty of acts of sabotage, the placing of bombs in mailboxes, and blowing up of public buildings.

AN HONOURABLE MEMBER: Is the honourable member condoning that?

DOUGLAS: The prime minister was minister of justice for three years and has been prime minister of this country for over two years. Why have we not been asked to supply the government with the powers to deal with the growing menace which it now says is so tremendous that we must invoke the War Measures Act to deal with an apprehended insurrection? The fact is, and this is very clear, that the government has panicked and is now putting on a dramatic performance to cover up its own ineptitude.

In the process of invoking the War Measures Act, I wonder if the honourable gentlemen opposite who are making so much noise have stopped to consider that today the prime minister holds more power in his hands than any prime minister in the peacetime history of Canada?

AN HONOURABLE MEMBER: Thank God!

SOME HONOURABLE MEMBERS: Hear, hear!

SOME HONOURABLE MEMBERS: Oh, oh!

DOUGLAS: Right now there is no constitution in this country, no Bill of Rights, no provincial constitutions. This government now has the power by Order in Council to do anything it wants—to intern any citizen, to deport any citizen, to arrest any person, or to declare any organization subversive or illegal. These are tremendous powers to put into the hands of the men who sit on the treasury benches.

If my friends will look at the regulations they will find that if the police in their judgment decide that some person is a member of a subversive organization—not just of the FLQ but of any organization that the police decide is subversive—

SOME HONOURABLE MEMBERS: Oh, Oh!

DOUGLAS: —or that he contributes to such a party—

AN HONOURABLE MEMBER: Why is the honourable member scared?

DOUGLAS: —or that he communicates any of the ideas or doctrines of such a party—

AN HONOURABLE MEMBER: What has changed you, Tommy?

DOUGLAS: —that person may be arrested and detained for ninety days. At the end of ninety days, he has the power to appeal to a superior court judge to set a date for his trial and that may be postponed for some time. He may be denied bail. A person in Canada may be held for ninety days or more without any opportunity to prove his innocence, to prove that he does not belong to a subversive organization or to prove that the organization to which he belongs is not subversive in spite of what may be in the minds of those who ordered the arrest. The regulations give the power to seize property and hold it for ninety days. It is a resurrection of the padlock law. These are very serious powers. If the government requires those kinds of powers, surely in a democracy they should have asked the democratically elected representatives of the people to give them these powers . . .

I say that the government's action today is an action of panic. In the hysteria which people feel, the government may, as the prime minister has said, get many letters and calls approving what is being done. But I predict that within six months, when the Canadian people have had time to reflect on what has happened today—the removal of all the protection and liberties presently on the statute books of Canada, a country placed under the War Measures Act, regulations introduced allowing persons to be detained for ninety days without a chance to prove their innocence—when that day comes, the Canadian people will look on this as a black Friday for civil liberties in Canada.

Joe Clark
19 April 1979

"We are fundamentally a community of communities"

Joe Clark had been involved in Progressive Conservative politics since childhood, and he won the party leadership in 1976. He proposed a federation much more decentralized than that of Pierre Trudeau and defined his concept of the country as a "community of communities" in this speech during the federal election campaign in 1979.

Let me start with a compliment to my opponent. The one important thing Mr. Trudeau has done well in his eleven years is to make the national government attractive to large numbers of able French Canadians. He did that well because he knew personally the discomfort that French Canadians have felt in not being active at the centre of their national government. That discomfort continues, of course, but Mr. Trudeau has reduced it considerably and that is one tradition of his on which I and my party intend to build. What is important is that in that case he understood the problem.

I think a central cause of the general failure of his government is that he did not understand, and sometimes did not try to understand, other aspects of Canada's very complex reality. Too often, he and the quite similar people he drew around him tried to change the country to fit their theory about what the country should be. In economic policy, in constitutional policy, in their attitude towards the instincts of the individual Canadian citizen, they have been governing against the nature of the nation.

To govern a nation, one must first understand it.

It's typical, I think, that our official emblem—the maple leaf—is not indigenous to two of our provinces and two of our territories. For there are thousands of happy and productive Canadian citizens who are most at ease when they speak neither of our two official languages. We are a nation that is too big for simple symbols. Our preoccupation with the symbol of a single national identity has, in my judgment, obscured the great wealth we have in several local identities which are rich in themselves and which are skilled in getting along with others.

If that truth has been lost on Ottawa's planners, it is not lost on the people of Canada, whether those people are artists like Alden Nowlan or Monique Leyrac or W. O. Mitchell or Gordon Lightfoot or Emily Carr or any of the Group of Seven, whose work evokes their locale, or whether they are citizens who are starting heritage societies, starting history clubs, organizing walks through their own back yards. In an immense country, you live on a local scale. Governments make the nation work by recognizing that we are fundamentally a community of communities.

Of course the national government has to be strong, particularly on economic questions. But it must also be sensitive to the damage that neat theories can wreak upon a diverse country. There is nothing new to that view. Indeed, the successful prime ministers of Canada have incorporated that idea into the makeup of their governments, ensuring that every region had senior ministers who were strong enough to keep the government in touch with local realities. That is a fact of life in Canada to which we must return.

A second thing that is important is my view, and that of my party, that our economy in Canada is potentially one of the strongest in the world. We have in abundance resources which are elsewhere in short supply, whether of food or energy or minerals. Capital will come to us, and come to us in ways that we can control. So will as much population as we want. Our challenge in this country is not to cope with scarcity; our challenge is to build on abundance. Other nations might well be forced, legitimately, to contemplate limits on growth, but our very different challenge here in Canada is to plan and to manage growth.

Finally, our people are ambitious. Whatever cultures we come from, whatever heritage we bring to these shores, we are all of us North American in aspiration. We want to build. We want to grow. Generally, the goals of Canadians are personal goals. A few people in our history have helped build our nation by consciously pursuing national goals, but many more have built this nation by pursuing the personal goals which the nature of this nation allows.

The personal goal of most Canadians has been freedom and some security for their family. That caused the settlement of new regions, caused the immigration of new citizens, caused the transplanting of old roots to new ground. A policy designed to make the nation grow must build upon and must not frustrate the instinct of most Canadians to build a stake for themselves.

So what we propose in this election campaign is not just a change in government, but a fundamental change in the very direction of this country, a change that would reflect the value of that cultural and regional diversity, that would build on the natural strengths of our economy, and would recognize that the best instrument of national achievement is the individual initiative of the private citizen and the private sector in this country.

Through the last decade, government has been properly concerned with services to citizens, and we now have a good basic system of services in place. But the challenge of this next decade is to make this nation grow in wealth and to make our people grow in understanding of the great good fortune that we have here in Canada.

We can do that . . .

We intend to create in Canada an atmosphere in which the innovator and the entrepreneur are encouraged to go out and to build in the world. No one who travels in this country, no one who knows it, can escape being impressed mightily by the great potential that is here, and by the knowledge on the part of the people of Canada that we are a fortunate nation, a fortunate people of unparalleled potential.

The prime minister, for reasons that I don't understand, has been suggesting that this is a time when people will have to lower their expectations.

He is dead wrong about that. He is selling Canada short when he says that. This is a time for Canadians to raise their expectations. Only if our expectations are high will we go out and go to work to build. There is a great deal in this country to be confident about.

There is no question in my mind nor in the minds of my colleagues. There is a tremendous potential upon which to build here in Canada. There is no doubt that the people of this country are seized with that spirit of potential. What we need is a government in Ottawa that will encourage and recognize how essential to our future it is that the policy, the attitude, the approach of government get in line with the attitude and the hopes of the people, that we have a government in Canada that is as confident and proud and as buoyant about the future of this country as are the people themselves.

Clark won the election with a minority government in May 1979, and Trudeau announced his retirement. But when Clark's government fell a mere nine months later, Trudeau staged a comeback.

René Lévesque

4 March 1980

"The time has come to choose the path to our future"

René Lévesque was born in Gaspé and studied at Jesuit schools, known for their strong tradition of classical education. He later dropped out of law school and became the most popular television journalist in Quebec. Jean Lesage recruited him as a Liberal candidate for the 1960 provincial election, and as a minister in that government Lévesque nationalized Quebec Hydro. He became increasingly frustrated by what he considered to be the futility of Quebec achieving its goals within Confederation. He bolted from the Liberals and helped form the separatist Parti Québécois. The PQ stunned the nation by winning the 1976 election on a platform of Quebec sovereignty. Lévesque was a consummate communicator, fluently and colloquially bilingual, and able to convey volumes with a mere shrug or a deep pull on his ever present cigarette. On 20 December 1979 Lévesque announced that there would be a referendum on "sovereignty association," an arrangement in which Quebec would become a state retaining a close commercial relationship with Canada. He made this major speech in the Quebec Assembly on 4 March 1980.

Fellow Quebecers, we have now all reached this deciding moment. After years of discussions, constitutional crises, inquiries, and reports, the time has come to freely and democratically choose the path to our future. The people must give the matter much thought when the moment comes to take this direction and commit to its collective destiny. We, Quebecers, where do we come from? Where do we stand and what are our chances of growing and developing? There are so many questions that we must ask ourselves in order to enlighten the vote . . .

The course of action that leads us to the referendum, the one that we propose, is faithful to Quebecers' most profound and most constant aspirations, and it is also the only one that will release us from the vicious circle that impedes our *crise de regime*. Only political ostriches or very naïve or presumptuous people would refuse to acknowledge that the repeated failures of all the governments that looked for a solution in the tinkering of the regime, and also that the gap between Quebec's reality and English Canada's is widening, inevitably lead us to the following conclusion: it is only a majority commitment, a massive majority as much as possible, for change in equality by Quebecers as a whole, that will ever allow us to initiate the indispensable process.

We must remember that opposite to us, in English Canada, there is also a very strong national sentiment . . . The Quebec government respects this national English Canadian reality and does not intend to impose any political system upon it. We will not reproach Canadians of the other provinces for being attached to the federal regime as it essentially is, for acknowledging its obvious advantages, and history proves that they were right to acknowledge them, and for always trying to conform this regime to their own aspirations.

But even though this system did work, and everyone acknowledges this, first and foremost to the advantage of the English Canadian majority, in particular Ontario, and that moreover Quebec finds itself increasingly in the minority, it is normal to seek new forms of co-operation by proposing an alternative solution that endeavours to respect the needs and the most central aspirations of both parties . . .

In fact, the only way we can hope for a new balance—and events have confirmed this for many years—is, on the one hand, through Quebec's recuperation of exclusive power to create our laws without having others step on our toes, to levy and use all our taxes here, all the public incomes that we pay, precisely, for our development; and on the other hand, in order to maintain a common economic space in which no one, from one side or another, would be deprived by this, the continuation of an economic association that would entail joint use of the same currency.

The government asks for a mandate to negotiate a new agreement that responds to these two demands, no more, no less. However, we are not asking for a blank cheque either. We are not asking citizens to approve in advance the outcome of this course of action. We commit to not making any definitive changes in political status without having again consulted the population because we are aware of the fact that no serious political change can be contemplated, and certainly not be realized, without the formal and unflagging support of the majority of citizens.

Moreover, this is the reason why—I have said this many times, and I want to repeat it—the government will respect, until the end of its mandate, the majority decision that will come out of the referendum, in no way disregarding the collective will. It would be desirable to have the same guarantee from those who are preparing to defend the negative option during the upcoming campaign. It would be good for such guarantees of democratic respect of the will of citizens to be given immediately, as of now, before intense debates take over.

Whereupon, we must honestly ask ourselves: What would be the impact of a yes or a no; what would one or the other bring in the foreseeable future? I think that many Quebecers—and every day there are more and more, if I am not mistaken—are already aware of what a negative response would mean. It would establish once again, and for a long time, Quebec's dependence on the English Canadian majority. It would establish once again, and for a long time, Quebecers' status of inequality and, even worse, an increasing minority situation within the federal unit. It would be the continuation and perpetuation of never-ending conflicts, federal-provincial dead ends, innumerable overlaps in which responsibility is diluted, and so much energy, resources and time is wasted in a constantly growing sterility . . .

The "yes" finally ensures a breakthrough. It is open to change within the scope of continuing development and maturing of an entire people. It is the clear proclamation of a desire for equality and for equality lived not only on paper. It is the certain and definite condition for cultural security with chances for this culture to fully blossom, for the identity it has formed through generations, and for the development of all this unlimited potential for which, like all societies, we will have to count on ourselves first. This "yes" is at the same time a better balance and a fairer sharing in the economic partnership with the rest of Canada. It would eliminate factors that hindered our development at many levels, and in particular, at the economic level . . .

We will persist until we forget what Mercier, in the last century, referred to as our fratricidal struggle. I am deeply convinced that those who will have done it, including some of our friends opposite, will be extremely proud the evening of the referendum when a solid majority of the population will have said yes—yes to Quebec, yes to its present maturity, yes to all its chances for a open and responsible future.

Pierre Trudeau

14 May 1980

"We are going to say a resounding, an overwhelming no"

René Lévesque and Pierre Trudeau had long been political foes who represented Quebec's historical and competing nationalist and federalist tendencies. Trudeau was defeated by Joe Clark and the Conservatives in May 1979, and announced his retirement from politics. The Parti Québécois referendum campaign was ready by December, but the Clark government fell that same month, and Trudeau was coaxed out of retirement. The scene was set for Trudeau and Lévesque to do battle. The PQ posed a referendum question that asked citizens to vote yes to sovereignty association, a sovereign Quebec that would form a close commercial and trade association with the rest of Canada.

Trudeau watched from Ottawa as the referendum campaign raged in Quebec during the spring months of 1980. He made only three campaign appearances, his last in the crowded, steaming Paul Sauvé arena in Montreal on 14 May 1980. He seized on a Lévesque quip that Trudeau wasn't a real Quebecer because his mother had been of Scottish descent. Trudeau had spent the better part of three days carefully drafting and revising this speech, in which he appealed to undecided voters, using some of his favourite techniques: Socratic questioning, crisp logic, and blunt attack.

I want to thank you for this warm welcome. I think it is obvious by this immense gathering, it is obvious that these are historic moments. There are very few examples in the history of democracy of one part of a country choosing to decide, for itself and by itself, whether, yes or no, it wants to be part of the country to which it has always belonged. There are very few occasions when this has happened in the history of democracy. And I believe that all those here this evening, all those who have worked for the No in this province for over a month, will be proud to reply when . . . our children and perhaps, if we are lucky, our grandchildren, ask us in twenty or thirty years: "You were there in May 1980. You were there when the people of Quebec were asked to decide freely on their future. You were there when Quebec had the option to stay in Canada or to leave. What did you do in May 1980?" "No, that was our answer" . . .

We know very well what they are doing, these hucksters of the yes vote. They are trying to appeal to everyone who would say yes to a new agreement. Yes to equality of nations. Yes at the same time to association. Yes at the same time to a common currency. Yes to a second referendum. Yes to a simple mandate to negotiate.

It is those who say yes through pride or because they do not understand the question, or because they want to increase their bargaining power, and to those among the undecided who are on the brink of voting yes, to whom I am addressing myself this evening, because what we have to ask ourselves is what would happen in the case of a yes vote, as in the case of a no vote.

And it is the undecided, those who are on the Yes side through pride, or because they are tired and fed up, who, in these last few days, must be addressed. So let us consider this: The government of Canada and all the provincial governments have made themselves perfectly clear. If the answer to the referendum question is no, we have all said that this no will be interpreted as a mandate to change the Constitution, to renew federalism . . .

And I make a solemn declaration to all Canadians in the other provinces, we, the Quebec MPs, are laying ourselves on the line, because we are telling Quebecers to vote no and telling you in the other provinces that we will not agree to your interpreting a no vote as an indication that everything is fine and can remain as it was before. We want change and we are willing to lay our seats in the House on the line to have change. This would be our attitude in the case of a no vote . . .

Here is a party whose goal was separation, then independence, then sovereignty, then sovereignty-association, and then they even said that sovereignty-association was only for the purposes of negotiation. Here is a party that, in the name of pride, said to Quebecers: Stand up, we are going to move on to the world stage and assert ourselves.

And now, this party, on the point of entering the world stage, gets frightened and stays in the wings. Is that pride? Should we use that as a reason to vote for a party that tells us it will start all over again if the answer is yes, that there will be another referendum?

Well, that is what we are criticizing the Parti Québécois for—not having the courage to ask a clear question, a question a mature people would have been able to answer, really a simple question: Do you want to leave Canada, yes or no?

The answer is no to those who advocate separation rather than sharing, to those who advocate isolation rather than fellowship, to those who, basically, advocate pride rather than love, because love involves challenges coming together and meeting others halfway, and working with them to build a better world. So then, one must say, leaving that whole convoluted question aside, one must say no to ambiguity. One must say no to tricks. One must say no to contempt, because they have come to that.

I was told that no more than two days ago Mr. Lévesque was saying that part of my name was Elliott and, since Elliott was an English name, it was perfectly understandable that I was for the No side, because, really, you see, I was not as much of a Quebecer as those who are going to vote yes.

That, my dear friends, is what contempt is. It means saying that there are different kinds of Quebecers. It means that saying that the Quebecers on the No side are not as good Quebecers as the others and perhaps they have a drop or two of foreign blood, while the people on the Yes side have pure blood in their veins. That is what contempt is and that is the kind of division which builds up within a people, and that is what we are saying no to.

Of course my name is Pierre Elliott Trudeau. Yes, Elliott was my mother's name. It was the name borne by the Elliotts who came to Canada more than two hundred years ago. It is the name of the Elliotts who, more than one hundred years ago, settled in Saint-Gabriel de Brandon, where you can still see their graves in the cemetery. That is what the Elliotts are. My name is a Quebec name, but my name is a Canadian name also, and that's the story of my name.

My dear friends, Laurier said something in 1889, nearly one hundred years ago now, and it is worth taking the time to read these lines: "My countrymen," said Laurier, "are not only those in whose veins runs the blood of France. My countrymen are all those people, no matter what their race or language, whom the fortunes of war, the twists and turns of fate, or their own choice, have brought among us."

All Quebecers have the right to vote yes or no. And all those no's are as valid as any yes, regardless of the name of the person voting, or the colour of his skin. My friends, Péquistes often tell us: The world is watching us, hold our heads high; the world is watching us, the whole world is watching what is happening in our democracy. Let's show them we are proud . . .

We are against independence. Of course the world is watching us. The world will be a bit astonished by what it sees. I admit, because in today's world . . . you see, things are unstable, to say the least. The parameters are changing, to use a big word. And that means that there is fire and blood in the Middle East, in Afghanistan, in Iran, in Vietnam, that means that there is inflation which is crippling the free economy; that means that there is division in the world; that means there is perhaps a third of the human race which goes to bed hungry every night, because there is not enough food and not enough medicine to keep the children in good health.

And that world is looking at Canada, the second largest country in the world, one of the richest, perhaps the second richest country in the world . . . a country which is composed of the meeting of the two most outstanding cultures of the western world: the French and the English, added to by all the other cultures coming from every corner of Europe and every corner of the world. And this is what the world is looking at with astonishment, saying: These people think they might split up today when the whole world is interdependent? When Europe is trying to seek some kind of political union? These people in Quebec and in Canada want to split it up?

(FROM THE FLOOR): No.

. . . they want to take it away from their children . . .

(FROM THE FLOOR): No.

. . . they want to break it down? No. That's what I am answering.

I quoted Laurier, and let me quote a father of Confederation who was an illustrious Quebecer: Thomas D'Arcy McGee: The new nationality, he was saying, is thoughtful and true; nationalist in its preference, but universal in its sympathies; a nationality of the spirit, for there is a new duty which especially belongs to Canada to create a state and to originate a history which the world will not willingly let die.

Well, we won't let it die. Our answer is no to those who would kill it.

We won't let this country die, this Canada, our home and native land, this Canada which really is, as our national anthem says, our home and native land. We are going to say to those who want us to stop being Canadians, we are going to say a resounding, an overwhelming no.

Peter Lougheed

20 October 1980

"The federal government is determined to move unilaterally"

There has been a long-standing struggle between Ottawa and the western provinces for control over natural resources such as oil and potash, and the benefits accruing from them. Spikes in the international prices for oil and other resources in the 1970s only increased the friction. Saskatchewan nationalized half of its potash industry, partly in response to Ottawa's tax policy on resources. Alberta was bitter about new taxes on oil, which subsidized consumption in eastern Canada. Alberta's Premier Peter Lougheed outlined the issues in this speech in October 1980. Lougheed had been a corporate lawyer, and his remarks to the legislature are factual and unembellished, much like a CEO reporting to his board of directors.

I think there's no need for me to emphasize to this Assembly the significance of oil and gas revenues to our province. We're aware that 55 percent of our budget comes from natural resource revenues. We're aware that we utilize 70 percent of natural resource revenues for current purposes and put aside only 30 percent for the Heritage Trust Savings Fund. I believe all members of this Assembly do not need any reminder about the economic significance of oil and gas, and an active petroleum industry in terms of job security and stability and prospects for advancement.

I'm sure all honourable members are aware [that] under the Canadian Constitution, Section 109, the provinces own the resources, and with the ownership go rights and jurisdictional positions. Of course that involves the determination of what resources should be developed, in what way, and the pace of that development. Those are clearly the rights of the provinces, who own resources under our Constitution. However, as we have said before, but important to repeat: when a province produces a resource and it moves from the wellhead into interprovincial trade, at that time the federal jurisdiction comes into play under the Constitution. So you have the obvious balance in our nation today, where you have federal jurisdiction over interprovincial trade and provincial ownership rights. Quite clearly they have to be reconciled, and that has been the way between 1974 and 1979: a reconciliation by way of agreement. Neither party can dominate the other, therefore, there has to be agreement. We've recognized that over the course of the years 1974–79 by agreeing to phasing in the price of oil to commodity value. We've agreed to selling our natural gas at less than the price at which we're selling our conventional oil, to encourage substitution, among other reasons. That has been the history of the Canadian energy scene in that period of time.

I'd like to remind members of the negotiations this government conducted last fall with the then-federal administration under Prime Minister Joe Clark. That negotiation was conducted essentially with the same civil servants in senior capacity who are in place today in the federal Department of Energy, Mines and Resources . . .

We're aware of the decision of the voters of Canada on February 18, which saw a shift in support for the Clark administration in Ontario and certain other parts of the country but certainly not in western Canada. The support in western Canada on February 18 for the whole concept of approach to the provinces as reflected by the Clark administration is illustrated by the results of that day. The present federal government, as we all know, has no representation at all in the provinces of Saskatchewan, Alberta, and British Columbia, and nominally in Manitoba, with two seats. That is a situation that any Canadian looking at this matter should not ignore. It's a message to be very much aware of . . .

In mid-June, after the Quebec referendum, because the federal minister was not prepared to get into discussions until that time, there was a meeting of some two days in duration in Ottawa between the minister of energy and natural resources of this province and the minister from Ottawa, with no progress whatsoever and no effort to negotiate or compromise by the federal government. That's a very strong statement, but an accurate one. The decision was then made to extend the pricing agreement until the end of July this summer, to give the premier of Alberta and the prime minister of Canada an opportunity to become involved in the whole matter of energy issues. I met with the prime minister for two days, on July 24 and 25.

The minister of energy and natural resources has tabled in the legislature today a very important document. I ask our honourable members to consider it very carefully. I believe it's important that it be reviewed here at this time. It starts with an oil-pricing proposal over a four-year period and sets as its target not 85 percent of the world price, which was the arrangement made with the Clark administration, but 75 percent of the North American price. That is a very major compromise and concession, if you like, by the government of Alberta in an effort to make an arrangement with the federal government . . .

The proposal was rejected in its entirety by the prime minister and the federal government. Many throughout all parts of Canada have assessed that proposal as being reasonable, generous, and in the best interests of Canadians. It was rejected in its entirety as a package proposal for energy self-sufficiency for Canada, in the interests of Canadian harmony, Canadian unity, and Canadian economic strength . . .

I want to assure the legislature that we have done and will continue to do everything we can to work out this situation on the basis of negotiations. However, indications are that the federal government is determined to move unilaterally in eight days, and try, no matter how it might be interpreted or presented, to take over control of Alberta resources to all intents and purposes. I sadly say that if they proceed on that basis, we will throw away, for as long as one could judge, our prospect of the economic potential for

Canada, and what that means for us in terms of jobs and reducing employment by being oil self-sufficient, when many other countries in the world
in the late '80s will not be able to. Throwing away an opportunity to create
activity in this country will have a multiplier effect across all of Canada, and
a very significant impact on the Canadian economy in all parts, with a
strong west and a multiplier effect in the manufacturing centre. We're on the
verge of throwing that opportunity away by the actions of the federal government. I hope I'm wrong, but today I can give this Legislative Assembly
no indication other than that analysis.

Soon after Lougheed's speech, Ottawa enraged Albertans by implement-
ing the National Energy Program, and the Liberals have never recovered politically in western Canada.

Pierre Trudeau
17 April 1982

"Bringing home our Constitution marks the end of a long winter"

Pierre Trudeau and the No side won the 1980 referendum, and Trudeau pushed ahead with constitutional change. He wanted a constitution that recognized Canada as a multicultural state, but one enshrining English and French language rights. He also wanted a charter to outline the rights and freedoms accorded to individuals. Trudeau did succeed in his goal, but only after a bruising process of brinksmanship and negotiations with the premiers, some of whom believed Trudeau's charter would take power away from elected politicians and give it to judges. When agreement was reached in November 1981, Quebec's long-sought veto over future constitutional change was absent, and the province refused to sign on. On 17 April 1982 the Queen was in Canada at a ceremony to proclaim the new Constitution, and Trudeau made these remarks.

Today, at long last, Canada is acquiring full and complete national sovereignty. The Constitution of Canada has come home. The most fundamental law of the land will now be capable of being amended in Canada, without any further recourse to the Parliament of the United Kingdom . . .

For more than half a century, Canadians have resembled young adults who leave home to build a life of their own, but are not quite confident enough to take along all their belongings. We became an independent country for all practical purposes in 1931, with the passage of the Statute of Westminster. But by our own choice, because of our inability to agree upon an amending formula at that time, we told the British Parliament that we were not ready to break this last colonial link.

After fifty years of discussion we have finally decided to retrieve what is properly ours. It is with happy hearts, and with gratitude for the patience displayed by Great Britain, that we are preparing to acquire today our complete national sovereignty. It is my deepest hope that Canada will match its new legal maturity with that degree of political maturity which will allow us all to make a total commitment to the Canadian ideal.

I speak of a Canada where men and women of Aboriginal ancestry, of French and British heritage, of the diverse cultures of the world, demonstrate the will to share this land in peace, in justice, and with mutual respect. I speak of a Canada which is proud of and strengthened by its essential bilingual destiny, a Canada whose people believe in sharing and in mutual support, and not in building regional barriers. I speak of a country where every person is free to fulfill himself or herself to the utmost, unhindered by the arbitrary actions of governments.

The Canadian ideal which we have tried to live, with varying degrees of success and failure for a hundred years, is really an act of defiance against the history of mankind. Had this country been founded upon a less noble vision, or had our forefathers surrendered to the difficulties of building this nation, Canada would have been torn apart long ago. It should not surprise us, therefore, that even now we sometimes feel the pull of those old reflexes of mutual fear and distrust: fear of becoming vulnerable by opening one's arms to other Canadians who speak a different language or live in a different culture; fear of becoming poorer by agreeing to share one's resources and wealth with fellow citizens living in regions less favoured by nature.

The Canada we are building lies beyond the horizon of such fears. Yet it is not, for all that, an unreal country, forgetful of the hearts of men and women. We know that justice and generosity can flourish only in an atmosphere of trust.

For if individuals and minorities do not feel protected against the possibility of the tyranny of the majority, if French-speaking Canadians or Native peoples or new Canadians do not feel they will be treated with justice, it is useless to ask them to open their hearts and minds to their fellow Canadians. Similarly, if provinces feel that their sovereign rights are not secure in those fields in which they have full constitutional jurisdiction, it is useless to preach to them about co-operation and sharing.

The Constitution which is being proclaimed today goes a long way toward removing the reasons for the fears of which I have spoken. We now have a charter which defines the kind of country in which we wish to live, and guarantees the basic rights and freedoms which each of us shall enjoy as a citizen of Canada.

It reinforces the protection offered to French-speaking Canadians outside Quebec, and to English-speaking Canadians in Quebec. It recognizes our multicultural character. It upholds the equality of women, and the rights of disabled persons.

The Constitution confirms the longstanding division of powers among governments in Canada, and even strengthens provincial jurisdiction over natural resources and property rights. It entrenches the principle of equalization, thus helping less wealthy provinces to discharge their obligations without excessive taxation. It offers a way to meet the legitimate demands of our Native peoples. And, of course, by its amending formula, it now permits us to complete the task of constitutional renewal in Canada.

The government of Quebec decided that it wasn't enough. It decided not to participate in this ceremony, celebrating Canada's full independence. I know that many Quebecers feel themselves pulled in two directions by that decision. But one need look only at the results of the referendum in May, 1980, to realize how strong is the attachment to Canada among the people of Quebec. By definition, the silent majority does not make a lot of noise; it is content to make history.

History will show, however, that in the guarantees written into the Charter of Rights and Freedoms, and in the amending formula, which allows Quebec to opt out of any constitutional arrangement which touches upon language and culture, with full financial compensation, nothing essential to the originality of Quebec has been sacrificed.

Moreover, the process of constitutional reform has not come to an end. The two orders of government have made a formal pledge to define more precisely the rights of Native peoples. At the same time, they must work together to strengthen the Charter of Rights, including language rights in the various provinces. Finally, they must try to work out a better division of powers among governments.

It must however be recognized that no Constitution, no Charter of Rights and Freedoms, no sharing of powers can be a substitute for the willingness to share the risks and grandeur of the Canadian adventure. Without that collective act of the will, our Constitution would be a dead letter, and our country would wither away.

It is true that our will to live together has sometimes appeared to be in deep hibernation; but it is there nevertheless, alive and tenacious, in the hearts of Canadians of every province and territory. I wish simply that the bringing home of our Constitution marks the end of a long winter, the breaking up of the ice jams and the beginning of a new spring.

For what we are celebrating today is not so much the completion of our task, but the renewal of our hope; not so much an ending, but a fresh beginning. Let us celebrate the renewal and patriation of our Constitution; but let us put our faith, first and foremost, in the people of Canada who will breathe life into it.

Trudeau was a nation builder, but at a cost. Quebec's absence from constitutional agreement led to another twenty years of abrasive Canada-Quebec relations.

Brian Mulroney

6 October 1983

"Bilingualism is a valued principle and an
indispensable dimension of our national life"

Brian Mulroney defeated Joe Clark for the leadership of the Progressive
Conservative Party in 1983. The Conservatives traditionally had little
appeal in Quebec, but Mulroney was a bilingual son of the province, and
he was determined to alter his party's fate. Early in his leadership, the
Liberals tried to trip him up on a question of minority language rights.
Protections accorded to the French language in Manitoba when the
province joined Confederation in 1870 had been stripped away. In 1890,
the legislature passed an act declaring English to be the province's only
official language, much to the chagrin of francophones and their
national champions such as Henri Bourassa. But ninety years later, the
courts ruled that the act of 1890 had been unconstitutional. That judgment was unpopular with many westerners and Ontarians, including
some in Mulroney's caucus. Trudeau and the Liberals proposed an

all-party resolution in the House of Commons supporting the minority language provisions. It was an immediate test of Mulroney's mettle. He worked long into the night of 5 October writing a speech that was both personal and political, and he delivered it on the following day.

I speak today on a resolution of consequence before this House. I do so with pride and in the genuine hope that our action will be helpful to our fellow Canadians in Manitoba as they search for an equitable solution to a problem which has troubled the soul of the nation for over one hundred years.

The purpose of this resolution is one which has touched the soul of Canada for decades. When I was very young in Baie-Comeau, we were taught at the local school the sad story about some of our francophone brothers outside of Quebec. Even at that young age, we knew that an injustice had been committed in Manitoba. We did not know why or how, but we knew that certain basic rules—which we Quebecers, anglophones as well as francophones, could benefit from—had been broken. A francophone minority, which had enjoyed an historical protection of its language in Manitoba, was suddenly cut off—amputated—from this guarantee which was so vital. We knew also, without being able to really evaluate its consequences, the less than glorious role some of our Quebec leaders had played in the outcome of this very painful situation.

I do not want today to go over all of the steps, again make all of the accusations, recite all of the injustices. Still less do I intend to blame anybody. The facts are clear and speak for themselves.

Our collective evolution has determined that two peoples speaking English and French were united in a great national adventure. This unique situation has given birth to our Canadian citizenship. This very noble outcome has not been without failings. Neither has it been protected from constant assault by those who wish that we give it up for a less grandiose vision, a more limited country, a less generous mentality. There is even a member of the PQ government who said that any such initiative to help the francophone minority in Manitoba was stupid.

This resolution compels us to remember our overriding commitments in this country of almost limitless space, overflowing with great opportunities for the future. These commitments comprise a respect for our linguistic and other minorities, a long-held desire to encourage their flowering, and the duty to protect the rights of our minorities—wherever they are.

Manitoba is going through a period of disturbance. In making this gesture today, I do not want to exacerbate the complexity of this situation. In the final analysis, it is up to Manitobans themselves to decide. I hope that Manitoba's leaders, who I assume are acting in good faith, will work together in a spirit of generosity to ensure that franco-Manitobans are treated with dignity and respect.

Thus we have today the occasion to state our position on this question here in the House of Commons. By this resolution before us, we are asked to make a gesture. The significance and the impact of this action relate first and foremost to profoundly human values, values which define to a large degree the kind of generosity of spirit typical of Canadian society.

It is with pride that I announce today, in the name of my colleagues in the Progressive Conservative Party, our unanimous support for the resolution which is before this House.

Years ago this House approved the principle of official bilingualism for Canada. Simply put, it means that English and French Canadians shall have equal rights and equal opportunities across Canada. It is a noble principle, one which is capable of enriching the life of this nation. By our stand today we reaffirm our commitment and that of our party given earlier in this same House of Commons by outstanding and distinguished Canadians such as the Honourable Robert Stanfield and the Right Honourable Member for Yellowhead (Mr. Clark).

Bilingualism is a valued principle and an indispensable dimension of our national life. The program, however, must be implemented with fairness and with equity. It is diminished if it comes to be perceived by large numbers of Canadians as an instrument of division or an instrument of unfairness. Governments must always be alert to this possibility. Excessive zeal and regrettable statements by public officials have seriously hindered worthy programs in the past. We do not want that to happen here.

We are all children of our environments. We bring to given problems the judgment that has been shaped by the realities to which we have been exposed in our lives. In Canada, particularly, in the area of language, these differ widely according to individuals and according to regions because of our sense of history. We must seek to understand these differences and consider them not as obstacles but as guides to the elaboration of sensible and realistic policies which will enhance rather than lessen the attractiveness of such policies in the minds of all Canadians. Sensitivity to people and the presumption of good faith should be the hallmarks of implementation. They will ensure for bilingualism a more durable character and more pervasive acceptance. In the larger sweep of history these qualities will have served the country better than a divisive gesture or an uncaring remark.

I want to say a word to the people of Manitoba. I am aware of the problems that have arisen in many of your communities. We do not seek today to make them more difficult. Sadness always results when there is division among us. Strong people take strong stands on major issues and have done so throughout our entire history.

Our days together as Canadians have not always been glorious, but neither have they been without absolutely splendid accomplishment. For all our imperfections, we remain in Canada a country of promise and a people of hope. We have come through so much together against overwhelming odds that our citizenship has become a privileged symbol in our lives. Our respect for the rule of law, our unparalleled record in civil liberties, our sense of tolerance, our respect for our neighbour and his property have combined to make Canada an admired nation in the world.

The issue before us today is one that must be approached in a spirit of conciliation. This is a quality for which Manitobans are renowned. It does honour to them and to their province. The issue before us today is also one of simple justice. There is no painless way to proceed. There is no blame to be apportioned. There are no motives to be impugned. There is only the sanctity of minority rights. There is no obligation more compelling and no duty more irresistible in Canada than to ensure that our minorities, linguistic and otherwise, live at all times in conditions of fairness and justice.

The Manitoba Members of Parliament in our caucus, along with many Manitobans at home, have been deeply troubled by this issue. I have shared with them their moments of anguish but they have responded with courage and with respect. In a great unifying gesture to all of Canada they stand with me and our party today in an historic and unforgettable endorsement of a fundamental tenet of this nation.

My friend Robert Cliche was a great humanist who sought, at all times, conciliation, the right approach, respect for the common man whose rights have been abused. He often quoted Felix Antoine Savard who once wrote: "Happy are those men and those peoples who get along together."

I believe that with this resolution we have helped the process of reconciliation which must take place in Manitoba . . .

This resolution is about fairness. It is about decency. It is an invitation for co-operation and understanding. It speaks to the finest qualities in this nation.

I say to you on behalf of my entire party on this or any great issue that affects this nation that we stand before you, united in the sunlight, ready to work for a better Canada.

Remi De Roo

13 December 1983

"An economy must serve the basic
needs of all the people"

The Canadian Conference of Catholic Bishops issued frequent statements in the 1970s and 1980s regarding Canada's most pressing social
and economic issues. Early in January 1983 the bishops' Social Affairs
Commission questioned the very moral underpinnings of the Canadian
economy. The statement prompted weeks of heated debate, including
angry denunciations from business and a sharp rebuke from Prime
Minister Trudeau, who said the bishops were meddling inexpertly in
economic matters. Bishop Remi De Roo of Victoria was deeply involved
in preparing the 1983 statement, and later that year he appeared before
a Royal Commission on the economy led by former Finance Minister
Donald McDonald.

We here are representing the Canadian Conference of Catholic Bishops . . . We attempt to be present to the experience of marginalized people who are the victims of the recession; we try to develop a critical analysis of the causes, not just the superficial effects, but the deeper root issues that underlie these situations; we discern or judge them in the light of gospel principles and the experience of social teaching of the Roman Catholic Church down through the centuries; and then we try to stimulate or encourage people to bring forward alternative visions; and we also try to act in solidarity with the popular groups, particularly the people that most are affected by the economic crisis.

We are not trying to the present dogmatic prescriptions. While we are confident that moral principles are universally valid and binding, their application to concrete situations allows for a great variety of options. So we limit ourselves, in the light of the gospel values, to offer suggestions about possible new orientations that might be tried so as to show, in a fairly concrete way, that we are aware that there are alternative visions and new orientations possible.

We understand that the goal of the economy is, briefly put, to provide people with bread, but we are also very conscious that people do not live by bread alone; they also need dignity and they need creativity . . . We are convinced that people are created in the image of God and consequently are called to be responsible, creative agents of their own history, not pawns to deterministic forces or to ideologies which so readily turn into contemporary idols.

We believe, as a result, that people should be the prime actors or subjects of their own history; in other words, called to shape their own economy. And we believe that an economy must serve the basic needs of all the people because our biblical heritage indicates that created things have a universal purpose and are meant to be used for everyone, and that is why for us an economy dominated by a powerful few is a poor economy in the light of gospel values because it does not respond to the very nature of its own being . . .

For us economics is based on certain assumptions and is guided by goals. That means it is not a value-free science, and our understanding is that the people themselves are the greatest resource that we have, even in terms of economics. Consequently, they should all participate in re-examining these goals, and we would hope that the continuing work of your commission will facilitate the participation by people in the setting of these goals . . .

Our principles, then . . . are: the priority of human labour or of work over capital and technology; the necessary participation by the poor, by the presently marginalized and powerless people in society; the development of self-reliant models of an economy that is also situated in a context of global solidarity . . .

We see that the current recession is symptomatic of a deeper structural crisis. In other words, capital and technology are being reasserted as the dominant organizing principles of our socio-economic order, and this to us is an assault on the human dignity of workers, as youth, the elderly, women, Native peoples, small business people, and farmers increasingly lose control of capital and technology which are meant to be instruments, not ends in themselves, and that increasingly their world is being shaped according to the plans and for the benefits of a small minority of powerful people. This inversion of capital and technology over labour is to us a structural disorder, a case of the means being put before the ends. Consequently, it is a moral issue or an ethical question, and it becomes our pastoral role to make our specific contribution by challenging this inversion in the light of gospel values . . .

We are really calling for the development of more creative social imagination, and we are hopeful that your commission will encourage people to participate in this process and not just see themselves as limited by a certain technological rationality that says that things are the way they are and they just have to continue roughly in the same direction.

The signs of the problems are all around us, and I will not go into detail here; you are already familiar with massive unemployment, social deprivation, labour devaluation, increasing marginalization, economic disparities and dislocations, export orientation, the increasing trend towards militarization, ecological damage, and social breakdown.

The consequences, as we suggested earlier, are a terrible social cost in terms of an assault on the human dignity of people.

We want to make it clear that we are not against progress or technology as such. On the contrary, we believe that technology can enhance the development of peoples here and throughout the world, but the critical question is: who controls this technology? What orientation will it have? How will these instruments be used?

Unless the people themselves have control over this orientation, technology tends to become a set of destructive forces rather than constructive instruments for authentic economic development. What happens then is that a human person becomes more and more redundant and increasingly a victim of impersonal economic forces ...

The primary task for us is not simply a question of how governments can better manage the economy in the new high-tech industrial age. It is not a question of making people adjust, accommodate, adapt, retrain, relocate, lower their expectations, or whatever. What we are facing are basic structural problems that reveal a moral disorder and call for serious change.

The challenge then, as we see it, is to search for alternative visions and models for the future development of our socio-economic order in the new industrial age. In other words, ways must be found for people to exercise more effective control over capital and technology so that they may become constructive instruments of creation by serving the basic needs of people ...

The Canadian bishops believe that as a country Canada has the resources, the capital, the technology, and above all else, the aspirations and skills of working men and women that are required to build an alternative economic future. Yet, the people of this country have seldom been challenged to envision and develop alternatives to the dominant economic model that governs our society.

We would hope that the work of your commission would help to promote this dynamic public process, one that is designed to stimulate social imagination, to develop alternative models and to forge a new cultural vision for our country ... It is imperative that conscious decisions be taken now to forge a human economy and a true community for the sake of future generations.

Bob White

2 February 1988

"This agreement is about more than the removal of some tariffs"

Bob White built his reputation as a hard-nosed leader with the Canadian section of the United Auto Workers. In 1986, he led a move to leave the international union and form the Canadian Auto Workers. White staunchly fought concessions demanded by business and when Brian Mulroney did an about-face and began negotiating a free-trade agreement with the United States, White was prominent in a labour and citizens' movement opposing the deal. He and others described it as being more about investment than trade, arguing that it would fundamentally undermine Canada's sovereignty and its ability to maintain social, health, and regional development programs. White made this speech to the convention of the United Fisherman and Allied Workers Union in Vancouver early in 1988.

I believe strongly and have been saying for over two years, that free trade with the United States goes beyond specific interest and gets to the fundamental question of what kind of a society we want to have and build. In other words, what kind of a Canada will we have in the future?

Is it going to be a Canada as shaped by the giant business interests of the large multinationals-dominated Business Council on National Issues; where competitiveness and profit is the only yardstick; where workers are a disposable commodity in a survival of the fittest dog-eat-dog society? . . .

Or is it going to be a kind of society that I believe most Canadians want: a continually developing and growing Canada with a mixed economy including government intervention when necessary; a Canada which recognizes the importance of trade, not just with the United States but with other countries of the world; a society that limits corporate power, that improves our identity as an independent nation, strengthens our sovereignty, and that maintains and strengthens our commitments to our social programs.

These issues, much more than a reduction of tariffs, is what the debate surrounding free trade with the United States is all about. Certainly the business community understands that very well. They know it goes well beyond a particular industry or narrowly defined interests . . .

If you think back fifteen or twenty years ago, it was a time of relative optimism about having both continuing economic growth and a steadily improving measure of social justice. Sure, there were tensions, conflicts and problems, but a kind of unwritten social contract emerged: we accepted that the economy was basically a capitalist one dominated by private corporations; business accepted that government regulation and intervention was legitimate to establish a measure of equity.

But as international competition intensified and as the U.S. in particular faced the implications of new competitive pressures, business began to opt out of this informal consensus. Even though so much of the potential of workers and the economy were not being used, even though technology was accelerating, the new message was that workers could no longer expect rising standards of living, and that continued progress towards social justice had to be derailed.

What we had before defined as progress, better wages, better and more responsive working conditions, improved social services, and a general increase in security was now being redefined as the "problem." Thatcherism and Reaganomics had arrived.

Attempts to spread this new gospel in Canada were, however, hitting some serious bumps. Here, workers fought against concessions and politically, Canadians were not ready to buy the new corporate agenda . . .

As significant as the corporate sector's single-minded support of free trade is, equally significant is the scepticism of virtually every organization that represents popular groups in this country: trade unions, women's groups, the churches, social advocacy groups. In spite of what the federal government is selling, in spite of what most of the premiers have bought, in spite of the unanimity and activism of the corporate community, a social movement opposed to free trade has emerged and developed . . .

This agreement is about more than the removal of some tariffs. It is about the control and use of our natural wealth, the control over the investment that shapes our industrial structure, and the ability to use popular pressure to influence the direction of the economy and how its benefits are distributed. The free trade debate is, therefore, not just about how we see Canada today, but about differing visions of what we hope to do about Canada's future.

Opposition to this agreement rests on two basic concerns. The first is nationalistic. Do we want to be more integrated into the United States? Can we further formalize our integration into the United States and really not expect a dramatic erosion of our social, cultural, and political sovereignty?

Whatever attractions the U.S. had in the past as a model representing steady economic progress, its dying cities, violent crime, hopeless poverty have seriously eroded this image. This also undermines the credibility of the free-market philosophy that is at its base.

The second and related concern is free trade as a cover for the neo-conservative agenda. Free trade has been called a leap of faith. But for the corporate sector, it is a leap with a very comfortable landing. It is hardly a leap of faith into uncertainty since it gets them what they are really after and it promises results that, once achieved, will have a strong degree of irreversibility.

It is this attempt to end, or at least decisively undermine, any future progressive alternatives that makes free trade so dangerous and so important to the rest of us. For us, unlike the corporations, there is indeed a blind "leap of faith." We are expected to believe that if we strengthen the power of the corporations over our lives and just leave things to the market, eventually and indirectly good things will rain down on us.

Why should we trust those selling this message? Just as the U.S. model has lost credibility, so is the credibility of business as speaking on behalf of the national interest now being questioned . . .

Do a review of a checklist of Canada's important social programs or progressive legislation affecting workers rights, and ask where was the support from the giant business community or the Canadian Federation of Independent Business? That will answer the question of what kind of a Canada we would have had in the past, had they been in charge of the agenda.

Why should we trust those telling us that free trade is really good for us if they are part of a team so determined to prevent us from having an election to make up our own minds?

We have a prime minister who opposed free trade in the strongest terms when he was running for head of the Conservative Party, who didn't mention free trade during his election campaign even though he subsequently labeled it as the most important policy development for decades, and who now lamely argues that he will put something in place, make it as difficult and costly as he can to reverse it, and then finally let us judge him when he ultimately does end up at the polls.

The prime minister speaks of confidence in the free-trade agreement and Canada's future but doesn't have the confidence in the people to decide the issue. The prime minister tries to assure us that our sovereignty is not in danger, but he himself is denying us a chance to exercise one of our most important sovereignty rights: democratically determining the crucial issues of our times.

We must defeat the free trade deal and defeat the attempt to both cement our economic integration into the United States and limit our future alternatives. We must begin to spend our energies on how, not if, we can develop an independent Canada that is compassionate, caring, dynamic, prosperous, and proud of the role we play in the world.

John Turner
and Brian Mulroney
25 October 1988

"I happen to believe that you sold us out"—John Turner

"You do not have a monopoly on patriotism"
—Brian Mulroney

The 1988 election was one of the most tumultuous in Canadian history. Brian Mulroney had defeated John Turner and the Liberals in the 1984 election. He had scored a personal coup in the televised debate that year by attacking Turner for making a series of patronage appointments left for him by the departing Pierre Trudeau. By 1988, Turner sensed Canadians' profound unease about free trade and decided to fight the deal in the election. Ironically, throughout Canadian history it was the Liberals who had supported free trade while the Conservatives opposed it. The centrepiece of Sir John A. Macdonald's National Policy was a tariff to protect Canadian industry, allowing it to supply the Canadian market. Wilfrid Laurier fought two elections on reciprocity with the United States and lost. In 1988, Mulroney, Turner, and NDP leader Ed Broadbent held televised debates in French and English. In the English debate on 25 October, Broadbent was the first to attack Mulroney regarding free trade. Turner launched his attack in the debate's final segment. The free trade exchange has become legendary in Canadian political folklore.

TURNER: The prime minister hasn't answered this really in five hours of debate. He hasn't answered why he changed his own personal mind against a bilateral agreement with the United States. The Americans can't believe their good luck. No wonder the Senate of the United States passed this deal in one day, no wonder the House of Representatives passed it in one day, no wonder President Reagan says that this is the fulfillment of the American dream.

We gave away our energy. We gave away our investment. We sold out our supply management and agriculture. And we have left hundreds of thousands of workers vulnerable because of the social programs involved, because of the minimum wages that we will have to start to compare and harmonize, because of the fact that they are in vulnerable industries. And really I think the time has come, after five hours of debate, for the prime minister to really answer those questions and tell us why he is where he is and why he did not pull out when he did not get what he thought he should have got.

MULRONEY: I have answered, Mr. Turner, every conceivable question that has been put to me both in English and in French directly on national television, and I don't think I need any lessons from you, sir, about answering questions . . .

TURNER: I think the Canadian people have a right to know why, when your primary objective was to get unfettered and secured access into the American market, we didn't get it. Why you didn't put clauses in to protect our social programs in this negotiation . . . Why did that not happen? Why also did we get a situation where we surrendered our entire energy policy to the United States, something they've been trying to achieve since 1956? Why did we abandon our farmers? Why did we open our capital markets so that a Canadian bank can be bought up and we don't have reciprocity in the American market at all? Why did you remove any ability to control the Canadian ownership of our business?

These are questions that Canadians deserve to have an answer to and we have not had an opportunity in six hours to deal with them in the way that would make you come out of your shell.

MULRONEY: Well, Mr. Turner, you're about two feet away from me. I've been with you for six hours. I've responded to everything that you had to say. I responded openly to all questions by Canada's most distinguished journalists in English and French. There has been a most vigorous and I think probably unprecedented exchange of views. And yet, notwithstanding that, simply because you have an idea that only you have a proper interpretation of a given agreement, it's difficult for anyone to persuade you of the opposite. And so you ought not to blame me or blame Mr. Broadbent for that or blame the journalists . . .

TURNER: I happen to believe you have sold us out. I happen to believe that, once you—

MULRONEY: Mr. Turner, just one second—

TURNER: Once any region—

MULRONEY: You do not have a monopoly on patriotism—

TURNER: Once—

MULRONEY: —and I resent your implication that only you are a Canadian. I want to tell you that I come from a Canadian family and I love Canada, and that is why I did it, to promote prosperity.

TURNER: Once any country yields its economic levers—

MULRONEY: Don't you impugn my motives or anyone else's—

TURNER: Once a country yields its energy—

MULRONEY: We have not done it.

TURNER: Once a country yields its agriculture—

MULRONEY: Wrong again.

TURNER: Once a country yields itself to a subsidy war with the United States—

MULRONEY: Wrong again.

TURNER: On terms of definition then, the political ability of this country to remain as an independent nation, that is lost forever and that is the issue of this election, sir.

MULRONEY: Mr. Turner, Mr. Turner. Let me tell you something, sir. This country is only about 120 years old, but my own father 55 years ago went himself as a labourer with hundreds of other Canadians and with their own hands, in northeastern Quebec, they built a little town, schools and churches, and they in their own way were nation-building. In the same way that the waves of immigrants from the Ukraine and Eastern Europe rolled back the prairies and in their own way, in their own time, they were nation-building because they loved Canada. I today, sir, as a Canadian, believe genuinely in what I am doing. I believe it is right for Canada. I believe that in my own modest way I am nation-building because I believe this benefits Canada and I love Canada.

TURNER: I admire your father for what he did. My grandfather moved into British Columbia. My mother was a miner's daughter there. We are just as Canadian as you are, Mr. Mulroney, but I will tell you this. You mentioned 120 years of history. We built a country east and west and north. We built it on an infrastructure that deliberately resisted the continental pressure of the United States. For 120 years we've done it. With one signature of a pen, you've reversed that, thrown us into the north-south influence of the United States and will reduce us, I am sure, to a colony of the United States because when the economic levers go, the political independence is sure to follow.

MULRONEY: Mr. Turner, the document is cancellable on six months notice. Be serious. Be serious.

TURNER: Cancellable? You are talking about our relationship with the United States—

MULRONEY: A commercial document that is cancellable on six months notice.

TURNER: Commercial document? That document relates to treaty. It relates to every facet of our lives. It's far more important to us than it is to the United States.

MULRONEY: Mr. Turner.

TURNER: Far more important.

MULRONEY: Please be serious.

TURNER: Well, I am serious and I've never been more serious in all my life.

Turner won the debate, the Conservatives plummeted in the polls, and they engaged in an aggressive advertising campaign to discredit Turner. Mulroney won the election with a reduced majority.

David Suzuki

8 December 1988

"We need a radically different notion
of society's priorities"

David Suzuki is Canada's most prominent environmentalist. He was a biology professor in British Columbia, but became first a radio broadcaster and later the long-serving host of CBC TV's *The Nature of Things*. He also created the David Suzuki Foundation, which has been active on a range of issues, including climate change. He has warned that human activity is changing the planet in harmful ways that cannot be reversed. Suzuki gave this speech to the Empire Club in Toronto in 1988, clearly aware that he was speaking to an establishment audience that would be skeptical about his message—continued high levels of economic growth are not environmentally sustainable.

We now are the most numerous, ubiquitous large mammal on the planet, but we are like no other animal that ever existed, because we are armed with the incredible muscle power of science and technology. Armed with that kind of muscle power, and our numbers and demands, we now assault the environment, and the environment can no longer take it and bounce back.

I think of the increase in muscle power out our way in the Queen Charlotte Islands where the people have lived for thousands of years. They tell me that before contact with Europeans, it took them up to a year and a half to cut down a single cedar or spruce tree. It took so long for those trees to fall, they would build cradles to cradle them as they were starting to lean. After contact with Europeans, two men and a saw and axe could take ten days. Now, one man and a chainsaw can repeat the job in minutes. It's that incredible increase in muscle power that is at the base of what we are facing today. We continue to attack the environment as if it were the way it has been for 99.9 percent of our existence.

There are historical reasons why we seem blind to what is going on. I think even more important than that, we continue as a society to cling to beliefs and values that are so deeply embedded in our culture that we never question them. I call them sacred truths. And yet, in many cases, these sacred truths are the very cause of the problems that we are trying to deal with, and I'd like to spend the rest of the time discussing a few of these sacred truths. I think the most important one that we have to face is that we now are driven by the priority of global economics. Global economics has become the reason why governments exist, to deal with global economics and to carve out our place in the market.

I would suggest that we have to look at the way that economics has changed in the last few decades. We have come as a society to equate progress with economic growth. If there is no economic growth, we say that we have stagnated, that we have a crisis, we have a recession. Growth and progress have become equivalent and most of the growth we deal with is in terms of profit. So growth, progress and profit have become interchangeable terms; growth has become an end in itself. If we don't grow, we don't progress. The problem with that is that nothing in the universe continues to grow in that way indefinitely, exponentially. It's a ludicrous kind of notion. If growth becomes an end in itself, then there is no further end.

I can tell you there is something fundamentally wrong with that, fundamentally wrong because, according to the Brundtland Commission, 20 percent of the planet's population—North America, Europe and Asia, or Japan at least—now consumes over 80 percent of the resources of the planet.

It produces the vast bulk of toxic waste . . .

Now I know your eyeballs are all rolling up and you think I'm nuts. But I would suggest that if you are seriously concerned with where we are going in the next few decades, you cannot continue to cling to the notion that we can have steady exponential growth in the coming years.

Let me just skim through some other sacred truths. We believe that we as a species lie outside nature, above nature; that we are somehow different from other creatures and it's easy to see why we believe that. Eighty percent of Canadians live in urban settings, in a man-made environment, and even those of us who live in the country live in what is essentially a "manscaped" landscape.

We have created the area around us the way that we want. It is easy to feel a sense or an illusion that we now are somehow controlling the world around us. We forget this at great peril. We forget that we are still, at its absolute fundamental level, animals. We are animals who for our health and longevity require clean air, clean water and clean food . . .

It's a ludicrous idea to think that we can use air, water and soil as a dumping ground for our effluents and not ultimately pay for that in some way. We live in a finite world in which all that we eat and depend on must derive its nutrition and survival out of the air, water and soil around . . .

When you then look at who are our elected representatives in Ottawa, and I did this last year, over 70 percent of cabinet members came from two professions. They came from business and they came from law. Now I have nothing against business people and lawyers. I'm not going to speak to a group like this and say I've got anything against lawyers and business people, but the fact that you have such a disproportionate representation from two professions skews government perceptions of priorities. It's not an accident that Meech Lake jurisdictional and free trade economics have dominated the thinking of our politicians. Most of them are business people and lawyers. And business people and lawyers are scientifically illiterate and they are the people who are going to have to make decisions about the future of our forests, about the atmospheric degradation, about the ocean pollution, about desertification, and so on.

How can you make a wise decision about that when you can't assess the technical advice that you get from your experts. We aren't led into the future by our leaders, we back into the future because the people we elect to office are scientifically illiterate.

I usually talk about what we can do about it, but I don't have time. I've tried to challenge you by saying that we face a massive unprecedented crisis, an ecological crisis, on this planet, that we are currently blinded to the immensity of it and the importance of it by many of our most deeply held sacred truths. And to challenge them, what I have tried to do in this time is to provide you with some insight into questions about those sacred truths.

We cannot continue to mortgage our children's futures by opting for short-term profit and power. We need a radically different notion of society's priorities, a redefinition of the word progress and of our relationship with nature.

George Erasmus
29 November 1990

"We have come to a fork in the road"

In June 1990, the Meech Lake Accord failed when provincial legislatures in Newfoundland and Manitoba chose not to approve it. In Manitoba, Aboriginal leader and MLA Elijah Harper held a white eagle feather
as he refused to give the necessary unanimous consent for his province
to approve. Despite support for the accord by most provinces and the
three major federal parties, other groups, including the Assembly of
First Nations, were opposed. Assembly of First Nations Chief George
Erasmus made this speech just a few months after an armed standoff
between the army and Aboriginal warriors at Oka in Quebec. He argued
that there are three nations in Canada, and one of them is Aboriginal.

Last summer, Native people in this country took a very firm stand against
the Meech Lake Accord. It was not a stand against Canada. It was not a stand
against Quebec. We took a look at the agreement, and as Native people we

found the agreement wanting. We were going to put into the Canadian Constitution the concept that there were two fundamental characteristics of Canada that should be entrenched, embedded in the Constitution. It was following from the concept that there are two founding nations, and one of those was not the original Native people. That was something we could not live with. We could not have further entrenched rights for other people in this country that would make us even less able to compete and try to protect our language and our culture. In Quebec, Native people could not live with a situation where Quebec was being recognized as a distinct society and there was no ability for the Native people there to be able to also protect and have their language and culture flourish. The balance was not there . . .

We have come to a fork in the road, where if we are going to continue to be immersed in a status quo, we're just not going to be together very much longer. Or else we are going to be so disgruntled across this country, we're not going to be able to live with each other. We have the ability to create a country that will be envied. We have the potential, but we also have the potential to fragment and create many smaller states, and that's absolutely not necessary. What we have here is the ability to bring together two European peoples, complemented by cultures from all around the world, with an indigenous population that has been here for tens of thousands of years. We have the ability to create a culture that will be different from others because we will take from each other and we will give to each other, but we will not have to crush each other. We will not have to make beggars of any of us. We will not have to make people orphans from their culture . . .

This country was not settled like the United States. I'm a Dene. No conquering army came to the Dene and defeated us. No conquering army came to the Mohawks and defeated them, or any other of the people across this country. We willingly, consciously, with our eyes open, thought we had enough resources. Being a peaceful people we arrived at an agreement that provided for our institutions to continue on part of our land and for the institutions of the people coming in to also be placed on our lands. Never in our worst nightmares did we ever imagine what was going to take place. That for nearly one hundred years, from 1867 until 1960, we would be so limited in our activity that we would need passes to get off reserves. We couldn't own businesses. We couldn't run for office. We couldn't vote. We never reached the age of majority. We weren't human beings really. The kind of apologies that Native people have watched being provided to other people has been kind of a joke. We provided our support to most of those people, whether it was the Japanese or others, who were seeking apologies. We're still waiting. We're still waiting for someone to tell us that they apologize for what has happened, what is happening, and how it will never happen again.

We want to put in place, once again, our institutions so that we will make decisions for ourselves. So that we will shoulder the responsibility of whether or not an education system is relevant for our people. We're not going to be satisfied with being provided with school boards that fall under someone else's jurisdiction, that fall under someone else's legislation. We're not going to be satisfied with putting Native people on school boards and hiring teachers and using someone else's curriculum and someone else's legislation. We're not going to be satisfied with taking over child care services, social services that belong to somebody else, somebody else's legislation. We want to make our own laws. And we're not talking about municipal governments. Obviously, we have many communities in this country and we have to have municipal governments, but what we are talking about is, as collectives, as nations, we must have—like Quebec, like Newfoundland—the kind of powers that are typically enjoyed by provinces that are free-standing . . .

We see a time, if this works out, when Native people will again control a large percentage of their original lands. No one is trying to go back. No one is trying to turn any clock back. We have no intention of making any attempt at that. But, we do want to nurture and to revitalize our culture. We know we cannot govern all of the land that we used to govern. We realize in real politics that we are the minority population in a country that has twenty-six/twenty-seven million people. So we are more than prepared to be practical. We think it is only just that with so few people living in Canada, with all of the land, all of the resources we have, that rather than having the open forests that you have, a large portion, negotiable portion, is back in the hands of Native people so that we can have some control over our lives. So that we can create a revenue base that will allow us to have some dignity, a revenue base that will allow us to pay our own way, so that we are not always beggars in our own land, and watching people from everywhere else get rich on our resources.

That's got to end. All across this country, people have been painfully, quietly, putting up with atrocities that should never have happened, whether it was residential schools where you could not speak your language and where virtually every value of your culture was being negated, or seeing your land being used by corporations from abroad, stripping your resources, shipping them out of the country and jobs with it, and nothing being returned to you.

Patience is coming to an end. The internal suffering is just so great, the loss of life amongst our young people, the internal alcoholism, the glue sniffing, the wife beating, child neglect, all of the social disorders of an oppressed people. Our frustration, our hurt, our pain, our anger, our hate, is forced inside. It cannot go on any longer. Imagine it like a pot on a burner that is burning on high constantly and you think, well, there's still some water in the bottom, there's still some water in the pot.

The time is here. We must now be sincere. Native people are not a threat to this country. We are not a threat to the sovereignty of Canada. We actually want to reinforce the sovereignty of Canada. We want to walk away from the negotiating table with an agreement that Canada feels good about and Native people feel good about, where we can say that we have strengthened the sovereignty of Canada . . . we're not a threat. We are only a threat if we continue to be ignored and taken lightly. We are only a threat if people don't understand that it is impossible for people to maintain the frustration level without the kind of actions that we've seen this summer . . .

We're not trying to get out of Confederation. We never were a part of it. We're still knocking on the door. Let's hope we get a wonderful reception when the door is open.

Preston Manning
6 April 1991

"Canada is a house divided"

Preston Manning, the son of former Alberta Premier Ernest Manning, had long dreamed of creating a conservative and western-based political party. Brian Mulroney defeated the Liberals in 1984 by creating a coalition of western Conservatives and Quebec nationalists. Manning's new Reform Party exploited what they saw as Mulroney's pandering to Quebec. Manning was also critical of a prime minister who talked like a neo-conservative but often acted like a liberal on issues like social programs and immigration. Manning, who maintained a keen interest in history, revived the debate about the intention of Canada's founding fathers. He balked at the concept of a historic partnership between English and French as founding nations. He proposed instead a "new Canada," with no special status for Quebec, and where provinces had much greater freedom to pursue their own ends, including leaner and meaner government. This is

Manning's address to the Reform Party convention in Saskatoon in
April 1991.

At our last party assembly, held in Edmonton in October 1989, I expressed
the view that under the constitutional policies pursued by both Liberal and
Conservative administrations over the past thirty years, Canada had become
a "house divided against itself," and a house divided along the most dangerous of cleavage lines, namely those of race, language, and culture.

I say to you tonight that nothing has happened in Canada over the past
seventeen months to cause me to change that view. To the contrary, the
events of the past seventeen months serve only to affirm it. The collapse of
Meech Lake, the clash between the Quebec government and the Mohawks
at Oka, the emergence of the Bloc Québécois, the Allaire Report from the
Quebec Liberals, the report of the Bélanger-Campeau Commission, and the
continued paralysis of the federal government and the traditional federal
parties in the face of these developments, all constitute continuing evidence
that Canada is a house divided.

And nothing has happened in the past seventeen months to change the
judgment of history, from the days of Christ to the days of Lincoln, that "a
house divided against itself cannot stand."

Reformers therefore say old Canada—the Canada defined as an equal
partnership between two founding races, languages and cultures, the English
and the French—is dying. And this approaching death of old Canada has serious, practical implications for every man, woman and child in the country.

In considering the foundations on which to build new Canada, there
will be those—the Mulroneys, the Chrétiens, the McLaughlins, the politicians of the old order—who will insist that we must continue to consider
French-English relations as the cornerstone of Canada's future constitutional development. And I say to you that no more damnable advice could
be given to the Canadian people at this point in time than that. The first
task, therefore, of genuine constitutional Reformers will be to vigorously
challenge that false assumption and replace it with something better . . .

The vision of Macdonald and his associates was clear. They sought not a
perpetuation of the "two nations" problem through a tighter political and
constitutional integration of French and English institutions, but the creation
of a new nation from sea to sea which itself would be part of yet a larger
entity, namely the British Empire. It was essentially left to the government of

Quebec to deal with the "two nations" problem at the provincial level.

Now, if subsequent generations of politicians had been content to resolve the French-English tension within the provincial confines to which the fathers of Confederation had relegated it, and to continue to expand and build on the new foundation of Canada as a federation of provinces rather than a federation of founding peoples, Canada would not be in the dilemma it is today. But unfortunately this was not to be.

As each new western province after British Columbia was added, in particular Manitoba, Saskatchewan, and Alberta, there was a controversy as to whether the constitutions of these provinces should include provisions to provide special status, in the areas of education and language, for the French minority. These provisions were promoted by federal politicians of the old two-nation school, and provincial politicians from Quebec, and generally resisted by western politicians who fully embraced the new vision of one nation from sea to sea.

And then almost thirty years ago, there arose the most serious challenge yet to this vision since 1867. After the disintegration of the British Empire, and the emergence of the Quiet Revolution in Quebec, Lester Pearson established the Royal Commission on Bilingualism and Biculturalism and revived the concept of Canada as an equal partnership between two founding races, languages, and cultures, the English and the French. Future historians will no doubt refer to this as the great leap backward.

A fateful decision was made to make the federal government, not the government of Quebec, the primary guardian of the French fact in Canada, and, in effect, to "nationalize" the very issue which the fathers of Confederation had "provincialized" in 1867. This vision was pursued with vigour by Pierre Trudeau who was its chief author, and continues to shape the unimaginative thinking of the current prime minister. It was affirmed in the Liberal Official Languages Act of 1969 and the Constitution Act of 1982. It is similarly reflected in the Conservatives' Official Languages Act of 1988 and the terms of the ill-fated Meech Lake Accord.

Reformers say that this revival of the concept of Canada as an equal partnership between founding races was doomed from the start. Even in the 1960s it was profoundly out of step with the times. What the Québécois were demanding was *maîtres chez nous*. Federal politicians responded by trying to bolster a national duality which had been in decline for ninety years. English-speaking Canada was more and more becoming a society with many heritages. Quebecers were calling for less bilingualism, not more bilingualism, in their own province.

Most importantly, outer Canadians, especially western Canadians, were beginning to fully realize the real significance of the "two nations" theory of Canada. A Canada built on a union of the English and the French is a country built on the union of Quebec and Ontario. And in this union the other provinces are, in a fundamental sense, little more than extensions of Ontario.

A Canada which gives special constitutional status to the French and the English as "founding peoples" also automatically relegates the nine million Canadians who are of neither French nor English extraction (including Aboriginal peoples) to the status of second-class citizens . . .

The issue of the future relationship of Quebec to new Canada must be resolved one way or the other in the next several years. We cannot go on as we have. We cannot stagger into the twenty-first century still fixating on English-French relations, a house divided against itself, foolishly hoping to survive or prosper as a first rank industrial nation . . .

I am saying that the great Canadian constitutional negotiation—the real thing, not a charade—cannot proceed in earnest until a Quebec provincial election and a federal general election have been held.

The principal issue in that Quebec provincial election will be "Who really speaks for the new Quebec, and who should be entrusted to negotiate on its behalf with the representatives of new Canada?"

The principal issue in the next federal general election will be "Who really speaks for new Canada, and who should be entrusted to negotiate on its behalf with the representatives of the new Quebec?"

Any political party leader who cavalierly seeks to occupy that position for purely partisan or personal reasons is a fool, for he or she will face a task even more difficult and dangerous than that which faced Macdonald in 1867.

But it is our task as Reformers, and my task as your leader, to so position and conduct ourselves in the months ahead that we will not be found wanting or deficient should Canadians ask us to shoulder a portion of that awesome responsibility . . .

And so I ask you, can we define a new Canada to replace the old Canada that is dying? Can we leap the barriers of narrow vision and negativism, and for once in our lives conduct ourselves like big Canadians worthy of this vast territory we call our home? Can we get on the road to new Canada by the next federal election, by electing genuine Reformers to the next Parliament?

These are the questions which I propose, with your direction and support, to ask every last Canadian who will listen over the next two years. And if Canadians show the resolve and enthusiasm that you have demonstrated, if enough of our fellow Canadians will not only say, "Yes, we can!" but also "Yes, we will!" then new Canada is much closer than we imagine.

Maurice Strong
3 June 1992

"We are a species out of control"

Maurice Strong is a Canadian Renaissance man who has played a major role in business and international development. He has held senior posts with the United Nations, was the first CEO of Petro-Canada, and served as a chairman of Ontario Hydro. Strong was secretary-general of the 1992 United Nations Conference on Environment and Development, the so-called Earth Summit. It brought together leaders from 180 countries in Rio de Janeiro, and succeeded in outlining a comprehensive set of measures to deal with global environmental problems. Strong, in the opening address to the summit, insisted that environmental considerations must become central in any consideration of economic policy.

This is not a single-issue conference. Rather, it deals with the overall cause and effect system through which a broad range of human activities interact to shape our future . . . We have been the most successful species ever; we are now a species out of control. Our very success is leading us to a dangerous future. The concentration of population growth in developing countries and economic growth in the industrialized countries has deepened, creating imbalances which are unsustainable, whether in environmental or economic terms. Since 1972, world population has grown by 1.7 billion people, equivalent to almost the entire population at the beginning of this century; 1.5 billion of these live in developing countries which are least able to support them. Each individual person is precious. We must honour, and the earth must support, all its children. But, overall, this growth cannot continue. Population must be stabilized, and rapidly. If we do not do it, nature will, and much more brutally.

During the same twenty-year period, world GDP increased by $20 trillion dollars. Yet only 15 percent of the increase accrued to developing countries. Over 70 percent went to the already rich countries, adding further to their disproportionate pressures on the environment, resources, and life-support systems of our planet. This is the other part of the population problem: the fact that every child born in the developed world consumes twenty to thirty times the resources of the planet than a Third World child.

The same processes of economic growth which have produced such unprecedented levels of wealth and power for the rich minority and hopes of a better life for everyone have also given rise to the risks and imbalances that now threaten the future of rich and poor alike. This growth model, and the patterns of production and consumption which have accompanied it, is not sustainable for the rich, nor can it be replicated by the poor. To continue along this pathway could lead to the end of our civilization.

Yet the poor need economic and social development as the only means of relieving the vicious circle of poverty in which they are caught up. Their right to development cannot be denied, nor should it be impeded by conditions unilaterally imposed on the financial flows or trade of developing countries.

The rich must take the lead in bringing their development under control, reducing substantially their impacts on the environment, leaving environmental space for developing countries to grow. The wasteful and destructive lifestyles of the rich cannot be maintained at the cost of the lives and livelihoods of the poor, and of nature.

For the rich, the transition to sustainable development need not require regression to a difficult or primitive life. On the contrary, it can lead to a richer life of expanded opportunities for self-realization and fulfillment, more satisfying and secure because it is sustainable, and more sustainable because its opportunities and benefits are more universally shared.

Sustainable development—development that does not destroy or undermine the ecological, economic, or social basis on which continued development depends—is the only viable pathway to a more secure and hopeful future for rich and poor alike. Fortunately, that pathway is still an option, but that option is closing. This conference must establish the foundations for effecting the transition to sustainable development. This can only be done through fundamental changes in our economic life and in international economic relations, particularly as between industrialized and developing countries. Environment must be integrated into every aspect of our economic policy and decision-making as well as the culture and value systems which motivate economic behaviour . . .

I want to pay tribute to those who have negotiated the Conventions on Climate Change and Biodiversity, which will be opened for your signature here. It has not been an easy process and some have important reservations about both instruments. They represent first steps in the processes of addressing two of the most serious threats to the habitability of our planet. Signing them will not, in itself, be sufficient. Their real importance will depend on the extent to which they give rise to concrete actions and are followed quickly by protocols containing the special measures required to make them fully effective and the finances needed to implement them.

For both these issues deal with the future of life on earth. Over the next twenty years, more than one-quarter of the earth's remaining species may become extinct. And in the case of global warming, the Intergovernmental Panel on Climate Change has warned that if carbon dioxide emissions are not cut by 60 percent immediately, the changes in the next sixty years may be so rapid that nature will be unable to adapt and man incapable of controlling them . . .

Perhaps the most important common ground we must arrive at in Rio is the understanding that we are all in this together. No place on the planet can remain an island of affluence in a sea of misery. We're either going to save the whole world or no one will be saved. We must from here on in all go down the same path. One country cannot stabilize its climate in isolation. No country can unilaterally preserve its biodiversity. One part of the world cannot live an orgy of unrestrained consumption while the rest destroys its environment just to survive. Neither is immune from the effects of the other.

There is an ominous tendency today to erect new iron curtains to insulate the more affluent and privileged from the poor, the underprivileged, and the dispossessed. Iron curtains and closed national boundaries provide no solutions to the problems of an interdependent world community in which what happens in one part affects all.

Like it or not, from here on in, we're in this together: rich, poor, north, south, east, and west. It is an exhilarating challenge to erase the barriers that have separated us in the past, to join in global partnership that will enable us to survive in a more secure and hospitable world. This industrialized world cannot escape its primary responsibility to lead the way in establishing this partnership and making it work. Up to now, the damage inflicted on our planet has been done largely inadvertently. We now know what we are doing. We have lost our innocence. It would be more than irresponsible to continue down this path . . .

Our essential unity as peoples of the earth must transcend the differences and difficulties which still divide us. You are called upon to rise to your historic responsibility as custodians of the planet in taking the decisions here that will unite rich and poor, north, south, east, and west, in a new global partnership to ensure our common future. The road beyond Rio will be a long and difficult one; but it will also be a journey of renewed hope, of excitement, challenge, and opportunity, leading as we move into the twenty-first century to the dawning of a new world in which the hopes and aspirations of all the world's children for a more secure and hospitable future can be fulfilled. This unprecedented responsibility is in your hands.

Lucien Bouchard
17 January 1994

"Quebec's future as a sovereign country
is just one step ahead"

Lucien Bouchard was another prodigy to emerge from Quebec's Catholic school system. He was brilliant, serious, and intense, even as a youth. He was raised in the Jonquière region, long a nationalist and later a separatist hotbed, but his political path was peripatetic. When he studied law at Laval, he emerged first as a supporter of Pierre Trudeau, later of René Lévesque, and finally of Brian Mulroney, his law school classmate. Mulroney recruited him as a Conservative candidate and promoted him to become environment minister. Bouchard was a good minister, but he didn't fit. He quit the party in 1990 to create the Bloc Québécois, dedicated to Quebec's independence. In the 1993 federal election, the Bloc won fifty-four seats in the House of Commons and became the official opposition. Bouchard was a passionate and mesmerizing orator, particularly adept at using metaphors to stoke a sense of grievance among Quebecers. In this, his first speech in the House of Commons as opposition leader, Bouchard left no doubt that his party would use its status in the federal Parliament to promote independence for Quebec.

The people of Quebec will soon decide their future, following a debate that we all hope to be marked by democratic spirit . . . The major change in this House is undoubtedly the massive influx of sovereignist members from Quebec. No one can trivialize the shift represented by the decision some two million voters have made to send fifty-four members here to pave the way for Quebec's sovereignty . . .

The voters have set the record straight. For the first time in contemporary history, this House, which is now beginning its work, reflects the very essence of Canada, its binational nature, and the very different visions of the future which flow from that. As General de Gaulle said, one may well long for the days of sailing ships, but the only valid policy one can have is based on realities . . .

More than thirty years ago, Quebec awakened to the world and decided to catch up. The quiet revolution transformed Quebec. It did not take long before the spirit of reform in Quebec collided with the spirit of Canadian federalism in Ottawa. Thirty years ago the horns were locked. Thirty years later we are still at it, as if frozen in a time warp. We should learn from the past, and this we should have learned: The political problem with Canada is Quebec, and the problem of Quebec is Canada.

However, many Canadians refuse to acknowledge the problem, which only serves to compound it. For example, the Bloc Québécois has been on the federal scene for more than three years, but until recently we were ranked alongside the bizarre and the outer fringes.

Our aim, of course, is not to win popularity contests in English Canada, but you have here in a nugget the essence of the political predicament which bedevils Canada. A new political party which had led systematically in the polls in Quebec for three years was regularly dismissed as a quirk on the charts or a manifestation of a temporary leave of the senses. Hugh MacLennan's powerful novel *Two Solitudes* was published in 1945. Half a century later the same title still mirrors the political landscape . . .

Canada and Quebec have both changed tremendously in the last 100 years, but they are travelling on parallel tracks and remain as different today as they were yesterday. By and large, they both continue to ignore the history and the culture of the other. This is no accident: language, geography, and history largely account for it.

However, Quebecers do not deny that English Canada constitutes a nation in its own right, with its own sense of community. Every single poll in the last few years has shown that the vast majority of the people in each of the nine provinces want to remain politically united after Quebec becomes sovereign. This small detail is conveniently neglected by all those who question the existence of an English Canada on the shaky basis of regional differences . . .

If one accepts the obvious, one must surely accept the consequences. Every nation has the right to self-government, that is, to decide its own policies and future. We have no quarrel with the concept of federalism when applied to the uninational states. It is a different matter when it comes to multinational states, particularly to the Canadian brand of federalism.

Canadian federalism means the government of Quebec is subordinate to the central government, both in large and lesser matters. Within the federal regime, English Canada, in fact, has a veto on the future development of Quebec . . .

The fact is that Quebec is the only nation of more than seven million people in the western world not to have attained political sovereignty. I invite members of this House to reflect upon this. As a political structure, Canada is the exception rather than the rule, an exception that is not working well, to understate the case . . .

Whether we like it or not, there will be a debate on our political future, and it will take place right here. The government is free to immure itself in silence as it has been the practice in this House with regard to the sovereignist aspirations of so many Quebecers. Is it out of fear or powerlessness that they are evading subjects that put into question the old political structures of Quebec and Canada, as well as their capacity to solve social and economic problems?

Whether fainthearted or resigned, this total silence is irresponsible and leads to paralysis. The Bloc Québécois has been sent here precisely to break this conspiracy of silence . . .

In reality, Quebecers want to live a normal life. They are tired of fighting for basic things that have been denied them. They are quite willing to confront the challenges of the day, but they want all of the odds to be on their side. On the one hand, they want greater economic integration and a stronger competitive position internationally, while on the other hand they want political sovereignty in order to face Quebec's competitive partners on a level playing field . . .

Let there be no mistake. Bloc members will not forget that their commitment to sovereignty constitutes the real reason for their presence in this House. One could say that, as far as we are concerned, the pre-referendum campaign has begun. Meanwhile, we will not let the recession be dissociated from its causes.

For the time being, and until Quebecers have made their decision in a referendum, members of the Bloc will seek to safeguard the future by averting present evils to the best of their ability. These evils include unemployment, poverty, lack of budgetary restraint, undue duplication, threats to our political programs, fiscal inequity, and loss of confidence in our political institutions and leaders.

All these issues have a direct impact on Quebec's interests, but are equally important for the rest of Canada. Our aspirations drive us apart, but our social, economic, and budgetary problems are the same . . .

I would like to repeat that, unlike the government, members of the Bloc Québécois will not evade any of the issues this Parliament will have to face. We will not tolerate the government's refusal to deal with Quebec's aspirations. Let it not be said that it was for nothing that the majority of federalists and all Quebec sovereignists struggled, each in their own way, for thirty years, to give Quebec the tools to develop as a people. What Quebec started in the Sixties must be allowed to come to fruition.

After the concept of a nation was established, after mobilizing Quebec society, after the efforts of Jean Lesage, the manoeuvering of Robert Bourassa, and courage of René Lévesque, there must be more than the evasive platitudes of the Prime Minister [Chrétien]. He should realize that the history of Quebec did not stop on a certain night in November 1981, behind closed doors in the Chateau Laurier. I suggest that he look at the fifty-four members of this party sitting here today and remember who sent us here and the mandate we were given.

Then he will realize that Quebec's future as a sovereign country is just one step ahead, a sovereign country that is Canada's neighbour and friend.

Paul Martin
27 February 1995

"This budget overhauls not only how government works but what government does"

The Liberals routed the Conservatives in the 1993 federal election. Paul Martin co-authored the Liberals' platform, published as the "Red Book," and it was brandished at every political whistle stop as proof of what the Liberals would do once elected. It promised to attack unemployment, lower interest rates, and reinvest in social programs. Martin became finance minister and was soon convinced that Canada's deficit and debt were unmanageable. In 1995 he introduced a draconian budget that chopped social programs, unemployment insurance, agricultural support, and transfers to the provinces for health care, education, and social assistance. The battle for public opinion was fierce. Martin, his advisers, and corporate Canada warned that the country was about to hit a deficit wall and that the dollar could become the "northern peso." Others argued just as passionately that it would be far better to attack unemployment and promote economic growth as a means of confronting the deficit. They accused Martin of manufacturing a crisis in an attempt to attack government programs and to keep labour in line through high unemployment. When Martin delivered his budget speech on 27 February 1995, he said that his aim was not only to reduce spending, but also to permanently change the role of government.

There are times in the progress of a people when fundamental challenges must be faced, when fundamental choices must be made, and a new course charted. For Canada, this is one of those times. Our resolve, our values, our very way of life as Canadians are being tested.

The choice is clear. We can take the path, too well trodden, of minimal change, of least resistance, of leadership lost. Or we can set out on a new road of fundamental reform, of renewal, of hope restored. Today we have made our choice. Today we take action . . .

The debt and the deficit are not inventions of ideology. They are facts of arithmetic. The quicksand of compound interest is real. The last thing Canadians need is another lecture on the dangers of the deficit. The only thing Canadians want is clear action. Therefore let me go directly to the bottom line . . .

Over the next three years, the actions in this budget deliver almost seven dollars of spending cuts for every one dollar of new tax revenue. This budget will deliver cumulative savings of $29 billion over the next three years, of which $25.3 billion are expenditure cuts. This is by far the largest set of actions in any Canadian budget since demobilization after World War II.

These measures will have a very significant impact on the level of government spending in the future. By 1996–97 we will have reduced program spending from $120 billion in 1993–94 to under $108 billion. Relative to the size of our economy, program spending will be lower in 1996–97 than at any time since 1951. The impact of these measures on the fiscal health of this country will be significant and substantial.

By 1996–97, our financial requirements, that is, what we actually have to borrow from the markets, will be down from $30 billion last year to $13.7 billion, or 1.7 percent of GDP. That percentage is lower than what is projected for the United States, for Germany, for Japan. In fact, it is lower than what is projected for all of the national governments of every country of the G-7 . . .

After extensive review this budget overhauls not only how government works but what government does. We are acting on a new vision of the role of government in the economy. In many cases this means smaller government; in all cases it means smarter government.

We are dramatically reducing subsidies to business. We are changing our support systems for agriculture. We will be putting government activities on a commercial basis wherever that is practical and productive.

We will be overhauling the unemployment insurance system as part of our social security reform, and reforming the system of transfers to the provinces—putting it on a basis that is more in line with the actual responsibilities of the two levels of government.

It is essential that our effort be guided by clear principles and values. First, we believe it is crucial that the government get its own house in order. Our budget must focus on cutting spending, not raising taxes . . .

If our purpose is to get the economy right, we need to redesign the role of the government in the economy to fit the size of our pocketbook and the priorities of our people. What is that role? It is to provide a framework for the private sector to create jobs, to see an aggressive trade strategy as central to Canada's industrial strategy. And it is initiatives such as the prime minister's, in Asia and Latin America, that will create opportunity for thousands of Canadians here at home.

What is the role of government in the economy? It is to ensure that the nation's finances are healthy. It is to do what only government can do best and leave the rest for those who can do better, whether they are in business, labour, or in the voluntary sector.

This budget puts our priorities into action. It does so after a top to bottom review of all departments of government led by the minister responsible for public service renewal. As a result we will be able to reduce departmental spending dramatically over the next three years while maintaining the services that are truly needed by Canadians.

For example, between this fiscal year and 1997–98, annual spending will go down by $1.6 billion at defence, $550 million for international assistance, $1.4 billion at transport.

Over the next three years spending will be cut by more than $600 million at natural resources, almost $900 million at human resources development, over $200 million at fisheries, almost $900 million in the industry portfolio, more than $550 million in the regional agencies, and nearly $450 million at agriculture. In short, overall departmental spending will be cut by almost 19 percent in just three years.

Let me emphasize, this is not a slowdown in the increase of spending masked as cuts. These are not the cuts of yesteryear. These are real cuts in real dollars.

In the last recession, every household, every business, every volunteer group in this country was forced to face up to hard choices and real change, but the Government of Canada did not. In this budget we are bringing government size and its structure into line with what we can afford.

As a result of the cut-back and reform of programs, the president of the Treasury Board has announced that the public service will be reduced by some forty-five thousand positions over three years, with twenty thousand being eliminated by the summer of next year . . .

In this budget, total spending on business subsidies will decline from $3.8 billion in this fiscal year to $1.5 billion by 1997–98. That is a reduction of 60 percent in three years. Remaining industrial assistance will be targeted on the key engines of economic growth: trade development, science and technology, and small and medium-size business.

Transportation and direct agricultural production subsidies are being eliminated or substantially reduced. This is historic change. Decades ago, even into the last century, those subsidies were put in place to respond to Canada's transportation and agricultural needs then existing. As time has passed, those needs have evolved but the subsidy structure has not. For years governments have known about the need for change but they have hesitated to act. But we cannot postpone action any longer.

To that end, subsidies under the Western Grain Transportation Act are eliminated effective 1995–96, resulting in savings of $2.6 billion over the next five years. This subsidy evolved from the Crow rate established in 1897. It has played a pivotal role in the development of the prairie economy, but in more recent years it has come to restrict the ability of prairie farmers and their industry to adapt and to compete. To facilitate this change we will make a one-time payment of $1.6 billion to prairie farmland owners to be provided for in this fiscal year 1994–95 . . .

The government is committed to privatizing and commercializing government operations wherever feasible and appropriate. Our view is straightforward. If government does not need to run something it should not, and in the future it will not.

Today we are announcing that the minister of transport will initiate steps this year to sell CN. He will also commercialize the air navigation system. When market conditions are favourable the minister of natural resources will sell our remaining 70 percent interest in Petro-Canada. The minister of public works and government services will examine divesting all or parts of the Canada Communications Group.

Let me be clear. This is not a one-shot exercise. Our effort to identify other candidates for privatization will continue. This is not ideology, it is simple common sense . . .

For too long, governments have known the need for reform and renewal—known the need, but not the will. That has been the problem with the governments of this country. This government has made its choice and it is against the status quo and in favour of a stronger country.

Within a few years Paul Martin's problem became government surpluses rather than deficits. Prior to the election in the year 2000, he announced some new spending, but also tax cuts of $100 billion distributed over the following five years. In December 2004, after a bitter internal power struggle, he replaced Jean Chrétien as Liberal leader and prime minister.

Denise Chong
19 April 1995

"How we tell our stories is the work of citizenship"

Denise Chong is an economist whose book *The Concubine's Children* won the Governor General's Award for non-fiction in 1994. In this speech she talked about her grandfather, who came to work in Canada, and his wife—his concubine—who used forged papers to get into Canada because immigration laws did not allow Asian men to bring their families along.

I ask myself what it means to be a Canadian. I was lucky enough to be born in Canada. So I look back at the price paid by those who made the choice that brought me such luck . . . The past holds some moral authority over us. Rather than forget it, we must acknowledge that we have one, and learn the lessons of it. We have to be vigilant about looking past the stereotypes and seeing the contrasting truths. It means understanding that someone's grandfather didn't change the family name from French to English to forsake his heritage, but to make it easier to find a job. It means lifting the charge against the early Chinese of having no family values by seeing how the laws and history cleaved their families in two. It means going to the Legion and looking at a Sikh and seeing the veteran as well as the turban.

If we don't, we won't see that the layers of injustice cut deep. It happened in my own family. My grandfather couldn't afford a concubine. To repay the cost of my grandmother's false papers and passage to Canada, he indentured her as a tea house waitress. In the bachelor societies of the Chinatowns of their day, a *kay toi neu* was seen as one and the same as a prostitute—both were there to woo men to spend money. My grandmother would spend the rest of her lifetime trying to climb up from that bottom rung of society. I, too, condemned my *Popo*, until I learned what she had been fighting against all her life.

Despite the luck of my mother's birth, discrimination continued to cast a long shadow over her growing-up years. Her parents separated. In neither of their lifetimes would either find work outside Chinatown. My mother knew too well the path to the pawn shop where she accompanied her mother to translate as she bargained her jewellery to pay her gambling debts. The wall on my mother's side of the bed at the rooming house was wallpapered with academic certificates. My mother wanted to become a doctor. She didn't know that it would be years after her time before the faculty of medicine at the University of British Columbia would admit its first Chinese student. Despite the narrow confines of her life, the opportunity of education gave my mother a chance to dream.

Eventually, exclusion against Chinese immigration was lifted and other barriers of discrimination began to fall. My mother's generation was the last to grow up in Chinatown. Gradually, the Chinese became part of the larger society. In 1947, my mother no longer had to call herself Chinese. With exclusion lifted, and the new citizenship act that Canada brought in that same year, for the first time in her life my mother could call herself Canadian.

My parents walked out from the shadow of the past. They were determined to raise their five children as Canadians. In our own growing-up years in Prince George, my mother wanted us to be as robust as our playmates; she enriched the milk in our glasses with extra cream.

My parents wanted us to take to heart the Canadian pastimes. They bought us skis to share among us. Every winter they bought us new used skates. There was a piano upstairs on which we learned to play "O Canada" for school assemblies. There was a hockey net in the basement so my brothers could practice for the pond.

My parents wanted us to understand that we were part of Canada's future. They instilled the importance of an education. They encouraged us to believe that individuals could make a difference. I remember when Mr. and Mrs. Diefenbaker came to Prince George. I remember when a dashing Pierre Trudeau made his first visit. My parents made sure we were turned out to greet every visiting dignitary. My grandparents, in their time, were barred from government jobs. I, their granddaughter, would come to work as senior economic advisor to Prime Minister Pierre Trudeau.

I am now the mother of two young children. I want to pass on a sense of what it means to be a Canadian. But what worries me as a parent, and as a Canadian, is whether we can fashion an enduring concept of citizenship that will be the glue that holds us together as a society . . .

How we tell our stories is the work of citizenship. The motive of the storyteller should be to put the story first. To speak with authenticity and veracity is to choose narrative over commentary. It is not to glorify or sentimentalize the past. It is not to sanitize our differences, nor to rail against or to seek compensation today for injustices of bygone times. In my opinion, to try to rewrite history leads to a sense of victimization. It marginalizes Canadians. It backs away from equality in our society, for which we have worked hard to find expression.

I believe our stories ultimately tell the story of Canada itself. In all our pasts are an immigrant beginning, a settler's accomplishments and setbacks, and the confidence of a common future. We all know the struggle for victory, the dreams and the lost hopes, the pride and the shame. When we tell our stories, we look in the mirror. I believe what we will see is that Canada is not lacking in heroes. Rather, the heroes are to be found within.

The work of citizenship is not something just for the week that we celebrate citizenship every year. It is part of every breath we take. It is the work of our lifetimes.

The world is changing, and changing fast. People's lives are on the move. We travel more. We move to take new jobs, to find a bigger house, to live next to the schools we want our children to go to, to find a smaller house when they've grown up and left home. Families are far-flung, even to different continents. Children may have more than one home, a parent in each. Few of us as adults live in or can even revisit our childhood home. Some of us cannot even return to the neighborhoods of our childhood and find the landscape familiar.

There are political pressures that could redefine Canada as we know it. Canadians continue to debate the future of the federation and question whether the country is governable. A growing regionalism could fracture the national interest. On a global scale, the trend is integration, economically and culturally. The availability and dominance of American culture crowds our ability as Canadians to find the time and space to preserve our own culture and to share it with each other. Clicking the remote control and finding the television show of our choice is a display of our consumerism, not our Canadianism. Somehow, in this rapidly changing, busy world, we have to satisfy the emotional longing for roots, for understanding who we are, and what we are . . .

In the late 1980s, I would find myself in China, on a two-year stint living in Peking and working as a writer. In a letter to my mother in Prince George, I confessed that, despite the predictions of friends back in Canada, I was finding it difficult to feel any Chineseness. My mother wrote back: "You're Canadian, not Chinese. Stop trying to feel anything." She was right. I stopped such contrivances. I was Canadian; it was that which embodied the values of my life.

Jean Chrétien
25 October 1995

"What is at stake is our country"

The Parti Québécois called its referendum for October 1995. Early in the campaign it appeared that federalists would win easily, and the strategy, as it had been in 1980, was to allow the provincial Liberals to take the lead. Jacques Parizeau, the pq premier, was unable to light a fire, so the separatists called on Lucien Bouchard, whose ringing speeches were a lightning bolt for the sovereignists. Polls indicated that the separatists might win. Belatedly, Prime Minister Jean Chrétien joined the fray, and on 25 October, appearing pale and sombre, he made this televised address to Canadians. Chrétien spoke in short, staccato sentences, many of them mere fragments, a rhetoric unlike Bouchard's torrent of words and images. And unlike Trudeau in 1980, Chrétien made no grand promises about constitutional change if Quebec voted no. Rather he played on love of country, and the serious economic consequences for Quebec if it chose to separate.

For the first time in my mandate as prime minister, I have asked to speak directly to Canadians tonight. I do so because we are in an exceptional situation.

Tonight, in particular, I want to speak to my fellow Quebecers because, at this moment, the future of our whole country is in their hands.

But I also want to speak to all Canadians because this issue concerns them, deeply. It is not only the future of Quebec that will be decided on Monday. It is the future of all of Canada. The decision that will be made is serious and irreversible, with deep, deep consequences.

What is at stake is our country. What is at stake is our heritage. To break up Canada or build Canada, to remain Canadian or no longer be Canadian, to stay or to leave—this is the issue of the referendum.

When my fellow Quebecers make their choice on Monday, they have the responsibility and the duty to understand the implications of that choice.

The fact is, that hidden behind a murky question is a very clear option. It is the separation of Quebec, a Quebec that would no longer be part of Canada. Where Quebecers would no longer enjoy the rights and privileges associated with Canadian citizenship. Where Quebecers would no longer share a Canadian passport or a Canadian dollar, no matter what the advocates of separatism may claim. Where Quebecers would be made foreigners in their own country.

I know that many Quebecers, in all good faith, are thinking of voting yes in order to bring change to Canada. I am telling them that if they wish to remain Canadian, they are taking a very dangerous gamble. Anyone who really wants to remain a Canadian should think twice before taking such a dangerous risk. Listen to the leaders of the separatist side. They are very clear. The country they want is not a better Canada, it is a separate Quebec. Don't be fooled.

There are also those Quebecers who are thinking of voting yes to give Quebec a better bargaining position to negotiate an economic and political partnership with the rest of Canada. Again, don't be fooled. A yes vote means the destruction of the political and economic union we already enjoy . . .

The end of Canada would be nothing less than the end of a dream, the end of a country that has made us the envy of the world. Canada is not just any country. It is unique. It is the best country in the world.

Perhaps it is something we have come to take for granted. But we should never, never let that happen. Once more, today it's up to each of us to restate our love for Canada, to say we don't want to lose it.

What we have built together in Canada is something very great and very noble. A country whose values of tolerance, understanding, generosity have made us what we are: a society where our number one priority is the respect and dignity of all our citizens.

Other countries invest in weapons, we invest in the well-being of our citizens. Other countries tolerate poverty and despair, we work hard to ensure a basic level of decency for everyone. Other countries resort to violence to settle differences, we work out our problems through compromise and mutual respect.

This is what we have accomplished.

And I say to my fellow Quebecers, don't let anyone diminish or take away what we have accomplished. Don't let anyone tell you that you cannot be a proud Quebecer and a proud Canadian.

It is true Canada is not perfect. But I cannot think of a single place in the world that comes closer, not a single place where people lead better lives, where they live in greater peace and security.

Why does Canada work? Because our country has always been able to adapt and change to meet the hopes and aspirations of our citizens. We've done so in the past. We're doing so today. And we will continue to do so in the future.

We must recognize that Quebec's language, its culture and institutions make it a distinct society. And no constitutional change that affects the powers of Quebec should ever be made without the consent of Quebecers. And that all governments, federal and provincial, must respond to the desire of Canadians, everywhere, for greater decentralization. And all that can happen quietly, calmly, without rupture, with determination.

To all Canadians outside Quebec, I say do not lose faith in this country. And continue to show the respect, the openness, the attachment, and the friendship you have shown to your fellow Canadians in Quebec all through the referendum campaign.

Continue to tell them how important they are to you, and how without them, Canada would no longer be Canada, how you want them to remain Canadian and you hope, deeply and profoundly, that they choose Canada on Monday.

In recent days, thousands of Canadians have taken the time to send messages of friendship and attachment to Quebecers. Keep them coming.

My friends, once again, our country is facing a crisis. And crisis and uncertainty exact a very heavy cost. We all pay a high price for political instability.

On Monday, once Quebecers have shown their commitment to Canada, I want to ask Canadian investors and foreign investors to show their commitment and confidence in return. Together, we will need to get our priorities back on track, on economic growth and jobs, and the time is long overdue.

My friends, we are facing a decisive moment in the history of our country. And people all across Canada know that decision lies in the hands of their fellow Canadians in Quebec.

As a proud Quebecer and a proud Canadian, I am convinced that a strong Quebec in a united Canada remains the best solution for all of us. I ask those Quebecers who have not yet made their decision to ask themselves these questions when they vote on Monday:

Do you really think that you and your family would have a better quality of life and a brighter future in a separate Quebec?

Do you really think that the French language and culture in North America would be better protected in a separate Quebec?

Do you really think you and your family will enjoy greater security in a separate Quebec?

Do you really want to turn your back on Canada? Does Canada deserve that?

Are you really ready to tell the world, the whole world, that people of different languages, different cultures and different backgrounds cannot live together in harmony?

Do you really think that ties of friendship and understanding . . . ties of mutual trust and respect can be broken without harm or rancour?

Have you found one reason, one good reason, to destroy Canada?

Do you really think it is worth abandoning the country we have built, and which our ancestors have left us?

Do you really think it makes any sense, any sense at all, to break up Canada?

These are the questions I ask each of you to consider. It's a big, very big responsibility.

In a few days, all the shouting will be over. And at that moment, you will be alone to make your decision. At that moment I urge you, my fellow Quebecers, to listen to your heart, and to your head.

I am confident that Quebec and Canada will emerge strong and united.

John Polanyi
13 March 1998

"Ideas are enormously powerful
and surprisingly scarce"

John Polanyi is a Canadian chemist, a Nobel Prize winner, and a peace
activist. He gave this speech in September 1997 to honour Nobel laure-
ate guest lecturers at the University of Toronto.

Ideas are enormously powerful and surprisingly scarce. Scientific ideas
change our lives, shape our future, and determine humanity's fate. It is scientists, not governments, who are best equipped to determine which scientific ideas to pursue. Scholarship is an investment in the future. As a result,
it is everybody's business, but, as we have noticed, not everybody's priority.

Perhaps we shouldn't be surprised. The universities are set apart from
society by their special function. They exist for exploration, the drawing of
intellectual maps. That is what we, faculty and students, do. We draw our

maps not because we can be sure who will use them, but because they fill us with delight. Who does not want to know where they live? We claim that our maps will come in handy. Later, we are flabbergasted to find that this is true.

Sometimes, happily, governments share our enthusiasm for the power of ideas. The establishment of what will be almost a billion dollar fund, the Canadian Foundation for Innovation, is a case in point. To foster innovation you need a public that is conscious of the power and value of ideas. I am thought once to have had an idea, but now I talk about them. There is an important moral to this, namely that ideas are scarce. Yet, far too often, our science policy is based on the notion that they abound.

On the face of it, the organization of the nation's science seems to acknowledge the centrality of ideas. Both federally and provincially, we set out to foster the very best we have through centres of excellence. But too often we deny the premise on which these centres were formed by reshaping them into centres of relevance, as if it was excellence that was plentiful, and relevance that was scarce.

This shift in emphasis from excellence to relevance will fail to deliver value for money, for two reasons. First of all, because excellence is, of its nature, rare. We cannot take our federal or provincial shopping cart and select the excellence we prefer. What we can do, and are driven to do, is to compromise excellence in the interest of supposed relevance.

That brings me to the second reason that this policy will fail. It is, most of the time, a very bad bargain to barter excellence for relevance since both the discovery that one wishes to see made and its application lie well in the future.

Of all things, the future is the hardest to predict. Historians, who struggle even to make sense of the past, will have to explain some day how it comes about that governments, having failed spectacularly to pick winners in the marketplace for goods, have persuaded us that they can be trusted to select winners in the marketplace for ideas . . .

The extremely risky decision as to what science to pursue is best made by the scientific risk-taker, who gambles his career in choosing the right research topic. However, modern governments, having quite properly (though insufficiently) taxed the privileged, are obliged to take on those of their functions that filled a social need, including the support of venturesome scientists where they are in short supply.

But when, I shall be asked, would I ever admit to there being a sufficiency of scientists, let alone too many? Again the test must centre on quality. When we in Canada have individual scientists (totaling one-tenth in number those in the U.S.) who can attract the very best students in North America, competitively with their counterparts at Harvard and Berkeley, then we shall indeed have achieved our goal of scientific sufficiency. It should be clear that we have some way to go . . .

There remains a nagging question, even for those on the side of the angels. Can excellence be judged? Does basic science have a bottom line? Could it be, for example, that when the stock market for ideas opens tomorrow, we shall discover that our scientists have nothing of value to say? I think it unlikely, and I will explain why. The procedures that we used in selecting them have long since shown themselves to be grounded in reality. The guiding principle for assessing value in basic science, now as in the past, has been excellence as perceived by the scientific community. We see the consequences of this around us.

For an annual investment of a fraction of 1 percent of the world's wealth in the generation of new knowledge, we have been rewarded in this century by insight into the nature of matter, of energy, of space, of time, of life, and of the cosmos, beyond anything that history has known.

And has this, you are entitled to ask, proved to be relevant? I would say, rather too much. Modern science has totally transformed our world. Our problem is not a lack of relevance, but a surfeit of it.

As a consequence of these changes, we can no longer wall ourselves off from one another, nor therefore have nations as we used to, nor make war as we did, nor squander resources, nor litter the globe or neglect the oppressed, as has so long been our custom.

By far the greater part of this transformation has been for the good. All of it represents a challenge unique in history. This challenge testifies to the power of ideas. Indeed, they will overpower us unless we continue to value them, rejecting mindless materialism and fanaticism.

There should be a grim humour for the all-seeing deity in our attempts to convince ourselves of the power of ideas. We shall shortly emerge from a century in which fifty million people died in the contest between the ideas of autocracy and democracy. Twice that number were in danger of being sacrificed on the altar of another idea: the pursuit of security through nuclear armament. We should take comfort from the fact that the more civilized notions of democracy and disarmament are in the ascendancy.

I began by speaking of the fear we have in Canada that ideas may prove irrelevant. I end by claiming that to have an idea is to be in the embrace of a tiger. In pursuit of an abstraction, Einstein, a devoted pacifist, gave the world nuclear weapons. In pursuit of a vision of shared concern for human suffering, three outstanding individuals, Canadian Generals Maurice Baril and Romeo Dallaire, and Secretary-General Kofi Annan of the UN, incurred some of the responsibility for the deaths of a multitude of Rwandan civilians. This was, in fact, the tragedy of an idea half-conceived; the three whom I mentioned were empowered to go to the scene of the crime, but not to deal with the criminals. The heavier burden of responsibility rests with us, we who failed to insist on the power of the idea that goes by the name of the United Nations, the idea that we owe an inescapable obligation to humanity. It is, I believe, on that simple but immensely powerful idea that all our futures rest.

Nelson Mandela
24 September 1998

"A personal farewell"

Nelson Mandela, the former president of South Africa, is one of only two people to have been granted an honourary Canadian citizenship. The second, Swedish diplomat Raoul Wallenberg, saved many Jews during the World War II prior to disappearing himself. His citizenship was granted posthumously. Mandela had first addressed the Canadian Parliament in 1990. He was nearing the end of his political career when he came to Canada in September 1998 to address Parliament for a second time. He thanked Canadians for their efforts to end apartheid and for helping to recast South Africa as a pluralist democracy.

When I stood before you in 1990, it was as a freedom fighter still denied citizenship in my own country, seeking your support to ensure an irreversible transition to democracy.

Today, I stand before you as the elected representative of the South

African people, to thank you once again, for helping us end our oppression; for assisting us through our transition; and now for your partnership in the building of a better life for all South Africans. We will forever be indebted to you.

Although we still have a long way to go before we have realised our vision of a better life for all, there has been a great transformation in South Africa since 1990, and solid foundations have been laid.

The experience of all peoples has taught that our democracy would remain secure and stable only if we could unite those who were once locked in conflict, and if our new freedoms brought material improvement in the lives of our people . . .

In order that the memory of historical injustice and violations of human rights should not remain as continuing obstacles to national unity, our Truth and Reconciliation Commission has helped us confront our terrible past. Painful and imperfect as the process has been, it has taken us further than anyone expected towards a common understanding of our history.

If we lay stress on uniting the different sections of our society, it is because unity and the partnership of all the structures of our society are critical to the reconstruction and development of our society in order to eradicate apartheid's legacy of poverty and inequality . . .

On my way here today, I had the honour of unveiling, at your human rights monument, a plaque dedicated to John Humphrey, author of the first draft of the Universal Declaration of Human Rights. I would like, if I may, to pay tribute to his contribution to the central philosophy of your country and his dedication to the cause of human rights worldwide.

This is an area in which your country and mine march hand in hand in practical action to make a living reality of the rights to which we subscribe. In this regard we think of Canada's hard work, together with other countries, to bring to fruition the anti-landmine convention. We were very proud, in December last year, to be the third country, after Canada and Norway, to sign that convention, here in Ottawa.

Canada and South Africa also together played a part in the recent establishment of the International Criminal Court. South Africa is increasingly being called upon to play a role in peacekeeping, in Southern Africa and in Africa as a whole. Our approach is that we will play whatever part we can within our limited means, and within a multilateral framework, whether it be the United Nations, the Commonwealth, the Non-Aligned Movement, the Organisation of African Unity, and the Southern African Development Community.

Essential to our vision of a new and more humane international order is the belief that inevitable as differences may be, they need not and should not be resolved by the force of arms. We look to peaceful resolution of differences because this is the only way in which humanity can prosper.

It is in this context that South Africa has in recent days found itself called upon to contribute its forces to a joint regional security initiative aimed at assisting, at its own request, the democratically elected government of a neighbour, by securing a measure of peace and stability.

Here too, we look to Canada as a partner. We recognize Lester Pearson as the founder of modern peacekeeping, because of his innovative intervention in the Suez crisis.

By the same token, we salute Canada's distinguished service over many years in Cyprus, Bosnia, and Somalia, and more recently in the disarmament process in Northern Ireland.

Canada's internationalist record gives us confidence that you understand and share our vision of an African renaissance. If history has decreed that our continent, at the end of the twentieth century, should be marginalized in world affairs, we know that our destiny lies in our own hands.

Yet we also know that we cannot bring about our renaissance solely by our own efforts, since the problems we face are rooted in conditions beyond the power of any one nation to determine.

Indeed, the turmoil in far off economies that we have had to weather has, we know, affected Canada too. In the interdependent world in which we now live, rich and poor, strong and weak are bound in a common destiny that decrees that none shall enjoy lasting prosperity and stability unless others do too.

These harsh lessons of our global economy were the focus of attention at the summit of the Non-Aligned Movement held in Durban earlier this month. They have forced themselves upon the attention of the whole international community. A debate about the global trade and financial system that has been too long in the making has now been joined.

We urge you to join with us in seeking to redirect the system and its institutions so as to cater for the needs of development and the interests of the poor. In so doing we would be affirming a fundamental principle of all human society, namely that the existence and the well-being of each of us is dependent on that of our fellows. In a globalized world, that is as true of nations as it is of individual men and women.

This occasion marks something of a farewell. I am deeply grateful that it has been possible, before my retirement from public life, to make this second visit to a people that has made our aspirations their own, who have insisted that the rights which the world declares to be universal should also be the rights of all South Africans. But though it is a personal farewell and in some sense an ending, I do know that it is also the beginning of a new and more profound relationship between our peoples.

Joe Gosnell
4 August 1998

"A cargo of hope"

Since time immemorial, the Nisga'a have inhabited the mountainous, fjord-indented region of what is now northwest British Columbia. The Nisga'a never signed a treaty or ceded their territory, but the province denied that anything called Aboriginal title ever existed. The stalemate persisted for more than a century, until Supreme Court Justice Emmett Hall wrote a judgment in the Calder case in 1973 saying that Aboriginal title did exist, had never been extinguished, and that the government would have to negotiate with the Nisga'a. But it was to take another twenty-five years before a treaty was completed. Joe Gosnell was president of the Nisga'a Tribal Council, and made this speech at a ceremony initialling the treaty on 4 August 1998.

Back in 1887, our ancestors, pressing to settle the Nisga'a land question, climbed into their canoes and paddled down the British Columbia coast to Victoria's inner harbour, where, on the steps of the Parliament buildings, they were sharply turned away by Premier Smithe.

Like a handful of politicians today, Smithe refused to discuss the Nisga'a land question, wrongly convinced the assimilation of Aboriginal people was inevitable. As a result, he plunged the province into one hundred years of darkness for the Nisga'a and other First Nations.

Today, that is changed forever, changed utterly. This ceremony is a triumph, for the Nisga'a people, the people of British Columbia, and the people of Canada. Today we make history as we correct the mistakes of the past and send a signal of hope around the world.

Today, let us talk of reconciliation and a new understanding between cultures. Today we join Canada and British Columbia as free citizens, full and equal participants in the social, economic, and political life of this country. That has been our dream for more than a century. Today it becomes a reality.

People sometimes wonder why we have struggled so long to sign a treaty. Why, we are asked, did our elders and elected officials dedicate their lives to a resolution of the land question? What is it about a treaty?

To the Nisga'a people, a treaty is a sacred instrument. It represents an understanding between distinct cultures and shows respect for each other's way of life. It stands as a symbol of high idealism in a divided, fractious world. That is why we have fought so long and so hard.

Has it been worth it? Yes, a resounding yes. But, believe me, it has been a long and hard-fought compromise. Some may have heard me say that a generation of Nisga'a men and women has grown old at the negotiating table. Sadly, it is very, very true.

Words can only hint at our feelings. I am talking here about a century of frustration, humiliation, and emotional devastation. We lived it every day. Devastated by smallpox, influenza, and other European diseases, our ancestors were torn from their homes, exiled to reserves, forbidden to speak the Nisga'a language and practise our own beliefs. In short, subjected to a system of cultural genocide for 130 years.

It still breaks my heart to see our young men and women sentenced to a life of seasonal, dead-end jobs, to see the despair and the disillusionment on the faces of my people.

Those are the reasons, ladies and gentlemen, I am still fighting to finalize the treaty, and will not stop until it is ratified and made into law. Look around you. Look at our faces. We are survivors. We intend to live here forever, and under the treaty, we will flourish.

The treaty represents a monumental achievement for the Nisga'a people and for Canadian society as a whole. It shows the world that reasonable people can sit down and settle historical wrongs. It proves that a modern society can correct the mistakes of the past and ensures that minorities are treated fairly. As Canadians, we should all be very proud.

We have detractors—oh yes—nay-sayers who say our interests should continue to be ignored, those who say Canada and B.C. are giving us too much, and there are others, particularly within the Aboriginal community, who say we settled for too little.

Our detractors do not understand, or, practising a wilful ignorance, choose not to understand. Or worse, using carefully coded language, they are updating a venomous attitude familiar to First Nations of the world.

They are wrong. By playing politics with the aspirations of Aboriginal people they are blighting the promise of the Nisga'a treaty, not only for the Nisga'a but for all Canadians.

No longer beggars in our own lands, we now go forward with dignity, equipped with the confidence that we can make important contributions, social, political, and economic, to Canadian society.

The Nisga'a treaty proves, beyond all doubt, that negotiations, not lawsuits, not roadblocks, not violence, are the most effective, most honourable way to resolve Aboriginal issues in this country.

Today, as you are my witness, the Nisga'a canoe returns to the Nass River with a cargo of hope and reconciliation.

Adrienne Clarkson
7 October 1999

"Canada is a forgiving society"

Adrienne Clarkson had a successful career in broadcasting and diplomacy prior to being appointed as governor general in 1999. Her speeches are elegantly written and skilfully delivered. In her installation speech, she talked about both Canada and her childhood experience as an immigrant from Hong Kong.

I take on the responsibility of becoming Canada's twenty-sixth governor general since Confederation fully conscious of the deep roots of this office, stretching back to the governors of New France and to the first of them, Samuel de Champlain. In our beloved Georgian Bay, which lies on the great water route he took from the French River to Huronia, there is a cairn, placed on a small island between a tennis court and Champlain's Gas Bar & Marina, which commemorates his passage and quotes from his journal: Samuel de Champlain, by canoe, 1615, "As for me, I labour always to prepare a way for those willing to follow . . ."

Champlain's successors have had many activists among them. Lord Elgin, who helped Baldwin and Lafontaine to anchor the Canadian model of democracy in 1848, stands out as somebody who appreciated the originality of a country which would promote such a project. He loved to wander about our few small cities, on foot, glorying in snowstorms, eschewing the formality of his office and speaking of his admiration for "this glorious country" and "its perfectly independent inhabitants." He also said that in order to have insight into the future of all nations, it was necessary to come here . . .

Allow me a moment of personal reflection. The Poy family, arriving here as refugees in 1942, was made up of my parents, my brother and myself. Three of us are in this Chamber today. We did not arrive as part of a regular immigration procedure; there was no such thing for a Chinese family at that time in Canadian history.

My mother's intense and abiding love is here in spirit today. My brother, Dr. Neville Poy, was seven when we arrived. And my father, Bill Poy, is here, extraordinary, in his ninety-second year. Lance-Corporal Poy, dispatch rider with the Hong Kong Volunteer Corps, received the military medal for his bravery during the battle of Hong Kong. Like many soldiers, he never speaks of those actions, but it is his bravery which is the underpinning of his children's lives. To have been brought up by courageous and loving parents was a gift that made up for all we had lost.

As I have said before, the city of Ottawa, then, was small and white, like most of Canada. Much of its psyche was characterised by what Mavis Gallant has called "the dark bloom of the Old Country, the mistrust of pity, the contempt for weakness, the fear of the open heart." But it was also the place where our family was befriended by the Molots, who owned the local drugstore, the Marcottes and the Proulx, among whom we lived in Lower Town, and our guardian angels, the Potters.

Because my father had a job with the Department of Trade and Commerce and because we lived among French Canadians, I became fixated, from the age of five, with the idea of learning French.

I remember the day when I was dressed up in my patent leather shoes and pink smocked dress, and was taken up the street by my parents to the convent of Ste. Jeanne d'Arc, where I was interviewed by a kindly woman wearing white all around her face, while a dim crucifix glowed in the background. Walking home, I sensed that there was dejection in the air and disappointment. It had been explained to my parents that it was not possible for a Protestant to receive French language education in Ottawa. In my lifetime, this has changed to such a radical degree that I don't even need to comment on it. But that early sense of something being impossible, which actually was nonsensical, put steel into me . . .

As John Ralston Saul has written, the central quality of the Canadian state is its complexity. It is a strength and not a weakness that we are a "permanently incomplete experiment built on a triangular foundation—Aboriginal, francophone and anglophone." What we continue to create, today, began 450 years ago as a political project, when the French first met with the Aboriginal people. It is an old experiment, complex and, in worldly terms, largely successful. Stumbling through darkness and racing through light, we have persisted in the creation of a Canadian civilization . . .

There seem to be two kinds of societies in the world today. Perhaps there have always been only two kinds: punishing societies and forgiving societies. A society like Canada's, with its four centuries of give-and-take, compromise and acceptance, wrongdoing and redress, is basically a forgiving society. We try—we must try—to forgive what is past. The punishing society never forgets the wrongs of the past. The forgiving society works towards the actions of the future. The forgiving society enables people to behave well toward one another, to begin again, to build a society in hope and with love . . .

In a 1913 photograph, a group of Scandinavian immigrants in Larchmont, Ontario, is huddled around a blackboard on which is written: Duties of the Citizen: understand our government; take an active part in politics; assist all good causes; lessen intemperance; work for others.

It would be easy to focus obsessively on all the pitfalls and prejudices that undoubtedly landmined this path of good intentions. But in examining the intent, you see the underlying central assumption. It was expected that the immigrant, along with everyone else, would join in the social process, which was democratic, co-operative and other-directed. The fact that it would take another fifty years for this kind of inclusiveness to become colour blind means, simply, that it took another fifty years. Too long, of course, far too long, but in other countries, it would take a hundred. In some, it has never come.

The essence of inclusiveness is that we are part of a society in which language, colour, education, sex and money need not, should not, divide us, but can make us more aware and sensitive to difference . . .

We must not see ourselves as a small country of thirty million people, floundering in a large land mass. We are among the healthiest, best-educated people in the world, with great natural riches. We have two of the world's great languages.

We must not see ourselves as people who simply react to trends but as people who can initiate them.

We must not see ourselves as people to whom things are done but as people who do things.

Our history demonstrates that we have the self-confidence to act and to act successfully. We can, when we trust ourselves, seize hold of the positive energy, flowing out of the choice we have made to be here and to continue what remains an unprecedented experiment . . .

As I take up this task, I ask you to embark on a journey with me. Together, I hope that we will be able to do it with the Inuit quality of *isuma*, which is defined as an intelligence that includes knowledge of one's responsibility towards society. The Inuit believe that it can only grow in its own time; it grows because it is nurtured. I pray that with God's help, we, as Canadians, will trace with our own lives what Stan Rogers called "one warm line through this land, so wild and savage."

And in the footsteps of Samuel de Champlain, I am willing to follow.

Justin Trudeau
3 October 2000

"Je t'aime, papa"

Pierre Trudeau died on 28 September 2000. Notre Dame Basilica in Montreal was filled to overflowing on 3 October for his funeral, attended by, among others, former U.S. President Jimmy Carter and Cuban President Fidel Castro. Trudeau's son Justin provided this eulogy to his father.

Friends, Romans, countrymen.

I was about six years old when I went on my first official trip. I was going with my father and my grandpa Sinclair up to the North Pole. It was a very glamorous destination. But the best thing about it is that I was going to be spending lots of time with my dad because in Ottawa he just worked so hard.

One day, we were in Alert, Canada's northernmost point, a scientific military installation that seemed to consist entirely of low shed-like buildings and warehouses.

Let's be honest. I was six. There were no brothers around to play with and I was getting a little bored because Dad still somehow had a lot of work to do. I remember a frozen, windswept Arctic afternoon when I was bundled up into a Jeep and hustled out on a special top-secret mission. I figured I was finally going to be let in on the reason of this high-security Arctic base.

I was exactly right.

We drove slowly through and past the buildings, all of them very grey and windy. We rounded a corner and came upon a red one. We stopped. I got out of the Jeep and started to crunch across towards the front door. I was told, no, to the window. So I clambered over the snow bank, was boosted up to the window, rubbed my sleeve against the frosty glass to see inside and as my eyes adjusted to the gloom, I saw a figure, hunched over one of many worktables that seemed very cluttered. He was wearing a red suit with that furry white trim. And that's when I understood just how powerful and wonderful my father was.

Pierre Elliott Trudeau. The very words convey so many things to so many people. Statesman, intellectual, professor, adversary, outdoorsman, lawyer, journalist, author, prime minister. But more than anything, to me, he was Dad. And what a dad. He loved us with the passion and the devotion that encompassed his life. He taught us to believe in ourselves, to stand up for ourselves, to know ourselves and to accept responsibility for ourselves. We knew we were the luckiest kids in the world. And we had done nothing to actually deserve it. It was instead something that we would have to spend the rest of our lives to work very hard to live up to.

He gave us a lot of tools. We were taught to take nothing for granted. He doted on us but didn't indulge. Many people say he didn't suffer fools gladly, but I'll have you know he had infinite patience with us. He encouraged us to push ourselves, to test limits, to challenge anyone and anything. There were certain basic principles that could never be compromised.

As I guess it is for most kids, in grade three, it was always a real treat to visit my dad at work. As on previous visits, this particular occasion included a lunch at the parliamentary restaurant which always seemed to be terribly important and full of serious people that I didn't recognize. But at eight, I was becoming politically aware, and I recognized one whom I knew to be one of my father's chief rivals. Thinking of pleasing my father, I told a joke about him, a generic, silly little grade school thing.

My father looked at me sternly with that look I would learn to know so well, and said: "Justin, on n'attaque jamais l'individu. On peut être en désaccord complet avec quelqu'un sans pour autant les dénigrer."

Et ce disant, il se leva, me pris la main, et m'amena rencontrer cet homme. C'était un gentil monsieur, qui mangeait avec sa fille, une jolie blonde un peu plus jeune que moi. Il me parla amicalement un moment, et ce fut dès lors que je compris qu'avoir des opinions différentes de celles d'une autre personne n'empêchait aucunement de leur porter le plus grand respect en tant qu'individu.

Parce que la simple tolérance, ce n'est pas assez. Il faut un respect réel et profond de chaque être humain, qu'importent ses croyances, ses origines, ou ses valeurs. C'est ce que mon père exgeait de ses fils, et c'est ce qu'il exigeait de notre pays.

Il l'exigeait par amour. Amour de ses fils, amour de son pays. Et c'est pour ça que nous l'aimons tant. Les lettres, les fleurs, la dignité des foules venus lui dire adieu, tout ça pour le remercier de nous avoir tant aimé.

My father's fundamental belief never came from a textbook. It stemmed from his deep love for and faith in all Canadians and over the past few days, with every card, every rose, every tear, every wave, and every pirouette, you returned his love.

It means the world to Sacha and me. Thank you.

We have gathered from coast to coast to coast, from one ocean to another, united in our grief, to say goodbye.

But this is not the end. He left politics in '84. But he came back for Meech. He came back for Charlottetown. He came back to remind us of who we are and what we're all capable of. But he won't be coming back anymore. It's all up to us, all of us, now.

The woods are lovely, dark and deep. He has kept his promises and earned his sleep.

Je t'aime papa.

Jean Chrétien
14 September 2001

"We will defy and defeat terrorism"

On 11 September 1991 terrorists crashed two hijacked jetliners into the twin World Trade Center Towers in New York City. Another was crashed into the Pentagon complex in Washington. Americans were shocked to have sustained such a massive attack on their own soil, and they were grief-stricken and angry. The Canadian government organized a memorial service on Parliament Hill, and Prime Minister Chrétien addressed the following brief comments to Paul Celucci, the U.S. ambassador to Canada.

Mr. Ambassador, you have assembled before you, here on Parliament Hill and right across Canada, a people united in outrage, in grief, in compassion, and in resolve; a people of every faith and nationality to be found on earth; a people who, as a result of the atrocity committed against the United States on September 11, 2001, feel not only like neighbours but like family.

At a time like this, words fail us. We reel before the blunt and terrible reality of the evil we have just witnessed. We cannot stop the tears of grief. We cannot bring back lost wives and husbands, sons and daughters, American citizens, Canadian citizens, citizens from all over the world. We cannot restore futures that have been cut terribly short.

At a time like this, the only saving grace is our common humanity and decency. At a time like this, it is our feelings, our prayers and our actions that count.

By their outpouring of concern, sympathy and help, the feelings and actions of Canadians have been clear. And, even as we grieve our own losses, the message they send to the American people is equally clear. Do not despair. You are not alone. We are with you. The whole world is with you.

The great Martin Luther King, in describing times of trial and tribulation, once said that: "In the end, it is not the words of your enemies that you remember, it is the silence of your friends."

Mr. Ambassador, as your fellow Americans grieve and rebuild, there will be no silence from Canada. Our friendship has no limit. Generation after generation, we have travelled many difficult miles together. Side by side, we have lived through many dark times, always firm in our shared resolve to vanquish any threat to freedom and justice. And together, with our allies, we will defy and defeat the threat that terrorism poses to all civilized nations.

Mr. Ambassador, we will be with the United States every step of the way, as friends, as neighbours, as family.

Sunera Thobani

5 October 2001

"U.S. foreign policy is soaked in blood"

In the aftermath of terrorist attacks in New York and Washington, U.S. President George Bush vowed to hunt down those responsible and to go to war against any states protecting them. He made it bluntly clear that no nation could remain neutral in the coming conflict. A central point in the debate in Canada was whether American foreign policy could in any way be linked to the attacks that had occurred. Sunera Thobani, a professor at Simon Fraser University and a former chair of the National Action Committee on the Status of Women, did make such a link, and her remarks precipitated a storm of controversy.

If we in the west are all Americans now, what are Third World women and Aboriginal women to do? If Canadians are Americans now, what are women of colour to do in this country? . . .

Living in a period of escalating global interaction now on every front, on every level, we have to recognize that this level and this particular phase of globalization is rooted in all forms of globalization in the colonization of Aboriginal peoples and Third World people all over the world. This is the basis. And so globalization continues to remain rooted in that colonization, and there will be no social justice, no anti-racism, no feminist emancipation, no liberation of any kind for anybody on this continent unless Aboriginal people demand for self-determination.

The second point I want to make is that the global order that we live in, there are profound injustices in this global order—profound injustices. Third World women . . . I want to say for decades, but I'm going to say for centuries, have been making the point that there can be no women's emancipation, in fact, no liberation of any kind for women will be successful unless it seeks to transform the fundamental divide between the North and South, between Third World people and those in the west who are now calling themselves Americans; that there will be no emancipation for women anywhere on this planet until the western domination of this planet is ended.

Love thy neighbour. Love thy neighbour, we need to heed those words, especially as all of us are being hoarded into the possibility of a massive war by the United States. We need to hear those words even more clearly today. Today in the world the United States is the most dangerous and most powerful global force unleashing prolific levels of violence all over the world.

From Chile to El Salvador, to Nicaragua to Iraq, the path of U.S. foreign policy is soaked in blood. We have seen, and all of us have seen, felt, the dramatic pain of watching those attacks and trying to grasp the fact of the number of people who died. We feel the pain of that every day we have been watching it on television. But do we feel any pain for the victims of U.S. aggression? Two hundred thousand people killed only in the initial war on Iraq, the bombing of Iraq for ten years now. Do we feel the pain of all the children in Iraq who are dying from the sanctions imposed by the United States? Do we feel that pain on an everyday level? Share it with our families and communities and talk about it on every platform that is available to us? Do we feel the pain of Palestinians who now for fifty years have been living in refugee camps?

U.S. foreign policy is soaked in blood, and other countries in the west, including, shamefully, Canada, cannot line up fast enough behind it. All want to sign up now as Americans and I think it is the responsibility of the women's movement to stop that, to fight against it . . .

Canada's approach has been mixed. It has said, yes, we will support the United States but with caution. It will be a cautionary support. We want to know what the actions will be before we sign on and we want to know this has been Canada's approach. And I have to say we have to go much further. Canada has to say we reject U.S. policy in the Middle East. We do not support it . . .

And we want to recognize—we have to recognize—that the calls that are coming from progressive groups in the Third World, and in their supporters, in their allies, in the rest of the world, the three key demands they are asking for: End the bombing of Iraq, lift the sanctions on Iraq—who in this room will not support that demand? Resolve the Palestinian question—that's the second one. And remove the American military bases, anywhere in the Middle East. Who will not demand, support these demands?

We have to recognize that these demands are rooted in anti-imperialist struggle and that we have to support these demands. We need to end the racist colonization of Aboriginal peoples in this country, certainly, but we need to make common calls with women across the world who are fighting to do this. Only then can we talk about anti-racist, feminist politics, only then can we talk about international solidarity in women's movements across the world.

And in closing, just one word, the lesson we have learned, and the lesson that our politicians should have learned, is that you cannot slaughter people into submission. For five hundred years they have tried that strategy; the west for five hundred years has believed that it can slaughter people into submission and it has not been able to do so, and it will not be able to do so this time either.

Stephen Lewis
21 June 2002

"We could save and prolong millions of lives"

Stephen Lewis spent his early life in politics and led the NDP in Ontario from 1970 to 1978. Brian Mulroney appointed him as Canada's ambassador to the United Nations in 1984. Lewis was Deputy Executive Director of UNICEF (1995–1999) and, since June 2001, he has been the UN Secretary-General's Special Envoy for HIV/AIDS in Africa. Lewis is a consummate orator who rarely speaks from a script. He frequently uses his persuasive powers to demand help for those, particularly in Africa, who are affected by the AIDS epidemic. He gave this speech at the opening ceremonies of the Group of Six Billion (G6B), a citizens' forum in Calgary held in advance of the Group of Eight (G8) meeting at Kananaskis, Alberta.

I live two lives: one is speaking within Canada to a variety of groups; the other is the role of UN Envoy on AIDS in Africa. Inevitably the two roles intermingle, but tonight, of all nights, I want to retain at least twelve degrees of separation. Tonight I'm speaking in what diplomacy elegantly calls my personal capacity . . .

Let me proceed to deal with the issues. The New Partnership for African Development (NEPAD) is a document driven by the fashionable current tenets of liberalized trade, governance, democratization and anti-corruption. They all sound fine in themselves, but I happen to believe that that prescription is faulty; indeed it is reminiscent of many similar analyses of Africa which have gone before, and have come to naught . . .

There is only a pro forma sense of the social sectors, only modest references to the human side of the ledger. And in a fashion quite startling, in fact, disturbingly startling, NEPAD hardly mentions HIV/AIDS at all. But how can you talk about the future of sub-Saharan Africa without AIDS at the heart of the analysis? The failure to do so leads to a curious and disabling contradiction.

NEPAD has a number of stunning goals. They are essentially the Millenium Development goals: an annual growth rate of 7 percent for fifteen years; cutting poverty in half by the year 2015; reduce infant mortality rates by two-thirds; reduce maternal mortality rates to three-quarters of what they were before; have every child enter school who is eligible, thereby re-enforcing the principle of gender equality. A more admirable agenda could not be imagined. But there's a dreadful conundrum . . .

I cannot put the case too strongly. There will be no continuous 7 percent annual growth rate in the twenty-five countries where the prevalence rate of HIV is above 5 percent, considered to be the dangerous take-off point for the pandemic, unless the pandemic is defeated. In fact, it is virtually certain that several of those countries will experience a negative rate of growth year over year under present circumstances.

There will be no cutting poverty in half by the year 2015 unless the pandemic is defeated; poverty exacerbates the pandemic, but the reverse is equally true. When family income is gutted as wage earners die, as plots of land are left untended, as every penny goes to the care of the sick and the dying, it is preposterous to pretend that poverty will be halved. There will be no reduction in infant mortality by two-thirds, unless the pandemic is defeated. How can there be? Two thousand infants a day are currently infected, a certain death warrant, maintaining or elevating the already impossibly high infant mortality rates. There will be no reduction in maternal mortality rates unless the pandemic is defeated. How can there be? We've learned over the years that maternal mortality is one of the most intractable health problems throughout the developing world; in a situation where the health systems are under assault, where hospitals and community clinics can't cope, there's no chance of reducing maternal mortality by three-quarters. Seldom has the word pipe dream been more applicable.

And there is certainly no chance of putting every eligible child in school, especially the girls, unless the pandemic is defeated. UNESCO has very recently released a study showing that four out of every ten primary school age children are now not in school in sub-Saharan Africa. Young girls are regularly pulled out of classrooms to look after ailing parents. There are thirteen million orphans in Africa, the numbers rising inexorably, huge cohorts of them living on the streets, or attempting to survive in child-headed households after the extended family is gone and the grandmothers are dead. These kids have nothing; they certainly have no money to afford school fees, or books, or uniforms. And it's not just the children, it's the teachers . . .

Last year alone, a million African children lost their teachers to AIDS. The government of Mozambique just issued a statement that 17 percent of its teachers will die of AIDS by the end of this decade. As I travel, when I speak to ministers of education, they haven't the faintest idea how they're going to replace the teachers that are gone, or how they will ever find trained or adequate substitute teachers to fill in for the regular classroom teachers who are off sick for extended periods of time. We're talking about an unprecedented calamity. There's nothing more noble than the objective of putting every child in school, but if the objective is not to be more than some kind of ephemeral mockery, then AIDS must be defeated.

In other words, quite simply, taken all in all, and I emphasize again, taken from NEPAD itself, the development goals of Africa are an impossible hope until we have turned the pandemic around.

I remember visiting a little Catholic community centre in Windhoek, Namibia, in February. It was a place where people living with AIDS could network, find a support group, have a meal, try to earn some money through an income-generating project. What was the project in that instance? The Sister running the centre took me out back to show me. A group of men were making miniature paper mache coffins for infants, and as they affixed the silver handles, they said to me with a mixture of pride and anguish: "We can't keep up with the demand."

I guess that was, for me, the nadir of this last year of travelling through Africa. It's simply self-evident truth that in country after country where the pandemic is grievously rooted, the development process has been dealt a mortal blow. The G8 Summit is, in a way, the last best chance for Africa. The G8 leaders, straightjacketed in the kind of denial that afflicted the African leaders for twenty years, must make a Herculean effort to break free and provide a binding commitment to the continent . . .

Let me be clear: while the situation feels apocalyptic, it can be addressed. AIDS has done and is doing terrible things to Africa, but we know how to defeat it. That's what drives me crazy, we know how to defeat it. We know all about voluntary counselling and testing; we simply have to train more counsellors and get rapid testing kits into the hands of those who administer the tests. We know all about the prevention of mother-to-child transmission. We know about the wonder drug nevirapine; one tablet to the mother at the onset of labour, one tablet during the birthing process, one dose of liquid equivalent to the baby within hours of birth and transmission of the virus can be reduced by up to 53 percent. We know about antiretroviral treatment, the so-called drug cocktails that keep people alive.

Largely as a result of competition from generic manufacturers in India, Thailand and Brazil, the cost of "ARVs" has dropped dramatically, but no matter how dramatic, the drugs are still beyond the capacity of Africans to afford when people live on less than a dollar a day. But it could be afforded through external financing, and it is one of the gruesome iniquities of the present situation that people are dying, everywhere, in huge numbers, unnecessarily.

We know about prevention, particularly in the key youth communities aged fifteen to twenty-four. Through what they call peer counselling and peer education, using music, dance, drama, drums and poetry, questions of sexuality and condoms and abstinence and behaviour change are confronted in a fashion so explicit, so real, so frontal as to take your breath away. What has to be done, of course, is to generalize prevention programs throughout any given country, that is, to take prevention to scale. And it's possible if only Africa had the resources . . .

To be sure, there are vexing, sometimes overwhelming problems of infrastructure, and overwhelming problems of finding the human capacity to do the job. When funerals are more pervasive than any other form of social gathering, when hospital wards are chambers of horrors, the life force of a society is slowly being strangled. But as I stand here, I genuinely believe, to the depths of my being, that we could save and prolong millions of lives, if only we had the resources to do so.

Roy Romanow
28 November 2002

"Medicare is sustainable if we want it to be"

Roy Romanow was premier of Saskatchewan from 1991 to 2001. Following his retirement, he was appointed by Jean Chrétien in 2001 to lead a one-man royal commission into health care in Canada. Romanow had been a youthful confidant of Saskatchewan premier Tommy Douglas, whose government introduced Canada's first public, tax-financed, medical care insurance plan. Later Romanow befriended Justice Emmett Hall, whose royal commission report in 1964 had recommended medicare for all of Canada. Ironically, it was Romanow who closed down many small Saskatchewan hospitals in the 1990s due to the province's financial crisis. After eighteen months of research and consultation in 2001–02, Romanow concluded that medicare should remain public, but must be reformed to provide prompt, quality service. He released his report at the National Press Theatre in Ottawa.

The changes I am proposing are intended to strengthen and modernize medicare, and place it on a more sustainable footing for the future. They are based on a vision of medicare as a national endeavour, where governments work together to ensure timely access to quality health care services as a right of citizenship, not a privilege. And they are designed to achieve a more effectively integrated and a more accountable world-class system that helps to make Canadians the healthiest people in the world.

Before summarizing the final report's recommendations, permit me to speak briefly on the issue of sustainability. After carefully reviewing the available evidence—hard facts, not unproven assumptions—I also make the case in my report that medicare is sustainable if we want it to be, that historically, single-payer health systems have proven to be significantly more cost-efficient than alternative approaches, and that despite the sometimes overheated rhetoric, Canada's health outcomes remain among world's best. Nor does a review of the evidence suggest that our health care spending is out of control . . . After several years of restraint, governments recognized the imperative to reinvest, to play catch-up. The result has been the sharp increases in health spending of recent years, a trend made all the more dramatic by the September 2000, $23.4 billion National Health Accord.

While I agree with those who argue that recent health spending trajectories cannot be sustained, I also note that the Canadian Institute for Health Information has reported that these growth trajectories have already begun to level off.

More to the point, my report also notes that despite this recent reinvestment, we are still spending less today on health as a share of our GDP than we did a decade ago, that our health spending is in line with that of other wealthy countries, and that there is a need for some immediate, targeted investments in some priority areas that are eroding public confidence in medicare's future . . .

But I want to make one thing absolutely clear. The new money that I propose investing in health care is to stabilize the system over the short term, and to buy enduring change over the long term. I cannot say often enough that the status quo is not an option! If the only result of these past eighteen months of collective effort by Canadians is simply more dollars for health care, our time will have been wasted.

Let me quickly summarize my report. In terms of modernizing the system's foundations, I propose establishing a Canadian Health Covenant that expresses Canadians' collective vision for health care and that outlines the responsibilities and entitlements of individual citizens, health providers, and governments in regard to the system. We need consensus on why the system exists, what it is intended to achieve and how its component parts should fit together. This is vital to restoring the public's confidence in the system.

I also am proposing to modernize the Canada Health Act by updating the principle of comprehensiveness to include priority diagnostic and homecare services, by clarifying the principle of portability to guarantee portability of coverage within Canada, and by adding a sixth principle of accountability.

Finally, I am proposing the creation of a Health Council of Canada. This intergovernmental council would serve as a meeting place and focal point for collaboration among governments, providers, and citizens in establishing overall system objectives, common indicators and benchmarks, criteria for measuring, tracking health, and reporting to Canadians on system performance.

These efforts are designed to help end the demoralizing long-distance hollering and bickering that passes as federal-provincial discourse on health care. Canadians want their governments to work together to make medicare better, not fight over it!

Now let's turn to funding. In recent speeches and press statements, I have described the "stop-go" approach that has characterized funding for our health care as deleterious. We need stable, predictable and long-term funding that is allocated in a way that makes it clear who is spending what, and with what results, so that we can understand where accountability rests.

Accordingly, my report recommends that the federal government commit to funding a minimum of 25 percent of the cost of insured health services under the Canada Health Act by 2005–06. I also recommend that the annual Canada Health and Social Transfer be replaced by a cash-only Canada Health Transfer that includes a built-in escalator to ensure more stable and predictable funding and greater accountability.

Because it will take time to negotiate a new transfer, and consistent with my overarching conclusion that any additional money invested in the health care system must achieve transformative change, I am also proposing provisional funding over the next two years . . . to an estimated additional $3.5 billion investment in health care in budget year 2003–04, rising to an additional $5 billion in budget year 2004–05. In 2005–06, these special funds and transfers will be subsumed within the proposed 25 percent federal funding base that should provide about $6.5 billion more for health care than is currently forecast . . .

Home care also figures in my final recommendations. With an increasing number of Canadians now receiving care at home, I am proposing we recognize this reality by creating a foundation for a national home care system . . .

I am also suggesting a new program for unpaid caregivers to relieve pressure on families and on the health care system by allowing informal caregivers to take time off work and to qualify for special benefits under Canada's Employment Insurance program.

It is also important that we acknowledge that prescription drugs are an increasingly important part of our health care system. But too many Canadians have no drug coverage at all, and existing provincial drug insurance coverage is uneven. I have therefore proposed a Catastrophic Drug Transfer. This transfer will enable provinces to protect Canadian families by increasing their capacity to expand existing drug coverage, while also fostering more effective medication management approaches.

I also believe Canada needs a new, independent National Drug Agency to control costs, evaluate new and existing drugs, and ensure quality, safety, and cost-effectiveness of all prescription drugs on behalf of all governments and all Canadians. Finally, I believe certain aspects of the drug patent legislation must be reviewed to ensure Canadians can have access to lower cost alternatives as soon as possible following the expiration of the statutory period of patent protection.

In completing this report, I am acutely aware that the support of Canadians for their health care system is not given freely. It is given in exchange for a commitment that their governments will ensure that high quality care is there for them when they need it. If Canadians come to believe that their governments will not honour their part of the bargain, they will look elsewhere for answers. And the grave risk we will face is pressure for access to private, parallel services—one set of services for the well-off, another for those who are not. Canadians do not want this.

Our reform agenda is an ambitious one, but at a time when one of our most cherished national programs is at a crossroads, Canadians expect no less than an ambitious plan.

I am always mindful of the lineage of Canada's medicare system—it began with the CCF party in my home province of Saskatchewan. It was a

Conservative Prime Minister who appointed Emmett Hall, and a Liberal government that introduced legislation to create modern medicare. And it was politicians of all stripes, and from all regions, who joined together to unanimously approve it . . .

Forty years ago, when visionary men and women came together to create medicare, we had private medicine in Canada. You paid out of pocket to receive medical services if you could afford them, or relied on the dole if you couldn't. If you needed an operation, you cashed in your savings, mortgaged your home, or sold your farm so you could pay, or you simply did without. If you had the resources or good fortune, you were able to pay your way to the front of the line; if you didn't, you waited and prayed for the best.

Many of the so-called "new solutions" being proposed for health care— pay-as-you-go, user and facility fees, fast-track treatment for the lucky few, and wait-lists for everyone else—are not new at all. We've been there. They are old solutions that didn't work then, and were discarded for that reason. And the preponderance of evidence is that they will not work today.

In the coming months, the choices we make, or the consequences of those we fail to make, will decide medicare's future. I believe Canadians are prepared to embark on the journey together and build on the proud legacy they have inherited.

It is now in their hands.

Thomas Homer-Dixon

4 December 2002

"We have to be aggressively proactive on multiple fronts"

Thomas Homer-Dixon is an expert in conflict studies at the University of Toronto, and author of the award-winning book *The Ingenuity Gap*. In his view our human society and ecological systems are under multiple stresses occurring at a rate that is too rapid and extreme to be met in customary ways. He gave this speech to the Elliott School of International Affairs at George Washington University, Washington, D.C.

Humankind, I argue, is on the cusp of a planetary emergency. We face an ever-greater risk of a synchronous failure of our social, economic and bio-physical systems, arising from simultaneous, interacting stresses acting powerfully at multiple levels of global systems . . .

Certainly, we must all acknowledge that many things are going very well in the world today. On average around the world, people are living far longer, healthier, and happier lives than they were even a generation ago. A larger proportion of the human population is living in democracies than ever before. Market-based economic policies are now accepted around the world. There is a general concert of views among the great powers. The spectre of nuclear cataclysm has largely vanished. In many ways, this is the best of times.

And yet, something tells me that this positive story is far from complete. I keep coming back to another set of unassailable facts. These are facts about a formidable array of powerful, underlying pressures, what I've come to call tectonic stresses, building beneath the superficial activity and buzz of human affairs . . .

The first is human population growth and the demographic imbalances that this growth is producing around the world. By the time our population stabilizes, we will see, almost certainly, at least 50 percent further growth from the current six billion. We will see, in fact, as much absolute growth in the next fifty years—about three billion people will be added to the world's population—as we saw in the last forty years. Conservative commentators are wrong: the population explosion is not over, by any means; indeed, we are probably just past its halfway point . . .

The second tectonic stress is the rising capacity of humanity to fundamentally perturb its natural environment and earth's biogeochemical systems . . . I'm going to talk about climate change for a moment. There is evidence, most notably in high latitudes, that climate changes are starting to occur very quickly. The signal of human-induced warming appears to be emerging from the noise of regular climate variations. For example, upward-scanning sonar used by the American military to determine the thickness of Arctic ice shows that the icepack has thinned by about 40 percent in the last forty years. The average thickness is now about 2 metres, and the thinning appears to be continuing at the rate of about a tenth of a metre every year.

Straightline extrapolation suggests that we could see in three decades or so the appearance of wide swathes of open water in the Arctic. Given that open water absorbs about 80 percent more solar energy than sea ice, this development alone could change the energy balance for the whole northern part of the planet.

But straightline extrapolation is a dangerous game in the climate business. One thing that we do know is that climate change, if it occurs, will likely come in sharp, nonlinear jumps, a form of change that human societies have great difficulty anticipating or adapting to.

Furthermore, the costs of climate change will be disproportionately borne by those who can least afford them, especially those in poor regions and areas of marginal agricultural productivity. Rapid climate change produces adjustment problems, and poor societies are least able to keep up.

The third tectonic stress is the critical problem of energy supply, especially of hydrocarbons, for a rapidly growing world economy . . .

The fourth stress is disease. Although not readily apparent to those of us in rich countries, the world is facing ferocious pandemics of tuberculosis and AIDS. Tuberculosis, the top killer among infectious diseases, has infected nearly a third of the human population; it kills three million people a year (a remarkable 5 percent of total deaths from all causes), and its incidence is growing fast.

AIDS has devastated the economies and military and civil infrastructures of many sub-Saharan African countries. It is literally eating the guts out of these societies. And AIDS is now making rapid inroads in India and China. While there has been recent grudging acknowledgment of the danger of AIDS in China, the problem has received little official attention in India. Let's be clear, though, about the implications: even if the infection rate peaks in these countries at 10 percent, which is only one-half to one-third of what we're seeing in southern Africa currently, we would be looking at two hundred million infected people in two countries alone, with incalculable consequences for the development of the world's largest southern economies . . .

The fifth stress is the widening wealth gap between rich and poor around the planet. UN data suggest that this gap has, in crude terms, roughly doubled in size in the last forty years. In 1960, the income of the richest 20 percent of the world's population was thirty times that of the poorest 20 percent; today, it's over eighty times greater. Research shows that highly unequal societies tend to be violent. Humankind is creating a grotesquely and increasingly unequal global society, and we can expect it to be increasingly violent . . .

The destabilizing social, economic, and political effects of these five tectonic stresses are powerfully boosted by two other factors that I call multipliers.

The first of these is the rising complexity, connectedness, and velocity of human technologies, institutions, and social interactions . . . This increase in connectedness and interdependence produces many benefits, but it can also result in unexpected system behavior, including cascade effects as damage in one part of a global network, whether caused by a new pathogen, a computer virus, or a financial shock, multiplies and spreads rapidly to other parts of the network. Good examples of such destabilizing cascades in the international economy include the Mexican peso crisis in 1994 and the Asian crisis of 1997 and 1998.

The second multiplier is the relentlessly escalating power of individuals and sub-groups, like terrorists and insurgents, to destroy things and people. Put bluntly, the bad guys are getting stronger, fast. They have better weapons: the trend over the centuries has been towards unremitting improvement in the lethality of all weaponry, which generally has meant that steadily fewer people could kill steadily larger numbers of people more quickly than ever before. In particular, small arms and light weapons, such as assault rifles, rocket-propelled grenades, mortars and the like, have become more lethal as their technology has advanced. They have become more rugged, cheaper, more portable, easier to use, and more accurate, and their striking range has increased. The result is extraordinary and unprecedented technological leverage. Now, as we've seen recently in this city, two people with one sniper's rifle can terrorize several million people for weeks . . .

The bottom line of the preceding analysis is the following: Demographic, environmental, technological, and economic pressures are producing two outcomes that have immense implications for global political stability. First, these pressures are contributing to social upheaval, dislocation, and unmet expectations that boost the grievances of a large fraction of the human population. Second, by undermining the capacity of governments and states, these pressures also boost opportunities for violence by aggrieved groups. In short, they produce exploitable resentments, political instabilities, and radicalized societies . . .

So what should we do? What are some possible policies or plans to prevent such an outcome? I believe it's entirely within human ability to prevent any form of synchronous failure. We must first recognize, though, that for the first time in our species' history, we have to be aggressively proactive on multiple fronts simultaneously. Each of the five tectonic stresses and two multipliers I've identified requires its own policy responses. There's no magic bullet, no single solution or institutional response that will cover all these problems.

We need to be increasing, not decreasing, our support for worldwide family planning; we need to boost efforts around the planet in soil, forest, and water conservation; we need to take climate change far more seriously and begin planning for a global transition to a suite of new energy technologies (including carbon sequestration, geologic storage, and hydrogen power) that will dramatically reduce our carbon emissions; we need to work out reasonable protection for intellectual property rights and then get anti-retroviral drugs into the hands of the millions of people infected with AIDS around the world; we need to reform the international financial system so that it no longer wrecks the economies of major countries like Indonesia and Argentina in response to the corrupt economic policies of their elites.

We also need to reduce the vulnerability of our complex economic and technological systems to cascade effects and nonlinear failures. This may require a radically different way of thinking about economic development and globalization. Sometimes the best policies may not be those that increase integration, interconnectedness, speed, and efficiency. Sometimes, in order to boost overall system resilience, it might be necessary to loosen the coupling within our economic and technological systems, for instance by making greater use of decentralized, local energy and food production, and by slowing the connection speed between system components, so that people have time to think before they act. And it might be necessary to increase buffering capacity of these systems, for instance by moving away from just-in-time production processes and by increasing inventories of feedstocks and parts for our factories.

It's on the matter of the increasing destructive power of small groups that I have most difficulty providing clear prescriptions. This multiplier is driven by technological trends that we can't derail without doing extraordinary damage to our overall economic progress, because the technologies that terrorists use, like laptop computers and the Internet, are often the same ones we use on a day-to-day basis.

To lower our vulnerability to attack, we will have to consider, in coming years, dispersing our high-value assets; in one hundred years, skyscrapers may seem like quaint anachronisms. But we also have to recognize that the war on terrorism is not a war in any conventional sense. It's more like a worldwide guerrilla conflict, in which the enemy chooses where to strike and then disappears into a vast crowd of passive supporters . . .

We especially need ideas on how to build governance capacity at the national and global levels, because, most fundamentally, the challenges we face are about the provision of public goods, like health infrastructure, well-functioning markets, protection of our common environment, and security from violence. The adequate provision of public goods requires capable institutions of governance . . .

We are clearly faced with immense political and intellectual tasks, in public policy, in public education and mobilization, and in scientific research. We need to be investing vastly greater resources in these areas. But if we're prepared to invest the necessary resources, and if we are prepared to back the right policies with the necessary political will, I'm convinced that my vision of synchronous failure will never be realized.

Speech Sources

Howe, 1835: Lawrence Burpee, ed., *Canadian Eloquence* (Toronto: The Musson Book Company Limited, 1909) 9–15.

Papineau, 1837: Desmond Morton and Morton Weinfeld, *Who Speaks for Canada* (Toronto, ON: McClelland & Stewart, 1998) 17–18.

Lafontaine, 1840: *Toronto Examiner*, 16 September 1840.

Howe, 1841: D. C. Harvey, ed., *The Heart of Howe.* (Toronto: Oxford University Press, 1939) 75–81.

Peau de Chat, 1848: Penny Petrone, ed., *First People, First Voices* (Toronto, ON: University of Toronto Press, 1983) 57–58.

McGee, 1860: *Canadian Eloquence,* 70–72.

McGee, 1862: *Canadian Eloquence,* 79–86.

Macdonald, 1865: *King's Printer,* 1865, 25–45.

Brown, 1865: *King's Printer,* 1865, 245–69.

Dorion, 1865: *King's Printer,* 1865, 245–69.

Cartier, 1866: *Who Speaks for Canada,* 36–38.

Macdonald, 1873: *House of Commons Debates* (3 November 1873) 759–772.

Mistawasis, 1876: Peter Erasmus, *Buffalo Days and Nights,* (Calgary: Fifth House Publishers, 1999) 246–49.

Laurier, 1877: Ulric Barth, *Wilfrid Laurier on the Platform, 1871–1890* (Montreal: Turcott & Mendard, 1890) 2–29.

Riel, 1885: Desmond Morton, *The Queen vs. Louis Riel* (Toronto: University of Toronto Press, 1974) 311–325.

Big Bear, 1885: William Beasdell Cameron, *Blood Red The Sun*

(Edmonton: Hurtig Publishers, 1977) 197–99.

Smith, 1888: "Speech of Mr. Goldwin Smith at the Banquet of the Chamber of Commerce of the State of New York," 20 November 1888. National Library of Canada. Microfilm. AMICUS Number 26090785.

Macdonald, 1891: "Address to the People of Canada by Sir John A. Macdonald," February 1891, Library of Parliament.

Laurier, 1891: *House of Commons Debates* (8 June 1891) 883–88.

Aberdeen, 1894: "National Council of Women of Canada, Meeting to Inaugurate the Local Council of Victoria and Vancouver Island," 8 November 1894, National Library of Canada. Microfilm. AMICUS Number 2938272.

Laurier, 1904: *The Globe,* 15 October 1904.

Bourassa, 1905: *House of Commons Debates* (5 July 1905) 8847–52.

Singh, 1912: Empire Club of Canada, *The Empire Club of Canada Speeches 1911–1912* (Toronto: The Empire Club of Canada, 1913) 112–116.

Borden, 1914: *House of Commons Debates* (14 August 1914) 11–19.

McClung, 1914: Nellie McClung personal papers, British Columbia Archives.

Meighen, 1917: Arthur Meighen, *Unrevised and Unrepentant* (Toronto: Clarke, Irwin and Company, 1949) 71–86.

Francoeur, 1918: *Les grands debats parlimentaires,* 25–27.

Meighen, 1921: *Unrevised and Unrepentant,* 109–10.

Parlby, 1921: Irene Parlby, "Progress or Reaction?" United

Farmers of Alberta, 1921.

Macphail, 1925, 1930: *House of Commons Debates* (26 February 1925; 4 June 1925; 9 May 1930) 570, 1950, 3864.

Aberhart, 1934: Lewis Thomas, ed., *William Aberhart and Social Credit in Alberta* (Toronto: Copp Clark, 1977) 67–69.

Bennett, 1935: http://collections.ic.gc.ca/canspeak/english/rbb/sp1.htm

Bethune, 1937: Ted Allan and Sydney Gordon, *The Scalpel and the Sword,* revised edition (Toronto: McLelland and Stewart, 1989) 158ff.

Heaps, 1939: *House of Commons Debates* (30 January 1939) 428–33.

Silcox, 1939: Claris Edwin Silcox, General secretary, Christian Social Council of Canada, *The Challenge of Anti-Semitism to Democracy,* 1939.
Woodsworth, 1939: *House of Commons Debates* (8 September 1938) 42–48.

Casgrain, 1941: Thérèse Casgrain papers, National Archives of Canada, MG-32, Series 325, Vol. 10.

King, 1942: William Lyon Mackenzie King, "Address on the national security plebiscite" (7 April 1942) www.collectionscanada.ca/primeministers/h4-4068-e.html.

Groulx, 1943: Abbé Lionel Groulx, Gordon O. Rothney, trans., *Why are We Divided?* An address delivered at the Monument National (Montreal), November 29, 1943, Ligue d'Action Nationale. Library of Parliament, FC 144 G76 1943e.

Douglas, c. 1944: "Mouseland" and "The Cream Separator," L. D. Lovick, *Till Power is Brought to Pooling: Tommy Douglas Speaks* (Lanzville: Oolichan Books, 1979) 78–81.

Kitagawa, 1945: Muriel Kitagawa, *This Is My Own: letters to Wes & other writings on Japanese Canadians, 1941–48* (Vancouver: Talonbooks, 1985) 226–32.

Smallwood, 1946: James K. Hiller and Michael F. Harrington, eds., *The Newfoundland National Convention 1946–48*, Volume 1 (Toronto: McGill-Queen's University Press, 1995) 93–96.

Cashin, 1948: James K. Hiller and Michael F. Harrington, eds., *The Newfoundland National Convention 1946-48*, Volume 1 (Toronto: McGill-Queen's University Press, 1995) 1089-92.

Coady, 1950: Alexander F. Laidlaw, *The Man from Margaree: Writings and Speeches of M. M. Coady* (Toronto: McClelland and Stewart Ltd., 1971) 47–49.

Diefenbaker, 1957: Diefenbaker Canada Centre Archives, University of Saskatchewan, Saskatoon, Saskatchewan.

Pearson, 1957:
http://www.nobel.se/peace/laureates/1957/press.html

Lloyd, 1962: Woodrow Lloyd, *Address to the Saskatchewan College of Physicians and Surgeons*, Regina: Queen's Printer, 1962.

Lesage, 1963: Frank Scott and Michael Oliver eds., *Quebec States her case: Speeches and articles from Quebec in the years of unrest* (Toronto: Macmillan of Canada, 1964) 19–30.
Aquin, 1967: *Debats de l'Assemblee legislative du Quebec* (3 August 1967) 4995–97.

Trudeau, 1970: Pierre Elliott Trudeau, "Notes for a national broadcast" (16 October 1970) www.collectionscanada.ca/primeministers/h4-4065-e.html

Douglas, 1970: L. D. Lovick, *Till Power is Brought to Pooling: Tommy Douglas Speaks* (Lanzville: Oolichan Books, 1979) 226-35.
Clark, 1979: Empire Club of Canada, 19 April 1979.

Lévesque, 1980: *Debates of the National Assembly of Quebec*

(1979-80, Vol. 21) 4962–69.

Trudeau, 1980: Pierre Elliott Trudeau, "Transcript of a speech given by the Right Honourable Pierre Elliott Trudeau at the Paul Sauvé Arena in Montreal" (14 May 1980) www.collectionscanada.ca/primeministers/h4-4083-e.html

Lougheed, 1980: *Who Speaks for Canada*, 270–76.

Trudeau, 1980: Pierre Elliott Trudeau, "Remarks by the Prime Minister at the Proclamation Ceremony" (17 April 1982) www.collectionscanada.ca/primeministers/h4-4024-e.html

Mulroney, 1983: *House of Commons Debates* (6 October 1983) 27818–20.

De Roo, 1983: *Royal Commission on the Economic Union and Development Prospects for Canada* (13 December 1983) 14408–44.

White, 1988: Bob White.

Turner and Mulroney, 1988: *Encounter 88* – verbatim transcript of televised leaders' debate (25 October 1988, StenoTran Services) 110–24.

Suzuki, 1988: Empire Club of Canada, 8 December 1988.

Erasmus, 1990: Empire Club of Canada, 29 November 1990.

Manning, 1991: Preston Manning.

Strong, 1992: Maurice F. Strong, Secretary-General, "Statement made to the United Nations Conference on Environment and Development," at the Opening of the United Nations Conference on Environment and Development, Rio de Janeiro, 3 June 1992.

Bouchard, Lucien: *House of Commons Debates* (19 January 1994) 32–40

Martin, 1995: *House of Commons Debates* (27 February 1995) 10094–102.

Chong, 1995: Denise Chong.

Chretien, 1995: Jean Chretien, "Address to the nation" (25 October 1995) www.collectionscanada.ca/primeministers/h4-4011-e.html

Polanyi, 1998:
http://www.utoronto.ca/jpolanyi/public_affairs/public_affairs4k.html

Mandela, 1998: *House of Commons Debates* (24 September 1998) 8380–84.

Gosnell, 1998: Tom Molloy, *The World is Our Witness*, (Calgary, AB: Fifth House, 2000) 138–39.

Clarkson, 1999:
www.gg.ca/media/doc.asp?lang=e&DocID=1379

Justin Trudeau, 2000: Justin P. J. Trudeau.

Chretien, 2001: Jean Chretien, "Address on the National Day of Mourning in Canada, Parliament Hill, Ottawa" (14 September 2001) www.patriotsource.com/wtc/intl/0911/canada.html

Thobani, 2001: Sunera Thobani.

Lewis, 2002: Stephen Lewis.

Romanow, 2002: Commission On The Future Of Health Care In Canada, "Statement by Roy J. Romanow, Q.C., Commissioner, on the Release of the Final Report of the Commission on the Future of Health Care in Canada" (28 November 2002) www.hc-sc.gc.ca/english/care/romanow/index1.html

Homer-Dixon, 2002: Thomas Homer-Dixon.

Other References

Bosc, Marc, ed. *The Broadview Book of Canadian Parliamentary Anecdotes*. Peterborough, ON: Broadview Press, 1988.

Burpee, Lawrence J., ed. *Canadian Eloquence*. Toronto, ON: The Musson Book Co., 1910.

The Canadian Encyclopedia, http://www.thecanadianencyclopedia.com

Canadian Speeches: Issues of the day. Woodville, Ontario.

Cmiel, Kenneth. *Democratic Eloquence: The Fight Over Popular Speech in Nineteenth-Century America*. Berkeley, CA: University of California Press, 1990.

Jamieson, Kathleen Hall. *Eloquence in an Electronic Age: The Transformation of Political Speechmaking*. New York, NY: Oxford University Press, 1988.

MacArthur, Brian, ed. *The Penguin Book of Twentieth-Century Speeches*. New York, NY: Penguin Books, 1992.

McLeod, A. L., ed. *Australia Speaks: An Anthology of Australian Speeches*. Sydney: Wentworth Books, 1969.

Miner, Margaret and Hugh Rawson, *The New International Dictionary of Quotations*. third ed. New York, NY: Penguin USA, 2000.

Morton, Desmond and Morton Weinfeld, eds. *Who Speaks for Canada: Words That Shape a Century*. Toronto, ON: McClelland & Stewart, 1998.

Morton, Desmond. *A Short History of Canada*. 5th ed. Toronto, ON: McClelland & Stewart, 2001.

Noonan, Peggy. *Simply Speaking: How to Communicate Your Ideas with Style, Substance and Clarity*. New York, NY: Harper Collins, 1998.

Petrone, Penny, ed. *First People, First Voices*. Toronto, ON: University of Toronto Press, 1983.

Safire, William, ed. *Lend Me Your Ears: Great Speeches in History*. New York, NY: W. W. Norton, 1997.

Scotland, Andrew, ed. *The Power of Eloquence: A Treasury of British Speech*. London: Cassell, 1961.

Wills, Garry. *Lincoln at Gettysburg: The Words That Remade America*. New York, NY: Simon & Schuster, 1992.

The publisher gratefully acknowledges the following authors, organizations, and publishers for permission to reprint material contained in this book. Every effort has been made to obtain permission to reprint the speeches in this book. The publisher would be pleased to adjust acknowledgements upon reprinting.

From Sir Wilfrid Laurier, "Sir John Macdonald now belongs to the ages." Copyright © *House of Commons Debates*, 8 June 1891. Reprinted with permission of *House of Commons Debates*. ★ From Henri Bourassa, "These territories were acquired in the name and with the money of the whole Canadian people, French as well as English." Copyright © *House of Commons Debates*, 5 July 1905. Reprinted with permission of *House of Commons Debates*. ★ From Dr. Sundar Singh, "Sikhs in Canada." Copyright © by the Empire Club of Canada. Reprinted by permission of the Empire Club of Canada. ★ From Robert Borden, "We stand shoulder to shoulder with Britain." Copyright © *House of Commons Debates*, 14 August 1914. Reprinted with permission of *House of Commons Debates*. ★ From Arthur Meighen, "A choice between fidelity and desertion." Copyright © by Senator Michael Meighen. Reprinted by permission of Senator Michael Meighen. ★ From Joseph-Napoléon Francoeur, "Quebec would accept the rupture of the federative pact." Copyright © L'Assemblée Nationale du Québec. Reprinted by permission of L'Assemblée Nationale du Québec. ★ From Arthur Meighen, "They rest in the quiet of God's acre with the brave of all the world." Copyright © by Senator Michael Meighen. Reprinted by permission of Senator Michael Meighen. ★ From Irene Parlby, "Strong party government does not interest us at all." Copyright © by the United Farmers of Alberta. Reprinted by permission of the United Farmers of Alberta. ★ From Agnes Macphail, "I want for myself what I want for other women, absolute equality." Copyright © *House of Commons Debates*, 26 February 1925; 4 June 1925; 9 May 1930. Reprinted with permission of *House of Commons Debates*. ★ From Claris Edwin Silcox, "Democracy must set its face like flint against anti-Semitism." Copyright © by Dr. Larry Weldon. Reprinted by permission of Dr. Larry Weldon. ★ From J. S. Woodsworth, "I cannot give my consent to anything that will drag us into another war." Copyright © *House of Commons Debates*, 8 September 1938. Reprinted with permission of *House of Commons Debates*. ★ From A. A. Heaps, "Never have human beings been treated so barbarously." Copyright © *House of Commons Debates*, 30 January 1939. Reprinted with permission of *House of Commons Debates*. ★ From Madame Thérèse Casgrain, "The right to vote is not an end in and of itself." Copyright © by Renée Nadeau. Reprinted by permission of Renée Casgrain Nadeau. ★ From William Lyon Mackenzie King, "The government asks you to give it a free hand." Copyright © *House of Commons Debates*, 7 April 1942. Reprinted with permission of *House of Commons Debates*. ★ From Canon Lionel Groulx, "Beware of the illusion of bilingualism." Copyright © L'action nationale. Reprinted by permission of L'action nationale. ★ From Tommy Douglas, "The Cream Separator" & "Mouseland." Copyright © The New Democratic Party of Saskatchewan. Reprinted by permission of the New Democratic Party of Saskatchewan.

Index

Rosanna Parry

About the Editor

Dennis Gruending is a former Member of Parliament from Saskatchewan. A journalist by profession, he has worked for three newspapers and as a producer and host for CBC Radio in western Canada. Gruending well knows the power of eloquence—not only has he delivered many speeches of his own, he has also written them for others. He is the author of four previous books, including biographies of Emmett Hall and Allan Blakeney, and *The Middle of Nowhere*, an anthology of non-fiction writing about Saskatchewan, from the fur trade to the present. His articles, stories, and poems have appeared in *NeWest Review*, *The Canadian Forum*, *New Internationalist*, *Maclean's*, and *Reader's Digest*.

Gruending is married to Martha Wiebe, who teaches at Carleton University; they have two daughters, Maria and Anna. He divides his time between Ottawa and Saskatchewan.